ISLAM DREAMING

PETA STEPHENSON specialises in the study of cross-cultural relationships between Indigenous and non-white immigrant communities in Australia. She recently completed an ARC Postdoctoral Fellowship in the Asia Institute, Faculty of Arts, the University of Melbourne, where she is now an honorary fellow. Her first book, *The Outsiders Within* (UNSW Press, 2007), traced the hidden story of centuries of trade and intermarriage between Indigenous and South-East Asian communities across Australia.

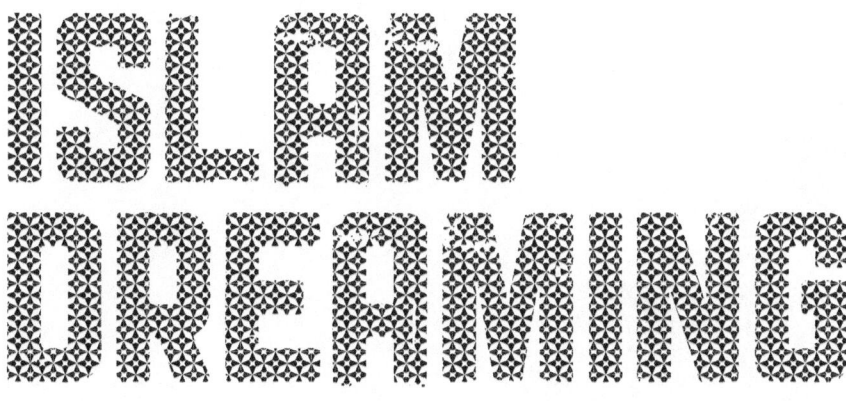

ISLAM DREAMING
Indigenous Muslims in Australia

PETA STEPHENSON

A UNSW Press book
Published by
University of New South Wales Press Ltd
University of New South Wales
Sydney NSW 2052
AUSTRALIA
www.unswpress.com.au

© Peta Stephenson 2010
First published 2010

10 9 8 7 6 5 4 3 2 1

This book is copyright. Apart from any fair dealing for the purpose of private study, research, criticism or review, as permitted under the Copyright Act, no part may be reproduced by any process without written permission. Inquiries should be addressed to the publisher.

Indigenous readers are advised that this book contains names, images and words of people who are now deceased.

National Library of Australia
Cataloguing-in-Publication entry
    Author: Stephenson, Peta.
    Title: Islam dreaming: Indigenous Muslims in Australia/
    by Peta Stephenson.
    ISBN: 978 174223 247 8 (pbk.)
    Subjects: Muslims – Australia – History.
        Aboriginal Australians6. – Religion.
    Dewey Number: 305.69794

Design Di Quick
Cover Design by Committee

CONTENTS

Acknowledgments   vii

Introduction   1

1 **The beginnings**   21

2 **Telling it like it was**   59

3 **Keeping it in the family**   90

4 **Marriage matters**   121

5 **Having faith**   150

6 **Speaking to the converted**   182

7 **Sisters are doing it for themselves**   213

8 **Malcolm X Down Under**   243

Conclusion   276

Interviews   294

Notes   295

Bibliography   309

Index   317

ACKNOWLEDGMENTS

This book would not have been possible without the generous contribution of the many Indigenous people who shared their personal and family histories with me. I feel privileged to have been taken into their confidence, and thank them for their warm hospitality, time and trust. I also give thanks to those interviewees who allowed me to reproduce photographs of themselves or their forebears. I owe a further debt of gratitude to the many other interviewees who shared their expertise and experience with me.

Philip Morrissey generously read and commented on an earlier version of the manuscript. For their feedback on individual chapters I likewise extend heartfelt thanks to Athol Chase, Philip Jones, Ian McIntosh, Balfour Ross, Anna Shnukal and Pamela Rajkowski OAM. I would also like to express my appreciation to Pamela for introducing me to many Afghan cameleer descendants, particularly Mona Wilson and Shirley Wilson. I give thanks to Simon Caldwell, Dilara Reznikas, Joan Staples and Ken O'Shea for providing access to interviews they had previously conducted. Thank you to Sandy Caldow, Aziz Cooper, Dexter Duncan, Soliman Gilany, Beylal Racheha, Kurander Seyit, Halima Binti Hassan Awal, Eugenia Flynn and Julie Nimmo for putting me in touch with other interviewees. I also thank Julie for allowing me to use the title 'Islam Dreaming'. I thank Muhammad Kamal for answering my queries along the way. Thanks to Tuba Boz for the copy of her honours thesis and to Edmund Carter for his help with the maps and cover image.

The staff at UNSW Press deserve special acknowledgment. In particular I would like to thank Executive Publisher Phillipa McGuinness for her continuing support and Cathryn Game for her careful editing.

Various sections of the book appeared in earlier versions in journals and edited collections. I thank the editors for the opportunity to have my work published and for their editorial advice. In particular, I give thanks to Peter Read (*Aboriginal History*), Tanja Dreher and Christina Ho (*Beyond the Hijab Debates*, Cambridge Scholars Publishing), Catriona Elder and Keith Moore (*Journal of Australian Studies*), Russell West-Pavlov (*Who's Australia? Whose Australia?*, WVT) and Carole Ferrier (*Politics and Culture*).

The research for this book was undertaken as part of an Australian Research Council Postdoctoral Fellowship. I thank the ARC for the grant and those, particularly Abdullah Saeed, at the Asia Institute, the University of Melbourne, for their support during the period of the fellowship and subsequently. This publication was also supported by grants from the Asia Institute and the Research and Research Training Committee, Faculty of Arts, the University of Melbourne.

Finally, I give loving thanks to my partner Paul Carter for reading and commenting on the manuscript from beginning to end, and for sharing my long journey of discovery with patience, grace and good humour.

INTRODUCTION

Islam Dreaming is a book about stories. It explores what Indigenous men and women from around Australia have to tell us about their varied encounters with Islam. Some of these stories come to us from Christian Aboriginal and Torres Strait Islander women who married Muslim men. Others are related by the 'mixed-race' children of these intermarriages. Still other stories are narrated by Indigenous Australians who have no Muslim forebears at all but who, for a variety of reasons, have been drawn to the Islamic faith. They are stories about travelling between cultures, between countries and families, and in learning about them I have become a traveller myself.

Collecting stories of Indigenous–Islamic contact has taken me on a five-year journey all over the country, from the bottom to the Top End of Australia, from east to west and back again, and from Perth to Thursday Island, from Broome to Brisbane, and Adelaide to Alice Springs. I've visited every mainland capital city (more than once) and countless regional towns in between. I've had the privilege to hear and record the stories of old people, young people, students, professionals, the unemployed, a multi-millionaire, some who don't want to be named and one whose name is known locally and internationally. I've met men and women who have high hopes for their communities, and some who feel they have no community at all. I have had the opportunity to interview husbands and wives, mothers and daughters, and brothers and sisters. I have entered a network of memories, experiences and aspirations that go back to a time before colonisation and look forward to a time of genuine decolonisation.

The almost fifty Indigenous men and women I interviewed exhibited great generosity in telling me their stories. They took time out of their day to recount personal and family anecdotes when perhaps the only previous contact we'd had was a telephone call or an email. Some respondents contacted me after hearing about my research through friends or family. Most did not know me at all. Nevertheless they made the decision to open their homes and their hearts, and for that I am tremendously grateful. They have also been immensely courageous and extremely trusting. Given the suspicion with which Indigenous and particularly Muslim people in Australia are often viewed, those I met took a risk in entrusting their experiences to me and in allowing me to communicate them publicly to the general reader.

Nearly thirty of the interviewees had Afghan or Malay heritage. The descendants of the so-called Afghan cameleers regularly organise and attend large-scale reunions, and I was fortunate to reconnect with former interviewees and meet new respondents at some of these events. The most recent Afghan Cameleers and Pioneers Cultural Festival, held in South Australia's Port Pirie in 2009 (and coinciding with the touring exhibition *Australia's*

Muslim Cameleers: Pioneers of the Inland 1860s–1930s), included camel rides, Afghani music and food, a photo exhibition and documentary films of the early cameleers as well as storytelling sessions with their Aboriginal and non-Aboriginal descendants. Dressed in clothes traditionally worn in their forebears' homelands, the descendants recounted, with visible pride, the contribution their fathers and forefathers made to Australia under very difficult circumstances.

The men and women of Aboriginal–Afghan heritage I met included Mona Wilson (née Akbar), the most active, committed and passionate octogenarian one is likely to meet. She and her siblings, unlike the majority of Afghan cameleer descendants, are first-generation Aboriginal–Afghans. Mona is devoted to telling her story and has done so in print and exhibitions, and on TV and radio. She is a consummate storyteller with an irreverent sense of humour and a wicked (and contagious) laugh. Mona has participated in many community events related to her Aboriginal–Afghan heritage. The fact that these rarely fund her petrol or accommodation costs doesn't daunt her. As she says, 'I sleep at nights in my vehicle to save on accommodation costs. This helps pay to fuel the car so I can get on with my work of creating understanding.'[1] Mona's younger sister Shirley Wilson (née Akbar) is an equally committed member of her local community. Like Mona, she too works indefatigably as a volunteer for countless community initiatives.

It is significant that the sisters' married names should both happen to be Wilson (their husbands are not related to one another). It is as if their close bond symbolically reaches beyond the Akbar nuclear family to encompass their own husbands, children and extended families. It is also a bond that responds defiantly to the many government-sanctioned attempts to tear their family apart. Their parents were forbidden from marrying by A.O. Neville, Western Australia's infamous Chief Protector of Aborigines. He sent the girls' Aboriginal mother Lallie off to Moore River Native Settlement but, after numerous attempts, she managed to escape, and together she and Peshawar-born[2] Jack Akbar fled the state, marrying in Adelaide in 1928. In a matter of months they were tracked down by the police and extradited to Western Australia where they were to stand trial for breaching the 1905 Aborigines Act. Insufficient evidence meant that the trial did not go ahead, and the pair was released from custody. They were exiled from Western Australia and sent back to South Australia (at their own expense), on the condition that Jack would care and provide for his wife and that she not be allowed to 'return to the land of her birth and her people'.[3]

When, almost twenty years later, Lallie returned to Western Australia to be reunited with her family and community, she was too old to be considered a ward of the Department of Native Affairs. However, this did not prevent Frank Bray, A.O. Neville's successor as Chief Protector of Aborigines (retitled Commissioner of Native Affairs in 1937), considering the removal of her second daughter Shirley, who had accompanied her. Luckily, Shirley returned to her home in Renmark (South Australia) before Bray could lodge the removal order. The Akbar siblings discovered these details only when, during her research, historian and author Pamela Rajkowski (who wrote about the Akbar family in her book *Linden Girl*) found that the Aborigines Department of Western Australia had a file on Lallie. The file, begun in 1926, was finally closed with Lallie's death in 1970. It is ironic that Mona, Shirley and their brothers Johnny and (the late) Jimmy learned of their parents' fight to remain together from the department that fought to keep them apart. Not wanting to risk their children's removal, Lallie and Jack had taken these stories with them to the grave.

In our interviews Azeem (Johnny), Beatrice and Marilyn, three members of the Aboriginal–Afghan Khan family, also spoke with evident pride of their close-knit family. Born in Oodnadatta in 1914, the late Aboriginal–Afghan Rameth (Rocky) Khan and his first (Aboriginal) wife Cissie did not have any biological children together, but they raised two of Rocky's sister's children (Marilyn and Philip). These children, too, were threatened with removal and, rather than see them become wards of the state, Rocky and Cissie married at an early age so that they could take care of them. After Cissie passed away her younger sister Esther married Rocky. This marriage was also largely contracted to keep the family intact. According to Marilyn, 'that was really amazing because they did it to keep us children together' (see figure 1).[4] Marilyn's biological mother Goolbegum had seven children. She raised two of her daughters but, yet again, the white authorities intervened, and a third daughter was taken away and brought up by a white foster family. Marilyn and Philip were raised by Goolbegum's brother Rocky, and the two oldest boys were raised by Goolbegum's parents. As Marilyn very movingly recalls:

> So at least we all were coupled, there were pairs, so at least we had a connection with our sibling. We were never all brought up as brothers and sisters under the same roof ever, but we've certainly made up for it over the years. We're very, very close. And that's something that no one can take away from us … Our family life is very distorted and fractured … and we were brought up as Muslims, [our family] did that to protect us, so that we wouldn't be taken away, because we were born at that time when children were being taken

away … but our family fought and kept us together, so we were very, very fortunate that way.

Those descended from the so-called Malay pearl-shell workers were also recently reunited at a community event. In 2007 Broome's annual Shinju Matsuri (Japanese for 'Pearl Festival') celebrated the contribution of the Malays to the pearl-shelling industry and the unique culture of Broome. During the week-long celebrations I renewed my connections with local Indigenous–Malay families and met others who had travelled from Darwin, Perth and elsewhere especially for the festival. The Merdeka party, which that year marked the fiftieth anniversary of the independence of the Federation of Malaya from British colonial rule, was a particularly emotional event. Through the storytelling of the (long-retired) Malay pearl-shell workers, the showing of a documentary and Malay dances, food, music and costumes, the early 'hard hat' pearling days were vividly evoked. Connections between first and subsequent generation Malays were reaffirmed as stories were swapped about the old Malay quarters and the celebrations marking the end of Ramadan.

Among the many Indigenous–Malay descendants I had the opportunity to meet was Halima Binti Hassan Awal. Halima, a grandmother in her late sixties, inherited a family history that includes generations of Indigenous–Muslim intermarriage. Originally from Thursday Island in Torres Strait, Halima is a third-generation Indigenous–Muslim. Her Darnley Islander maternal grandmother married a Muslim man from Singapore in the Straits Settlements.[5] Halima's mother married a Muslim from the Dutch East Indies (Indonesia), and Halima's late husband was a Muslim from Lebanon. Today Halima lives with one of her sons, his Muslim (Fijian–Indian Australian) wife and their three daughters. I was treated with much kindness and hospitality when I first met Halima at their house in Brisbane in 2005. The first thing I noticed was that shoes were not worn inside. Leaving mine at the door, I was promptly lent a pair of house slippers and invited into the immaculately clean and beautifully furnished house. The impressive wall hangings that depicted Makkah (Mecca) and calligraphy-based artwork immediately caught my eye. These sat side by side with the ornamental mother-of-pearl shells, trochus shells, copies of the *Torres News* and other memorabilia from Halima's island home.

We spoke at a table outside trying to catch the afternoon breeze. Halima informed me that the family home suited their needs well because the backyard was surrounded by a high fence. This meant Halima could walk around in the yard without being seen by any (unrelated) men while not wearing her hijab. It also helped to protect the modesty of the female residents while they swam in the pool. Halima described a recent celebration in which the ample yard provided enough space for the male guests to fraternise together while the women, sitting separately from the men, had their own space in which to socialise.

I was fortunate to sample Halima's hospitality (and fabulous halal cooking) on more than one occasion. A further indication of Halima's generosity was her willingness to invite me to come and meet her siblings on Thursday Island (known as TI or Waiben). In early 2007 I flew to Cairns, and from there over the Great Barrier Reef to Horn Island (or Narupai) before taking the bus and ferry to TI. I distinctly recall flying over Cape York Peninsula, perceiving the shape of the coastline against the bright blue of the sea. The sense that I was *leaving* Australia was certainly dispelled at the Australia Day celebrations I attended on TI. During my stay I spent much time with Halima, her brother Karim and sister Noreen. Despite failing eyesight Karim hand-carved several mother-of-pearl and trochus shells for me as gifts. I brought them back with me to Melbourne along with four woven rattan mats that Karim insisted I take. Noreen kindly gave me a beautiful blue and white beaded necklace that I wear to this day.

Karim, who had formerly worked as an engineer on the pearling boats (known as luggers), was an animated storyteller, and he recalled many a time when his skills and ingenuity had saved crews from disaster. Halima and Karim walked with me to the local cemetery and, in a spirit of piety, drew my attention to their forebears' headstones among the many graves that made up the Malay section, a number of which had Arabic inscriptions (see figure 2). Halima introduced me to many other Torres Strait–Malay descendants. I met members of the local Ahmat, Bin Doraho, Ketchell and Shibasaki families and took a day-trip to nearby Hammond Island to spend the day with the late Ambrose (Binjie) Bin Juda and his mother Rosemary (Mary).

The celebrations held on TI marking Australia Day were unlike any I had seen before. There was plenty of sunshine and just a hint of tropical rain as people of all ages turned out to hear Torres Shire mayor Napau (Pedro) Stephen announce the winners of the Torres Shire Council Australia Day Awards. A strong sense of camaraderie and abundant goodwill were evident as locals were acknowledged and thanked for their contribution to the community. The national anthem was proudly sung by men and women wearing brightly coloured floral shirts, dresses and sarongs. Countless Australian flags fluttered, small children swam in the pool, sausages sizzled on the barbie. The obvious racial and cultural diversity was matched only by the vast range of acoustic guitars, hip-hop and other musical styles and sounds on offer. Their patriotic fervour was all the more touching, I thought, when it is considered that most Australians, particularly those living outside Queensland, are not fully aware that the islands in Torres Strait are, indeed, part of Australia.

During the time of my research I also interviewed nearly twenty Indigenous men and women who have formally converted to Islam. Those who have embraced the faith without any Muslim family ties are similarly engaged in a process of community building. One interviewee, Eugenia Flynn, has established the Indigenous Muslim Support Network to advise and encourage Aboriginal people who want information about Islam, or who would like to share their experiences with other Aborigines and Torres Strait Islanders who have become Muslim. Eugenia was inspired to create the network because of the difficulties she encountered in embracing Islam. Her family initially found her decision hard to accept, and she was accused by some Aboriginal people of renouncing her Aboriginality. Aware that other Indigenous Muslims have faced similar criticism and that some have withdrawn from Islam as a result, she supports the members of her informal network with regular email and phone contact, holding gatherings and sending out copies of the Qur'an or other information members solicit from her. She currently plans to produce a monthly newsletter.

Rocky Davis, another interviewee (who was formerly based in Redfern), started the Koori Muslim Association.[6] This, too, was set up to combat negative stereotypes of Islam. The association also sought to provide support for Indigenous Muslims, counselling for Aboriginal prisoners, and a range of classes designed for Indigenous youth, including a gym program, cooking classes, anger management and drug and alcohol counselling. Members of the association have been invited out to New South Wales Aboriginal communities in Boggabilla, Walgett and Moree to act as mentors for their local youth. The elders in these communities were concerned that their younger generation were losing touch with their Aboriginal culture and becoming increasingly dependent on drugs. They recognised that the drug- and alcohol-free Aboriginal Muslims might act as a positive role model for their children.

A further ten interviewees were neither Indigenous nor Muslim. Experts in their various fields of inquiry, they ranged from prison chaplains and historians, anthropologists and curators to filmmakers, writers and community workers. They, like their Indigenous Muslim counterparts, were extremely generous in giving me their time and in bringing their considerable knowledge and expertise to bear on my enquiries. Some had researched, written about or exhibited material artefacts related to the Afghan cameleers. Their knowledge of the material heritage of Indigenous–Muslim communities in Australia provided important information that placed in a wider historical context the oral testimonies I collected from the Afghan descendants. Others informed me about areas of practice and spheres of personal travail and transformation that would not otherwise have been open to me. My interviews with three Muslim prison chaplains were critical in helping me understand the motivations and experiences of an increasing number of young Indigenous men who have converted to Islam while imprisoned.

Of course the contributors to this book live outside the book. I was very conscious of this when speaking with Aboriginal–Malay descendant Semah Mokak-Wischki. She not only agreed to an interview but also very kindly prepared a delicious dinner at her house in Tarragindi (in Brisbane). What an act of kindness, particularly when Semah was, understandably, preoccupied by the thought of her son's surgery the following day. Semah spends about half the year living with her Romanian-born husband in Singapore. They are extremely committed to providing their son, who has severe disabilities, with a range of experiences and opportunities. When my partner and I joined them for dinner at their house on a subsequent occasion they spoke passionately about their plan to set their son up (in a purpose-built bungalow on their property) in a business of his own. Semah, who is a visual artist, is now studying documentary filmmaking so that she can tell her story.

If I could, for a moment, overlook champion boxer and Muslim convert Anthony Mundine's life beyond this book, his many fans reminded me otherwise. During our conversation at Anthony's Boxa Bar, a café in Sydney's Hurstville (at which I enjoyed a complimentary lunch and was introduced to Anthony's mother and his manager Khoder Nasser), countless fans, young and old, stopped to ask Anthony for his autograph and to have their photograph taken with him. Anthony was always ready with a smile and a handshake and seemed more than happy to oblige the passersby. Despite the many demands on his time Anthony was willing to speak with me about his pre- and post-conversion experiences (Khoder Nasser said it was a reward of my dogged determination in contacting him so many times that got me the interview). Anthony bore no resemblance to his media image and graciously introduced me instead to a life humbly dedicated to his family and his faith.

While working on this book I encountered a range of responses. Answering the always uncomfortable question, 'What do you do?' almost invariably produced shock. 'You're writing a book on

Aboriginal Muslims?' the inquirer would respond, adding incredulously, 'Are there any?' Many seemed unable to grasp the concept. One thought I'd said I was writing a book about 'Aboriginal woodlands'. Another thought the topic must be 'environmental Muslims'. Those aware of Australia's most famous Aboriginal Muslim convert, Anthony Mundine, usually assumed he was the only one in the country. Others asked whether the growing number of Indigenous Muslims was politically inspired, reflecting the influence of Malcolm X. This surmise is not, as we shall see, wholly inaccurate. Unknown writers responding to Andrew Bolt's *Herald Sun* blog on my research made alarmist predictions about the threat Indigenous Muslims posed to Australian national security. Needless to say, similarly groundless scaremongering is the stock-in-trade of the many anti-Muslim websites that seek to patrol our electronic shores.

Imagine, then, my delight when, instead of disbelief, the subject started to elicit: 'Oh, there's one of those in the new Christos Tsiolkas book.' It was my turn to react with surprise. A visit to the bookshop confirmed that, in Tsiolkas's multi-award-winning 2008 novel *The Slap*, there is indeed an Aboriginal Muslim character. Significant, too, is the *name* of the character who, on converting to Islam, adopts the Muslim name Bilal. Although Tsiolkas does not explain why, this choice of name is highly significant. Historically, Bilal was a black Abyssinian (Ethiopian) former slave chosen by the Prophet Muhammad to be the first Muslim *muezzin* (the person who leads the *adhan* or call to prayer). One of the Prophet's closest companions, Bilal is revered by Muslims today as a symbol of the racial plurality and equality that characterise Islam. The fictitious Bilal's transformation from an angry, violent young man who 'found Islam, changed his name, and stopped drinking, dedicating himself to his new faith and to protecting his family'[7] in many ways parallels the experiences of the Indigenous Muslim men I interviewed.

In 2007 my book *The Outsiders Within* was published.[8] It was a study of the cross-cultural connections between Indigenous Australians and those from South-East Asia. It traced the enduring legacy of Asian contacts with Indigenous people in language, food, material goods and family genealogies as well as in song, art, dance and other cultural production. But it did not engage with the particular ways in which this cultural sharing also included the borrowing, adoption and adaptation of the outsiders' religious beliefs. I wrote about the pre-colonial Makassan (Indonesian) visitors who came to the Arnhem Land and Kimberley coasts in search of a marine slug known as trepang. I considered the 'Malays' who worked in the northern Australian pearl-shelling industry. But I did not discuss the fact that they were both Muslim. I emphasised that people of South-East Asian descent had begun making annual journeys to 'Australia' long before white settlement, but I overlooked the fact that Islam had therefore arrived here decades before Captain Cook's landing.

To be honest, the religious beliefs of these early sojourners and settlers had not fully registered with me. The product of a largely atheist upbringing, religion was a blind spot in my analytical vision. It was only after finishing my book that I began to ponder whether early Makassan visitors had also influenced Indigenous religious life. Did the 'Malays' – that is, Indonesian, Singaporean and Malaysian indentured labourers who came to Torres Strait and mainland Australia to work in the pearl-shelling industry – practise their religion here? I also started to wonder about the religious dimension of the migration to Australia of the 'Afghan' cameleers. What influence did their spiritual beliefs, codes of ethical behaviour and world views have on the

Indigenous people they met, worked with and married? And how, equally importantly, did these patterns of immigration, adaptation and economic innovation collide with, or converge upon, a variety of Indigenous systems of social obligation and environmental custodianship?

Previous authors have written about the Makassans, Malays and Afghans in Australia but, for the most part, have studied these groups individually. Valuable social and economic histories exist of relations between Makassan trepangers and Yolngu people,[9] of the alliances forged by indentured Malay pearl-shellers and northern Australian Indigenous people,[10] and of the cross-cultural partnerships that Afghan cameleers brokered with Aboriginal communities in Queensland and Central, Western and South Australia.[11] But these are local accounts in time and place. Nor, with the exception of Ian McIntosh, do they look specifically at the role Islam has played in these hybrid communities. *Islam Dreaming* is, then, the first book to consider Islam in Indigenous Australia across historical time and geographical space. It is the first to attempt a national assessment of Indigenous engagements with Islam, not only surveying the contemporary experiences of people located as far apart as Perth and Thursday Island but also placing them in their uniquely Australian context – one defined by a heritage of encounter and exchange extending down two centuries or more.

Chapter 1 offers an overview of the long and complex history of Indigenous engagement with Islam. It focuses on three early waves of Muslim sojourners and immigrants, the Makassans whose trepang harvesting along Australia's northern coastlines might have begun as early as the early eighteenth century; the Afghans who, as cameleers, were instrumental in opening up the Australian interior from the mid-nineteenth century; and the Malays, employed in the northern Australian pearl-shelling industries from the late nineteenth century into the last century. To select these groups is not to discount other early immigrant Muslim communities, notably the Javanese who arrived on the north Queensland sugar cane plantations in the 1880s, and the Albanians who came in the 1920s. However, Makassan, Afghan and Malay incursions are followed because they involved perhaps the greatest range and depth of encounter with Indigenous societies. The cross-cultural alliances formed, and the complex religious accommodations these entailed, make an account of these lineages particularly informative.

In the second chapter the focus is on the external evidence of the influence of Islam on the everyday lives of Indigenous people: habits of cleanliness, patriarchal authority (and its circumvention), the prohibition on pork. Anecdotes from family histories make up much of the material in this chapter, so the tone is altogether more intimate – yet the focus is still on the externals of what it meant and means to be part of an Indigenous–Islamic heritage. This becomes evident in succeeding chapters, where we start to probe progressively more inward aspects of the influence of Islam on Indigenous lives.

Islam Dreaming introduces readers to a broad spectrum of Indigenous identification with Islam. At one end are men and women patrilineally descended from Islamic fathers and forefathers and whose connection with Islam is intimately linked to their attempt to recover and maintain family histories and genealogies. Chapter 3 alludes to this phenomenon as *kinversion*; that is, the kin-based or informal absorption of Islamic values that occurs particularly among those with Muslim forebears. Kinversion does not involve formal conversion (or, as some Muslims prefer, reversion), but rather a capacity to absorb and respect inherited values and to reconcile them with other competing cultural expectations. Nor does kinversion imply a sentimental or uncritical view of the past, or of the problems associated with cross-cultural union. As chapter 4 illustrates in detail, the lives of kinvert women married to Muslim men involved remarkable adaptability, tenacity and goodwill. These qualities seem to have rubbed off on the children of these marriages, and chapter 4 presents often amusing and always captivating accounts of kinvert sons' and daughters' attempts to avoid the watchful eyes of chaperones, of arranged marriages, and of the gender segregation observed at family and community celebrations marking the end of Ramadan.

Amplifying the spiritual quest, chapter 5 turns to the other end of the Indigenous Muslim spectrum. It passes from relatively informal and circumstantial accounts of the kinvert's life to a more formal description of the experience of conversion. This chapter also marks a transition from the primarily historical material discussed in the earlier chapters to an investigation of the contemporary experience of Islam in Indigenous Australian lives, notably as it expresses itself in those whose embrace of Islam is first time, without family or community precedent. Although a convert goes through various stages on his or her pilgrimage to Islam, conversion is experienced inwardly as an ongoing process. Also, although it is in one sense a private experience, my interviewees emphasise that it ushers them into a world community. Further – and I noticed that this contrasts with the way non-Indigenous converts talk about their conversion – my interviewees consistently stressed that their conversion was an event of social significance, as it gave them a new sense of identity and agency that found expression in family and community-building.

As Islam is among the fastest growing religions in the world today, an increased rate of conversion to Islam among Indigenous

Australians might simply be a sign of the times. This is not, however, the case, as chapter 6 explains; and even where a trend is being followed, there are uniquely Australian circumstances that inform it, stemming from the immense disruption caused to Aboriginal cultures in Australia by the combination of colonial land theft, mission-mediated institutionalisation and subsequent government policies aimed at the assimilation and eventual disappearance of Indigenous peoples and cultures. Against this background Islam presents itself as a religion of liberation and decolonisation: in other parts of the world, of course, it is very different and, in an instance of structural homology, the role assigned to Islam by Indigenous Australians in this country is ascribed by colonised peoples elsewhere to the Christian faith.

Approaching the more private reaches of the Indigenous convert's experience of Islam is, paradoxically, also to find oneself increasingly in the realm of public controversy. The very act of turning inward, of seeking to take agency over personal conduct, seems to elicit in the media an unholy suspicion. In chapters 7 and 8 two very different expressions of Indigenous Muslim identity that attract public opprobrium are discussed: the veil or hijab, and the phenomenon of prison conversion inspired by the writings of Malcolm X. Indigenous women have been stereotyped as sexually available, and they suffer disproportionate levels of sexual abuse. Wearing the hijab is a practical as well as symbolic deterrent to unwanted attention. As a public expression of the importance Islam accords the family, it also appeals to Indigenous female converts who, against the backdrop of a long history of family break-up, want to offer their children security and stability.

A similarly nuanced and subtle set of arguments surrounds the supposed political radicalisation of Indigenous men in prison.

As chapter 8 reveals, while many Indigenous men, including or perhaps particularly those in the prison system, are initially drawn to Islam through the rhetoric of Malcolm X, the Islamic notion of 'universal brotherhood' and its disavowal of racial distinctions leads to a growth in self-esteem that has a significant influence on the way they think about their roles as husbands and fathers. Indigenous Muslims consistently emphasise the redemptive power of Islam. Despite this they have been stereotyped in recent media reportage as a serious threat to national security. Some would have us believe, particularly in a post-9/11 context, that Indigenous Muslims are not religiously but politically motivated. They are out to right historical wrongs, and Islam is going to help them do it – accusations that are examined in the book's Conclusion.

Some Muslims will question whether one can legitimately use the term '*Indigenous* Muslim'. In theory, at least, Islam does not recognise race as a category and people 'are simply Muslims or non-Muslims'. However, if one believes in a God who made human beings ethnically diverse, it can be argued that this heterogeneity is significant and needs to be recognised and affirmed.[12] The importance of this diversity has a particular significance in the present context for, while Anglo-Australians often locate conversion to Islam in terms of their own individual needs, seeing it as a means of addressing their private pain, Indigenous Australian Muslims (in common with black Britons and African-Americans), understand conversion as a means of repairing the deep psychological scars they suffer *as a people*. An Indigenous Muslim's description and interpretation of conversion to Islam is shaped by their prior understanding of their own situation, but the dimensions of that situation are understood to be primarily social and historical, not simply personal.[13]

This is not to suggest that Indigenous people turn to Islam merely as a form of defensive reaction. Islam also offers many positive social and spiritual attractions. In my conversations with Indigenous men and women it was clear that their resolution to become Muslim was as much a rational, cognitive decision as a spiritual experience or encounter with God. It was obvious that their identification with Islam owed 'as much to the head as the heart'.[14] The Islamic framework adopted by the individuals interviewed in this book enables them to formulate a strong critique of Australian culture, but none harboured any hostility towards Australia. Indigenous Muslims do not so much reject as creatively bypass many of mainstream society's values, and 'not necessarily the core liberal values – but the excesses that flow from them'.[15] They oppose aspects of Australian culture, including materialism, consumerism, secularism, the sexualisation of society and familial breakdown, that seem to perpetuate the destructive values historically associated with colonisation and Christianisation. They do not reject *all* Australian values. Far from it: they appreciate living in a pluralistic society where they can freely practise their religion. They value the equality of women and men and their entitlement to freedom of speech. Indigenous Muslims who have been born, socialised and educated in Australia contribute both to the Islamisation of Australia and to the Indigenisation of Australian Islam.

ONE

THE BEGINNINGS

Far from being an exclusively present-day, let alone post-9/11, phenomenon, Islam in Indigenous Australia has a long history. Indigenous and Muslim people traded, socialised and intermarried in this country decades before its white 'discovery' and settlement. This chapter looks at the exchanges that 'Makassan' (Indonesian) fishermen negotiated with northern coastal Aboriginal communities in the pre-colonial and early colonial eras; considers the diverse alliances and partnerships forged by the 'Afghan' cameleers and the Aboriginal people they encountered in the later nineteenth century; and, finally, examines the cross-cultural negotiations between Indigenous people and the 'Malays' who came to northern and north-western Australia to work in the pearl-shelling industry in the late nineteenth and early to mid-twentieth centuries. These different experiences of cross-cultural encounter have left their traces in the law, in language, in material culture and in economic organisation. Above all, Indigenous engagement with Islam has bequeathed to Australia a largely unknown human heritage in the form of memories, precious belongings, bicultural or multicultural identities and spiritual identifications that continue to be proudly invoked by descendants across the country.

An important point to bear in mind is that these three great histories of Indigenous–Muslim encounter have their own distinctive characteristics. These unique Muslim communities arrived and were dispersed at different times in history and across divergent geographical spaces. It is also important to acknowledge the diversity of doctrinal interpretation that exists between and within different Muslim communities. While Islam (the faith) provides Muslims (the believers) with an ideological framework for life conduct, it is one element among other loyalties, including ethnic and national identification.[1] We cannot assume that all Makassan, Afghan or Malay Muslims held the same religious views or an equal level of commitment to them – let alone imagine that Muslims from different countries adhered to the same form of Islam. Nor, as the testimonies in this book vividly illustrate, can we discard the role that individual personalities and circumstances played in the way encounters, at first involuntary and unlooked-for, were incorporated into their future lives and those of their descendants.

Aboriginal and Makassan alliances

Coastal contact

The earliest reliably documented records of Muslim activity in this country depict the annual visits of Indonesian fishermen to the north and north-western coastline. Early accounts, including navigator and explorer Matthew Flinders' *Voyage to Terra Australis*

(1814), commonly refer to these Muslim fishermen as 'Malays', but a more accurate term is 'Makassan'. The old port city of Macassar (now Makassar), located at the south-western tip of the Indonesian island of Sulawesi (formerly Celebes), was the major port of origin for most of the boats. But even the label 'Makassan' is somewhat inadequate because the fishing fleets were comprised of ethnically diverse crews with Makassans from Makassar, Bugis, Javanese, Ceramese, Sumawese and the Bajau 'sea-gypsies' among others.[2]

Using the winds of the north-west monsoon to sail their boats (called *perahu*), the Makassan fishermen made seasonal voyages to the northern Australian coast in search of trepang, a kind of sea slug, variously known as bêche-de-mer or sea cucumber. In December each year a fleet of up to fifty or more vessels would

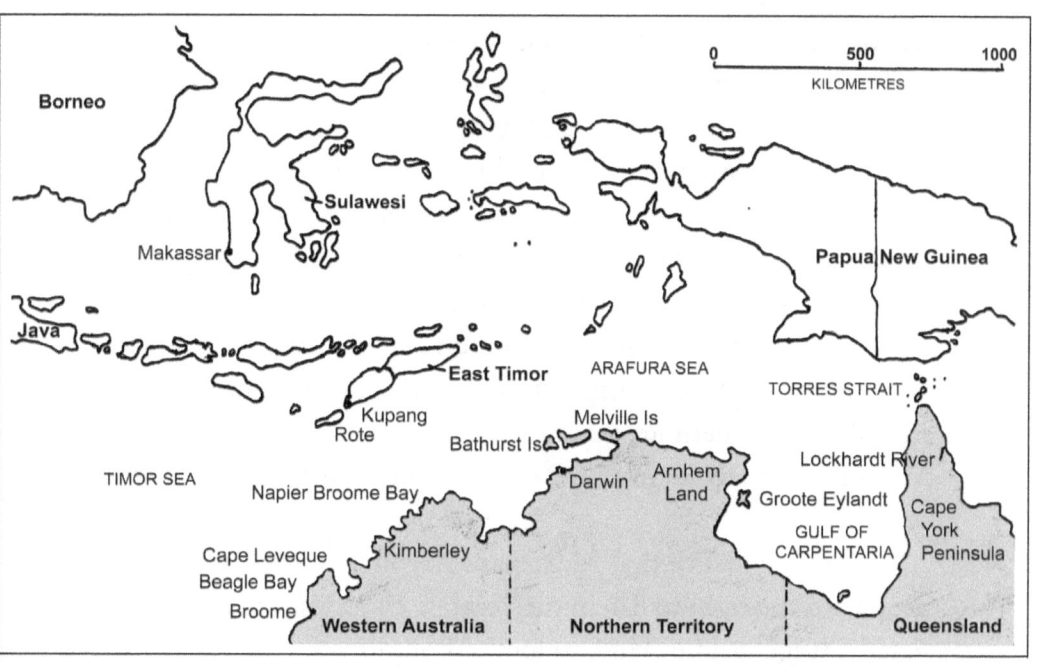

Eastern Indonesia and northern Australia

make the journey to either the northern shores of Arnhem Land, known to the Asian visitors as Marege, or the beaches on the Kimberley coast, which they called Kayu Jawa.[3] The Arnhem Land trepanging area extended from Melville Island east to the Gulf of Carpentaria, usually reaching the Sir Edward Pellew Group, more than 1100 kilometres to the south-east.[4] The Kimberley trepanging sites stretched south-west from Napier Broome Bay to Cape Leveque.[5] Approximately four months later, with the south-east winds behind them, the fishermen returned to Makassar with their cargo of trepang. There they traded it with Chinese merchants, who considered it a great delicacy for its culinary, medicinal and aphrodisiacal qualities.

A conservative estimate puts the number of fishers to arrive from Makassar each year at about a thousand.[6] Once here the crew would break up into smaller groups of around two to six *perahu*, working different locations along the coast. A *perahu* usually carried around thirty crew members, so that a beach encampment could have included up to 200 men at any one time.[7] Trepang processing camps (with large cauldrons to boil the trepang and bamboo smoke houses to dry them) were temporarily established along the coast and on nearby islands. A form of pidgin Makassarese was widely spoken by coastal Aboriginal communities, which also facilitated communication between different tribal groups who could not speak each other's language. Aboriginal crew sometimes accompanied the Asian visitors back to Makassar, usually returning to their clan estates the following season.

There is evidence that Makassans negotiated with Aboriginal people for the right to fish in their waters.[8] The visitors also negotiated a wage, paid in kind, to local Aborigines for the work they performed (with the Makassans) in procuring and processing the trepang, fishing, cutting firewood and digging wells.⁹ In exchange for Aboriginal labour and goods, which included pearls, pearlshell, tortoise shell, fresh water and timber, the Makassans traded cloth, metal hooks, axes and knives, rice, clay smoking pipes, tobacco, dugout canoes and alcohol. Given the wide range of economic and social interactions they engaged in, it is unlikely that one side benefited at the expense of the other. A mutually profitable relationship is more plausible, notwithstanding the fact that pockets of exploitation and violence from both sides occurred during some of the time and at some places.[10]

There is consensus among archaeologists and historians that the Makassan trepang trade was well established by the eighteenth and nineteenth centuries. But there is still conjecture over when these Muslim visitors first began arriving here. Even if we accept, as scholars Gerrit Knaap, Heather Sutherland and Campbell Macknight have recently concluded, that the Makassans began harvesting trepang in northern Australia no earlier than 1720, it was still another 160-odd years before European Australians started fishing for trepang.[11] But it was not long before they forced the Makassans to pay licence fees, fines, taxes and import duties on provisions carried.

In 1906, following the European trepangers' successful lobbying of the South Australian Government (which was then responsible for the administration of the Northern Territory), the Makassans were refused fishing licences altogether, effectively closing down their trepang industry. The banning of the Makassan visits was a serious blow to coastal Aboriginal people. The highly prized goods these communities were accustomed to receiving from the Makassans were no longer available.[12] These, in turn, could not be traded with inland Aboriginal communities — trade that fulfilled ceremonial and social obligations and significantly enhanced the prestige of coastal Aborigines. Close family and social ties were also severed.[13]

Islamisation

The Makassans left their mark, not only on Aboriginal social institutions and customs but also, importantly for our purposes, on their religious and spiritual practices. It is essential to keep in mind that the various coastal Aboriginal communities the Muslim Makassans encountered were not only culturally, linguistically and socially diverse but also lived in geographically dispersed locations. The ways in which different Aboriginal communities related to the Makassans also varied greatly. The Tiwi of Melville Island were reportedly so hostile to Makassans (and other outsiders) that they did not fish there.[14] Maung elders from the nearby Goulburn Islands, on the other hand, shared very close

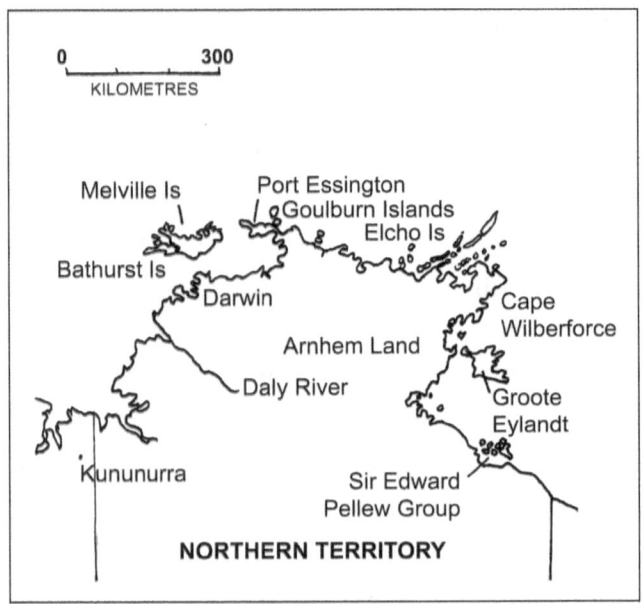

Arnhem Land

relations with the Makassans and eagerly awaited their annual visits.[15] Given this variety we cannot assume that different Aboriginal communities, or even those within a particular Aboriginal language group, were equally influenced by the religious beliefs of the Muslim visitors.

Today Islam is the majority religion in Sulawesi. Precisely how and when Islamic religion and religious practice were introduced to the Indonesian archipelago is debated. Some historians argue that it came via Muslim traders and missionaries from the Indian subcontinent, while others claim it was brought to the region directly from Arabia.[16] Some contend that by 1700 the process of Islamic conversion in the Indonesian archipelago had absorbed virtually all pre-existing animistic beliefs, including belief in the power of the spirits of one's ancestors and the spirits of nature.[17] Others believe that during the early phase of conversion not all rulers and their subjects were totally devoted to upholding all of the tenets of Islam. While Islamic influence was present, evident through ruling elites' renunciation of the consumption of pork and the pronouncement of the five daily prayers, some combined Islam with animistic beliefs.[18]

This is consistent with the observations of the anthropologists Ronald and Catherine Berndt, who, in their research on Groote Eylandt (which means 'large island' in Dutch and lies off the east coast of Arnhem Land), noted that the Makassan traders were 'nominally Mohammedan [Muslim] but retained a great many of their indigenous beliefs'. The Makassans' placing of offerings on local rocks that they proclaimed to be sacred is a case in point. When the *perahu* passed these rocks they would slacken their sails and, travelling in one of the canoes kept on the vessels, some Makassans would place food, goods and money on them 'to appease the spirits of the sea'. Significantly, the Berndts note,

The beginnings 27

'The Aborigines, who respected this custom and looked upon rocks as sacred, would never remove or steal [the offerings].'[19]

Their understanding that the Makassans also regarded the sea as a spiritual realm might have made coastal Aboriginal communities more open to the religious customs of the visitors. According to the Berndts, Arnhem Land Aborigines 'took careful notice of ... the religious customs of these [Muslim] traders'. Through their daily contact with the Makassans, Aboriginal people would have been conscious of Muslim prayer times, burial practices (wherein the corpse was buried facing Mecca) and other Islamic rites. Muslim prayer-men accompanied the *perahu* to Marege and Kayu Jawa. Recounting the oral testimony of Arnhem Land Aboriginal people, the Berndts report: 'At sunset, the prayer-man would emerge from his hut and bow towards the west, repeating the name of Allah. This prayer-man ... [would] look towards the sunset ... Then he would bow his head to the ground, calling out, "*walata 'walata!*"'[20]

As Alan Walker notes, the imam (someone who leads the prayers during Islamic gatherings) was clearly praying to Allah. The Berndts' Aboriginal informants recall that the Muslim prayer leader addressed Allah, the Arabic word for God, with the words *walata 'walata*. This is no doubt from the Arabic *Allah ta'ala*.[21] The stem verb *ta'ala* means 'to be sublime' or 'to be exalted'. *Allah ta'ala* therefore means 'God the exalted' or 'God, may he be exalted'.[22] Significant, too, is the fact that the imam 'bow[ed] towards the west'. According to Islamic tradition, every time Muslims pray, anywhere in the world, they must orient themselves towards the Kaaba, a cube-shaped shrine in Makkah (or Mecca). From Sulawesi, and the northern coast of Australia, Makkah is virtually due west. The Berndts' Aboriginal informants also recalled the imam 'bow[ing] his head to the ground'. The prayer leader was no doubt engaged in *sujud*, an Arabic word meaning prostration or bowing in reverence (to God). While in *sujud* a Muslim's hands, forehead, nose, knees and all toes must touch the ground. The Berndts' interviewees further recalled that the imam offered up his prayers 'at sunset'. Performed just after the sun dips below the horizon, the sunset or *maghrib* prayer is the fourth of the five daily prayers conducted by practising Muslims.

Spiritual legacies

Through their belief in the Dreaming creation figure *walata'walata* (or, as he writes it, *Walitha'walitha*) anthropologist Ian McIntosh confirms the Islamic religious legacy of the Makassans among the Warrimiri people of Galiwin'ku, the main township on Elcho Island (in the Arafura Sea, about 550 kilometres north-east of Darwin). McIntosh worked closely with the immediate past leader of the Warramiri clan, the late David Burrumarra MBE, whose father was known as 'Rajah' by the Makassans. The Makassans often bestowed the title Rajah (king) on certain Aboriginal elders. These leaders acted as brokers for the Makassans in negotiating the right to procure trepang from Aboriginal territories and the payment (in the form of exchange) for Aboriginal labour in harvesting and processing it. Burrumarra's father Garimbirrngu was the last Rajah of Melville Bay and Dholtji (or Cape Wilberforce, the north-easternmost point of mainland Arnhem Land).[23] He was close friends with Husein (Using) Daeng Rangka, the last Makassan captain to visit Marege (in 1907, a year after the Makassan trepang trade had been outlawed).

According to Burrumarra, Using gave a mast and a white calico flag to his father and the Warramiri 'as a sign that each had an agreement and were friends and would remember each other'.[24] Today the Warramiri continue to remember the Makassans through their reference to Cape Wilberforce, or Dholtji, as 'Mecca'. According to McIntosh, this is not only because of the many Islamic references in Warramiri cosmology but also because 'Dholtji once attracted Yolngu and outsiders from far and wide'.[25]

Burrumarra was born after the end of the Makassan trepang trade, but he nevertheless possessed considerable knowledge of the Asian visitors, and he shared this information with many prominent anthropologists, including Donald Thomson, Ronald and Catherine Berndt, Campbell Macknight, John Cawte and others.[26] It is because of the early work carried out by these researchers and, in particular, that performed by McIntosh between 1987 and 1992 that we have a clearer picture of the religious influence of the Makassans on the Warramiri clan than other language groups in the Top End and in the Kimberley region.[27]

The Aboriginal people of north-eastern Arnhem Land and its neighbouring islands are now known collectively as Yolngu. Yolngu society is divided into patrilineal halves or moieties that classify under two main headings almost everything in the Yolngu universe: an individual's descent line, their totems, animal and plant species, ancestral beings of the Dreaming, areas of land and individual human beings and clans.[28] In Arnhem Land the moieties are *yirritja* and *dhuwa*. Members of both moieties were involved in the Makassan trepang trade but, given that the *yirritja* moiety is concerned explicitly with strangers, with people and events that reside outside Yolngu day-to-day social life, it developed the body of Law explaining the origin, purpose and significance of the Makassan visitors.[29] Burrumarra's Warramiri clan is *yirritja*, and the fact that they were at the forefront of dealings with the Makassans is reflected in both their belief in *Walitha'walitha* and performance of the *wurramu* ritual.

According to Burrumarra, his ancestors must have wondered why Makassans had so much and Aborigines so little in the way of material wealth.[30] They speculated that something must have gone wrong at the beginning of time, and narrated Dreaming stories that explained this obvious disparity. In the beginning, according to one Dreaming account, a single law united Aborigines and Makassans.[31] Each was under the direction of a mythical being named *Birrinydji* – who was in the image of an all-powerful boat captain. But in their insatiable appetite for material possessions, Aboriginal people became greedy and jealous, fighting among themselves and sometimes killing each other and the Makassans. When Aborigines turned their back on the law of *Birrinydji* they lost everything and *wurramu* (an evil figure also known as the spirit of the dead) entered their lives.[32] The forgoing of the law of *Birrinydji* explains why only Makassans (and now Europeans) enjoy the wealth that was once also shared by Aboriginal people.

The role of *Walitha'walitha* (Allah) is to come down to earth to restore peace and harmony so that everyone can share in the wealth of the land. According to Warramiri clan members *Walitha'walitha* is a universal entity that looks down on *yirritja* lands from the heavens above. In Burrumarra's words: 'Yolngu have two bosses, *Birrinydji* and *Walitha'walitha*. Each limits the other. *Walitha'walitha* is Allah. He dwells on top ... *Walitha'walitha* tells us of right and wrong. It's sort of a sixth sense. It can judge a situation. It tells you what is going on in people's minds, like a warning.'[33]

This legacy is reflected in a *yirritja* mortuary ceremony, performed as part of the *wurramu* song cycle, also known as the 'Collection', 'Crook' or 'Stealing' man cycle.[34] During the funeral the corpse is lifted by two or more men who move it up and down as though they are lifting a mast. The Makassans lifted their masts in preparation for departure at the end of each trepanging season. The lifting of the mast by the Makassans communicated to Yolngu people that they were leaving, and the departure of the Makassan ship has been transferred to the idea of the departure of the soul of the dead.[35] According to the American anthropologist W. Lloyd Warner, who recorded his observations at Elcho Island and Milingimbi (500 kilometres east of Darwin) in the 1920s, 'the chorus sings "Oh-a-ha-la!!" [Allah] while the "mast" is laid down. When it is picked up again they sing: "O-o-o-o-a-ha-la!/A-ha-la!!/A-ha-la!!"'[36]

The Yolngu then chant in Makassarese pidgin over the corpse. When it is raised from the ground to be taken to the grave a Makassan prayer is recited.[37] Part of this Makassan prayer, according to Warner's informants, includes the words 'Ra-bin-a-la la-ha-ma-ha-ma', which they understood was the Makassans asking 'for something from that man God who lives in the moon'.[38] It is tempting to speculate that there is a relationship between these remembered prayer words and the Arabic phrase, transliterated in English as *Bismillah al Rahman al Rahim* ('in the name of God, most Gracious, most Compassionate').[39] If the Makassans repeated this phrase over and over, it is easy to understand how the Yolngu could interpret it as starting with Ra-bin (rather than ending with *Rahim*).

The day after the body is buried a *wurramu* or carved wooden grave post is erected and a mast of Makassan design is placed over the grave (see figure 6).[40] The carved *wurramu* figures might have been seen by Aboriginal people in Makassan burial rites in Australia, or by Yolngu who visited Makassar. Before it is erected the man who made the post, in company with his friends, takes it to the surrounding camps and collects any loose belongings that are lying about. All the food, tobacco, clothes and other goods then become his property. It is for this reason that the *wurramu* figure is called a 'crook' or 'collection' man.[41] He symbolises both Dutch customs officials who collected their dues from the Makassan fleets upon their return from Australia and the antisocial Aboriginal behaviour that followed the chaos associated with the arrival of outsiders.[42] The loot is placed in a heap with the *wurramu* in the centre, and when the songs are finished the belongings are distributed among the participants.[43]

The wooden *wurramu* figure is at once representative of the 'crook', of social disruption, *and* of salvation in *Walitha'walitha*.[44] Outside forces caused great disorder in Aboriginal people's lives, but the *wurramu* ceremony communicates their desire for a return to the social harmony that only *Walitha'walitha* can provide. For the Warrimiri, *Walitha'walitha* promises not only a return to the status quo but also dreams of an idyllic future in the hereafter.[45] In Ian McIntosh's words, the religion of the Makassan visitors, that of Islam, 'became the vehicle of an Aboriginal Dreaming in which there are visions of a return to inter-racial harmony'.[46]

While there is some overlap in meaning between the Yolngu Allah and Islamic understandings of Allah, the two are also quite separate. The dances associated with this being are known to have been performed by Makassans in the past, and the words for the songs stem from the Makassar language, but *Walitha'walitha* is an Aboriginal creation entity associated with particular Aboriginal territories and clans.[47] There is much evidence of Islamic influence in Yolngu belief in *Walitha'walitha* and in aspects of particular mortuary rituals, but it is not appropriate to say that Aborigines in north-east Arnhem Land were or are followers of Islam.[48] It is interesting that our earliest English-language documentary record of the Makassans (in an unspecified area of northern Australia) can be interpreted in the context of Islam. Using information collected in the 1760s, Alexander Dalrymple of the British East India Company reported the trepangers describing the Aborigines of 'new Holland' (Australia) as 'Mahometans'. But, according to Macknight, this was almost undoubtedly a reference to their being circumcised.[49] It is also interesting to speculate on George Windsor Earl's 1841 assertion that 'a few [Aborigines] have been converted to Mohammedanism; one of these, Caraday, a chief of one of Goulburn's Islands, visited us soon after our arrival at Port Essington.[50] He had been circumcised, and refused to eat pork.'[51] Even if there were some basis to these claims historically, today the evil spirit of *wurramu* is roughly equated with the devil, and *Walitha'walitha* is associated with the Christian God.[52] Belief in the Dreaming figure *Walitha'walitha* 'is not seen to be the same as belief in the religion of the [Makassan] other'.[53] Rather, like Makassan material culture and social institutions utilised by coastal Aborigines, aspects of Islam were creatively adapted to suit their own needs.

The adoption and adaption of Islamic terminology by contemporary Yolngu communities is a further indication of this cross-cultural borrowing. According to McIntosh, another ceremony performed at Yolngu funerals today, the *Djambayang*, takes its name from the Indonesian word *Sembayang*, meaning worship or Islamic prayer.[54] Similarly, John Algar, who lived in Arnhem Land for nine years, reports that at Numbulwar in south-east Arnhem Land the local school's Nunggubuyu dictionary includes the word *Ramadan*. For Nunggubuyu speakers *Ramadan* means 'singing'.[55] The meaning of the word has been changed to suit local conditions, but its usage is another reminder of the Islamic legacy that continues to resonate in northern coastal Australia.

Aboriginal and Afghan alliances

Desert encounters

The first Muslims to settle permanently in Australia were the so-called Afghan cameleers. These skilled camel-handlers were often members of any of several different tribal, nomadic clans that travelled across the border between Afghanistan and northern India. When they arrived here they were indiscriminately lumped together as 'Afghans' or simply 'Ghans', regardless of whether they came from Afghanistan, Baluchistan or the North-Western Frontier of the Indian subcontinent (now Pakistan).[56] With the exception of some Hindus and Sikhs, all of the so-called Afghans were Muslim.[57] Michael Cigler suggests that their being Muslim (or Musselmen or Mahommedans, as they were called in the nineteenth and early twentieth centuries) was what, 'in the eyes of ordinary Australians, made [the Afghans] look and behave as members of one ethnic group'.[58]

From the 1860s to the 1920s an estimated 2000 to 4000 camelmen (no official records were kept) provided a vital lifeline for the developing continent.[59] Camels and their attendants were initially shipped to Australia to participate in the ill-fated Burke and Wills expedition in 1860 and accompanied many other expedition parties throughout the rest of the nineteenth century. During the 1880s they arrived in much greater numbers. They came on a contract basis for two- or three-year periods, and the majority returned to their homelands after fulfilling their work agreements. Afghans used their camels to transport food, water, building materials, furniture and equipment to isolated pastoral stations, mines and government camps and returned loaded with

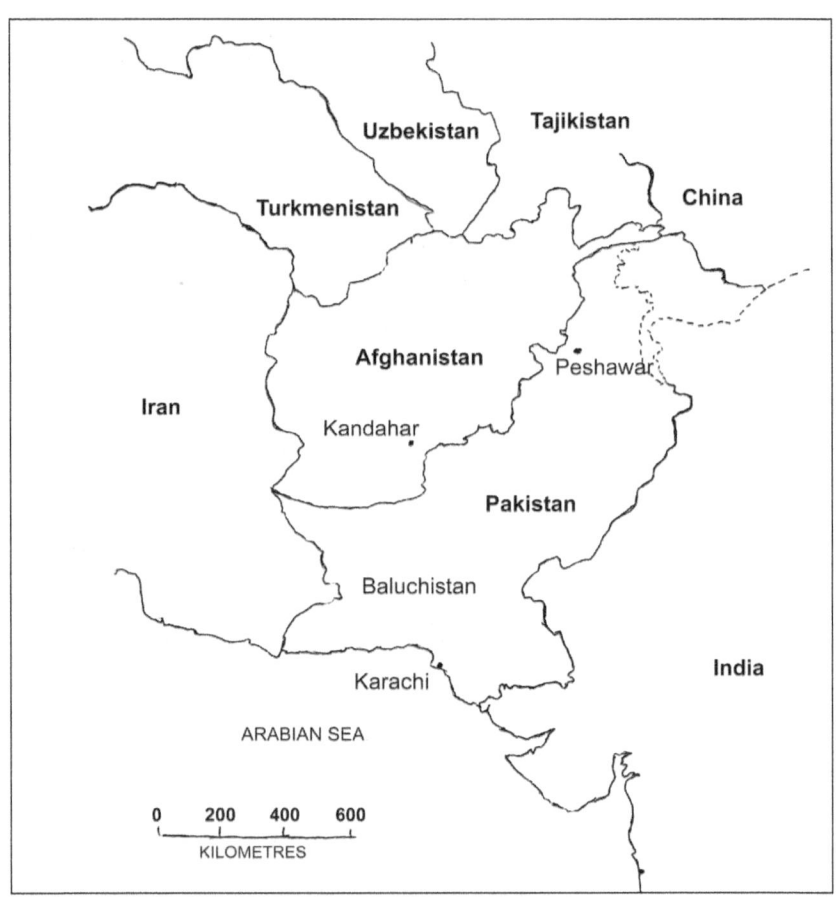

Homelands of cameleers

baled wool, ore and other commodities destined for southern and British markets. Unlike horses, bullocks and donkeys, camels could survive the extreme heat in the arid interior and could travel long distances without water, carry heavier loads, and eat foliage that other pack-animals found inedible.[60]

By the early 1930s, when the advent of motorised transport into the interior of Australia heralded the demise of the camel industry, Afghans had covered about three-quarters of the continent and their camels had carried goods in every mainland state except Victoria.⁶¹ The cameleers forged a network of desert trails, or 'camel pads' as they were called, which later became roads.⁶² According to Peter Scriver, the camel tracks that navigated 'the forbidding bush and deserts' were a 'palimpsest of the age-old migratory pathways of the Aboriginal custodians'.⁶³ These migratory pathways followed waterholes crucial to the survival of Aboriginal people, and it was from these trails that the Afghans developed their camel tracks.

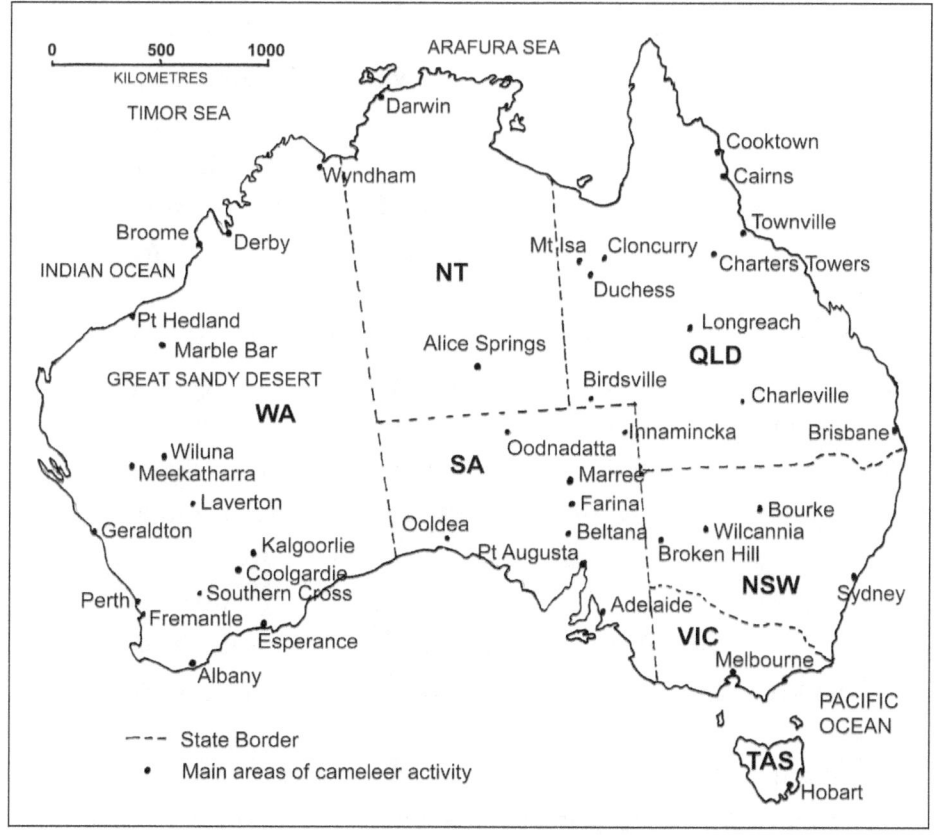

Main areas of cameleer activity

During their travels through the arid interior the Afghans came into contact with a variety of Aboriginal communities, each with distinct languages and cultures. Like their coastal counterparts, desert Aboriginal people, while coming together periodically for important ceremonies, maintained tribal divisions by protecting their own well-defined territories. Among others the Afghan cameleers encountered speakers of Arabana, who held the country to the west of Lake Eyre; the Dieri, who lived east of the lake; Wangkangurru speakers from the Simpson Desert (in the north-east of South Australia); the approximately eleven tribal groups now often referred to as Yammatji, a general name for Aboriginal people from the Gascoyne and Murchison districts of Western Australia; the Walmajarri, whose traditional lands are in the Great Sandy Desert, south of Fitzroy Crossing in the north of Western Australia; and Wardaman, a label used to describe the language, land and people traditionally associated with an area of land to the south-west of what is now Katherine in the Northern Territory.

Aboriginal people were initially extremely wary of the dromedaries they had never encountered before. According to Peter Horsetailer, a Kaytetye man whose traditional country is about 300 kilometres north of Alice Springs, his people thought camels were devils: 'Yes, they were camped there and they heard a bell. A camel had a bell on its neck, and it was eating from bean trees ... Well, one old fella said, "See that one ... It might be a devil!" ... The people decided to go back. "All you women go to the top of that big hill with the little children. We men will go to try and kill it."'[64]

In the early days some Aboriginal women and girls were also frightened of the Afghan camelmen. Any strangers in their sacred sites were to be feared. As far as Aboriginal people were concerned the Afghans, like Europeans, were outsiders.[65] Immigration restrictions prevented the Afghans who came here from bringing their wives and families, and some Afghans sought the sexual favours of Aboriginal women. Nguwauirr, a Walmajarri woman, recalled that as a teenager (possibly in the 1920s or '30s) she ran away from a group of her people (who had gathered for an initiation ceremony), not only because she feared the bell-wearing camels: 'those animals that make tinkling sounds as they move along', but also 'because I had heard that the Afghans were offering food in exchange for women. They wanted women. After hearing that I just took off.'[66]

Arabana woman Mona Merrick was told a story by her mother about two Aboriginal girls in the 1890s who thought they were being eyed off by some Afghans as tasty treats. The young women were at Alberrie Creek railway station, waiting for the train to Marree, when two Afghans came past with their camels. They instructed the girls to show them their breasts, legs and thighs. The women, frightened, did as they were told. According to Mona, 'The two Afghans liked what they saw: the girls had brownish-red bodies, not absolutely black, and they were both very plump.' She continues: 'both went on showing, they were frightened: "What will these two ask us next? ... Why do they keep looking at our breasts, while we've undone our clothes – they are not laying a hand on us: now we know they want to eat us."'[67]

When the train finally arrived the girls boarded it, relieved to get away from the two Afghans. Despite their fears about being eaten, Mona understood that the men 'only wanted a girlfriend'.[68] The fact that the girls were relatively light-skinned was perhaps another reason the Afghans showed such interest in them. Luise Hercus notes that the Afghans preferred women with fair skin, perceiving it as more beautiful. The camelmen's predilection for plumper women may also have been a result of cultural conditioning, because in their 'northern Indian homeland thinness was regarded as a sign of poverty and low status'.[69]

Mutual benefits

In time Aboriginal people became accustomed to the tall, turbaned figures in their midst. The Arabana used various words to denote the Afghans, all of which made reference to their turbans. The label *Abigana*, for instance, means 'white fellows with hair-string'.[70] Arrernte people, also from Central Australia, used the words *Apagana* and *Matawalpala* to refer to the Afghans.[71] They even devised a hand-sign wherein the hand was moved in a circular motion around the top of the head, another reference to the turbans the Afghan men invariably wore. Interestingly, as German missionary Carl Strehlow discovered at the turn of the twentieth century, another part of this hand-sign included a gesture that meant 'black', an indication that the Arrernte seemed to have perceived the Afghans as black people.[72] While they understood the Afghans to be distinct from themselves, we might assume that the Arrernte also understood these outsiders to be in some ways like them.

There was a considerable degree of cultural convergence or overlap between the Muslim camel drivers and the Aboriginal communities they encountered. Like their Aboriginal counterparts, Afghan cameleers were peripatetic. As noted, the majority were free-ranging herdsmen who came from nomadic tribal clans. Once here they continued to practise nomadism within discrete areas and, as with Aboriginal people, were simultaneously 'fixed' and mobile. The Afghans could recognise the lifestyle and outlook of the Aboriginal peoples they met, 'more so, certainly, than the resource dependent European settlers they served'.[73] Other points of cultural convergence between Afghan and Aboriginal communities included the practice of revisiting particular areas at certain times. Aboriginal people returned to specific sites for religious reasons or to gather foodstuffs that were seasonally available, while Afghan cameleers made return journeys to bush mosques and to other sites of religious or other significance along the various inland tracks.

Afghans and desert Aboriginal people shared many other social practices, cultural traits and experiences. Each was accustomed to surviving in a climate of extreme heat and aridity where the occupants had resisted invasion and, more recently, modernisation.[74] Although Afghanistan was never incorporated into the British Empire, the Afghans had some experience of British invasion of their homeland. Both came from vigorously determined tribal cultures where the avenging of injustices with violence or murder was understood.[75] Each observed spiritual and sacred sites; eating with the hands was customary, and both practised the circumcision of young boys as a rite of passage. In Afghan and Aboriginal societies great respect was shown towards their spiritual leaders and other elders, and they observed their obligation to provide food and other resources for newcomers and fellow countrymen.[76]

During the many years that Afghan camel handlers carted goods along inland tracks they observed the habits and customs of local Aboriginal people and, in many cases, developed trusting relationships with them. There is evidence that Aboriginal people incorporated camel hair into their string artefacts and that the cameleers assisted them by carrying traditional exchange goods, including red ochre, to other Aboriginal clans along ancient trade routes such as the Birdsville Track.[77] With their usual sources of food in short supply, Aboriginal people bought or bartered foodstuffs and other commodities from the Afghans. In the event that they were unable to pay the Afghans, Aboriginal boys and men worked for them, or temporarily loaned the visitors their wives for sexual favours.[78]

Some Aboriginal men were employed by the Afghans on a more formal basis. They accompanied the Afghans on their long desert treks, keeping the camels moving at a steady pace; hobbling, fetching, watering and saddling them, mending saddles and fixing snapped noselines.[79] The Afghans sometimes paid their Aboriginal workers in cash (although at a rate considerably lower than that offered to their own compatriots), but often payment was made in kind only. Perhaps of most value to Aboriginal people were the camel-handling skills they acquired. The use of camels enabled them to extend 'their mobility and independence in a rapidly changing frontier society'.[80] Aboriginal women sometimes accompanied their menfolk on their journeys with the Afghans, learning many skills in the process (see figure 4). At other times Aboriginal women were employed as domestics and nannies back in the 'Ghantowns' (described below).

The Afghans also benefited greatly from their interactions with Aboriginal people. Aborigines instructed the cameleers on a variety of plants and their uses. Personal testimony from Walmajarri man Malyapuka confirms that they not only shared the location of many of their precious sources of water with the Afghans but also gave them directions to outlying pastoral stations.[81] Malyapuka acted as the Afghans' guide within his own country, but he also accompanied the men into neighbouring tribal lands and, reassuring the elders there that the Afghans came in peace, they were able to travel into new territories safely. It is doubtful whether the Afghan camelmen could have contributed so effectively to the development of inland Australia without the vital assistance, labour and expertise they received from Aboriginal people.

The few studies that have considered the history of Aboriginal and Afghan meeting offer mixed accounts of how these groups interrelated. Pamela Rajkowski notes that while the 'two races respected one another, and there was no competition for land', the Afghan influence on Aboriginal people was minimal,[82] although given our foregoing discussion of what Philip Jones and Anna Kenny have labelled the 'exchange of skills, knowledge and goods' between Aborigines and Afghans, this assertion might need to be tempered.[83] Christine Stevens claims that Afghans considered themselves to be far superior to Aborigines: 'From their earliest encounters, Australian Afghans considered Aborigines inferior; their simple, very basic life-style, lack of material comforts or possessions … and their seemingly undeveloped religious life indicated to the Afghans an inferiority and lack of status.'[84]

According to Miriam Dadleh, whose father came from Peshawar (in what is now Pakistan) and whose mother was an Arrernte woman, despite the fact that a lot of cameleers married Aboriginal women, 'Afghans were prejudiced against Aboriginal people'. Later in her personal testimony, though, Dadleh notes that it might not have been prejudice *per se* but a reluctance to expose their children to non-Muslim ways: 'I don't know about prejudice, though, a lot of white people's ways too they didn't want us to know.'[85]

Artist Julie Dowling is the descendant of a rich cultural heritage that includes two generations of Afghan marriage into her extended Badimaya Aboriginal family (from Western Australia's southern Gascoyne region). According to Julie, her family's oral history describes the close relationships between the two groups (see figure 5). Julie's ancestors made connections with the Afghans because of what she called their 'respect for people's place and area'.[86] This is corroborated by Rajkowski, whose interviewees of Afghan descent in Adelaide, Marree and Alice Springs in the 1980s were 'unanimous in the positive opinion they had of Aborigines'.[87] According to Sallay Mahomet, the Afghans treated the Aborigines well because 'their religion taught them that all humans are equal'.[88]

It is important to remember that Afghans also often exploited Aboriginal people. Rajkowski admits that feelings of 'difference' between Afghans and Aborigines could be detected in conversations with her Afghan interviewees. There is evidence that some Afghans sexually exploited Aboriginal girls and women,[89] and Afghans clearly perceived Aborigines as a readily exploitable source of labour. In the case of one cameleer family their Aboriginal workers were not permitted to eat in the house with them.[90] Another of Rajkowski's Afghan descendant interviewees made a distinction between what she called 'full-blood' and 'half-caste' Aborigines, asserting that the latter were more 'cunning'.[91] The multifaceted relationships that Afghans and Aborigines shared are perhaps best summed up by long-term Marree resident Reg Dodd, a senior Arrernte–Arabana man: 'You see, the Afghans were sort of belittled by the whites. They sort of tended to degrade them. So the Afghans they used to kick the Aboriginals in the guts because they were the lower class. I think in all, the relationships between them, they both were discriminated against.'[92]

'Ghantowns'

The Afghans gradually established Muslim settlements on the outskirts of railhead towns where they could live and work according to their own religious and social conventions. The Muslim settlements, variously known as 'Afghan camps', 'camel camps' or 'Ghantowns', were dotted throughout the Australian interior, and included mosques, religious leaders and teachers, halal butchers, vegetable gardens and date groves.[93] 'Ghancamps' were often separated from the rest of a town because European colonists found the smell of the camels offensive and argued that they frightened the horses. The camelmen also found it more convenient to remain outside town centres in order to depasture their camels. In Marree the railway line physically and culturally divided the townsfolk. European Australians occupied the western side of the tracks, and on the east was a collection of irregular corrugated iron Afghan huts and sheds. Slightly further east were the humpies of Aboriginal fringe-dwellers.[94] The Aboriginal and Afghan communities associated with each other, but there was little interaction between either group and Europeans. Cigler suggests that the separation of Afghans from Europeans was, to a large extent, a result of the Afghans' feeling of affinity for and intermarriage with Aborigines.[95]

Some Afghans believed that Aboriginal women made more suitable wives than European women.[96] A few white women married Afghans, usually those living marginalised lives as deserted wives or widows with children, but many viewed them with contempt. Aboriginal women were accustomed to the basic, demanding life of the bush and more amenable to living in remote 'Ghancamps'. They helped with the loading of camels and were capable of looking after themselves while their husbands were away for long periods of time carting along desert tracks. Aware that they might face harsh penalties, Aboriginal women who grew up among their extended kin group were used to accepting decisions from the council of elders without protestation. Rajkowski suggests that 'Aboriginal women did not protest their lot, due to the way they were raised, which was in many ways similar to the expectations and duties placed on Moslem women'.[97] According to Stevens, obedience was for Muslim women a religio-cultural requirement, and lack of compliance was likely to attract severe punishment.[98]

In both Afghan and Aboriginal cultures husbands were usually considerably older than their wives. According to Islamic tradition, it is a man's responsibility to support his wife and children financially. Before marriage a Muslim man would often work for years saving the money to support his young wife, while Aboriginal men had to go through initiation before they were deemed ready to take a wife. In Aboriginal and Islamic communities it was also customary for a man to have more than one wife (a form of marriage known as polygyny). In each culture a girl would be betrothed to her husband at a very early age, with the arranged marriage occurring when she reached puberty.[99]

After marrying an Afghan cameleer a woman would often go to a remote settlement to live in the camelmen's community where she was quickly drawn into her husband's Muslim code and lifestyle. Since the 'Ghantown' mosques did not have areas set aside for women, Afghan wives, unlike their husbands, did not attend the daily prayer periods.[100] In other spheres of their lives, however, the women embraced Islamic codes of behaviour. They prepared meat in the halal fashion, avoided pork and alcohol, dressed modestly and did not leave home without a chaperone or their husbands. Writing about women married to Afghan men, Stevens observes that 'Islam was such a dominant force' in their husbands' lives and in their family life that there was neither space nor tolerance 'for a rival theology to co-exist'.[101] However, this claim might be overstated because there is evidence to suggest that Aboriginal wives embraced aspects of Islam while maintaining a connection not only to their Indigenous spiritual beliefs but to Christianity as well (a point we return to in chapter 3). This was especially the case for 'mixed-race' Aboriginal girls who were brought up in missions or native settlements.[102]

By the time the cameleers arrived in the late nineteenth century it is probable that a high proportion of the Aboriginal girls they came in contact with were of mixed parentage. It is likely that the Aboriginal wives of Afghan Muslims had been taken from their Aboriginal families as children and brought up on reserves and missions where they were exposed to Christian teachings. Nameth Khan's 'half-caste' Aboriginal wife Alice (or Alison) Mabunka, for instance, adhered to the strict Muslim lifestyle of her husband while simultaneously maintaining her faith in the Lutheran religion – a legacy of her upbringing at Hermannsberg mission in the Northern Territory.[103] Similarly, Lallie, the 'half-caste' wife of Akbar Khan (known in Australia as Jack Akbar), took on her Muslim husband's religious values while maintaining the Christian beliefs she had learned at Mount Margaret Mission (in Laverton, WA). In later chapters I look in more detail at the different ways Aboriginal wives and their Aboriginal–Muslim children embraced Islam. The key point here is that a remarkably flexible response to the challenge of a new faith is discernible. Aboriginal women often displayed great ingenuity, tact and understanding of context in negotiating marriage partnerships – partnerships that were themselves contracted in economically and politically precarious circumstances.

Indigenous and Malay alliances

From across the seas

Decades before the last Makassan *perahu* departed Australian waters 'Malays' were employed in the pearl-shelling industry, the major source of Malay employment in Australia for almost a century from the late 1860s.[104] Like 'Afghan', 'Malay' is another all-encompassing term. Anthony Milner suggests that it is best understood as an umbrella or 'cover' term to be compared with 'European'.[105] In Australian historical records the term 'Malay' was used to refer, as we have seen, to Makassans, and at other times to those who arrived in north and north-western Australia from Java, Timor, Koepang and elsewhere in the Indonesian archipelago. It was also used to denote those from the Straits Settlements (including Singapore) and the Federated Malay States (now Malaysia).[106]

The majority of the Malay-speaking pearl-shell labourers who came to Australia were Muslim.[107] But, given that they came from different countries, we cannot assume that each identified with his faith in the same manner, or to the same extent. Nor can we assume that the Indigenous communities the Malays met were homogeneous. Most Malays were employed in Broome in Western Australia, but they also gained employment in the pearl-shelling industries operating out of Port Darwin in the Northern Territory and Queensland's Thursday Island (see figure 4). As such they came into contact with a variety of Aborigines and Torres Strait Islanders. On the north-west Kimberley coast alone, the Malays met a number of different communities, including the Karajarri, Nyulnyul, Bardi, Yawuru, Jawi and Warrwa peoples.[108]

While each distinctive language was derived from a common base, marriage within one's own group was preferred, and tribal divisions were carefully observed. Contact history, whether it involves Makassans, Afghans, Malays or any other non-Indigenous foreigners, has to be understood with these cultural, social and linguistic differences in mind.

By 1875 there were close to a thousand indentured Malay divers, tenders and labourers working at various points along the north-west coast.[109] Malays comprised the greater part of the Asian labour force recruited for the pearl-shelling industry in the late nineteenth and early twentieth centuries, but by the time the industry reached its peak in 1911 the Japanese began to outnumber Malays. The Japanese, who were considered to be both temperamentally and physically better suited to diving than their Malay and other Asian counterparts, became the favoured divers. Thereafter few Malays worked as divers, but they continued to be employed on the pearling boats (or luggers) as crew, cooks, and pump- and deck-hands.[110] During the lay-up season when the threat of cyclones kept the luggers on shore (roughly December to March), Malays were employed as boat-builders, carpenters, shell-sorters and packers, and sail-makers. Aboriginal men worked on the boats as deckhands and kept an eye on the rest of the crew to make sure they did not steal any pearls.[111] On shore they worked at jobs including the opening and cleaning of shells, and as cooks, servants, gardeners and general labourers.[112]

The various jobs that Asian and Aboriginal workers performed attracted different levels of income and social status. According to Anna Shnukal and Guy Ramsay, the hierarchy that existed among so-called Asiatics was only partly based on 'their specialised status and earnings within the pearling industry'. They note that it was also supported ideologically by 'the supposedly scientifically proven "hierarchy of races"'.¹¹³ European pearling masters were at the apex of this racialised hierarchy. Aborigines, with Torres Strait Islanders just above them, were, perhaps unsurprisingly, relegated to the bottom. Located in between, in descending order, were the Japanese divers – upon whom the industry relied and who were the highest paid; the established Chinese and Japanese shopkeepers and merchants; and the 'Manillamen' (Filipinos), Koepanger (from or recruited from the port of Koepang in west Timor) and Malay indentured workers, who were accorded very little prestige and were treated poorly by whites and other Asians alike.¹¹⁴

The different nationalities of indentured labourers, particularly those at the higher end of the racial and social hierarchy, preferred to associate with their compatriots. Those at the bottom, especially the Malays, Koepangers and Filipinos, mixed more freely. In Broome and Darwin they also tended to associate much more readily with the local Aboriginal people. This was also the case in Torres Strait where the Malay and Filipino immigrants, unlike the Chinese and Japanese, tended to marry local Indigenous women.¹¹⁵ It was no doubt partially a result of the common (but qualitatively different) racial and economic discrimination that both Indigenous people and the lowest classes of Asians experienced.¹¹⁶ Speaking of Broome, Aboriginal–Malay local Sherena Bin Hitam recounts: 'Broome in those early pearling days, it was very segregated, and it was class … thus Aboriginal, Malay, Koepangers and Japanese were separate, Chinese were separate … [but] the Koepangers, Malays and Indonesians … were more inclined to mix with the local Aboriginal people and … most of the Malay men here have got wives, Aboriginal wives … simply because of their mixing.'¹¹⁷

Christine Choo suggests that the generally positive relations between Aboriginal people in the West Kimberley and 'brown-skinned Muslims' might also have stemmed from a sense of cultural affinity borne of the fact that the 'Asians of Malay background ... had dark brown skins, not unlike the colour of Aborigines of mixed background'.[118] This is corroborated by research conducted by Athol Chase on north Queensland's Cape York Peninsula. In his interviews with senior Kuuku ya'u, Umpila and Kaandyu men from the Lockhart River region, Chase found that what he called 'Asian Moslems, Malayans' were referred to by his informants as *tungkupinta*, a term used to describe them (and other Asians and alien 'coloured' people more generally), which translates as 'having dark skin'. This categorisation, which could also include Aboriginal people, distinguished them as a human group separate from Europeans. As Chase remarks, coastal Aborigines welcomed 'the Asian visitors, having learned from experience that it was the Europeans who wished to dispossess them of their lands'.[119]

As noted, Malays were generally paid substantially less than their Japanese and Chinese counterparts, but their average income was still far in excess of anything they could hope to earn in their homelands.[120] Most had come from extremely poor rural families and villages, and they empathised with the Aboriginal people they met. According to 'Patricia', a Broome-based Aboriginal woman whose husband is Malay, the Malays 'felt sorry for [Aboriginal people] ... so they'd give them tinned meat or something off the boat and help them feed their children, and probably they met each other and liked each other and had children from them. That's how it all started. That's why you see a lot of Asian children around today, multicultured children around Broome today.'[121]

According to Shnukal and Ramsay, unlike many white townsfolk and officials, Malay and other Asian sojourners and settlers were on the whole remarkably tolerant of cultural, linguistic and religious difference in everyday life. The members of the multicultural communities that emerged in Broome, Darwin, Thursday Island and many other regional centres across the Top End mutually accommodated each other's traditions and beliefs. This acceptance was even more pronounced among the second and subsequent generations of locally born children of Indigenous–Asian descent.[122] Halima Binti Hassan Awal, a third-generation Malay–Islander, recalls her post-war upbringing on Thursday Island in this way: 'On Thursday Island even though we were Muslims, we mingled, everyone was a big whole community ... Even though we all had different beliefs, we respected each other's religions ... they knew we were Muslims and we knew the Islanders, they were Church of England, Catholics, whatever. But everyone was still an Auntie.'[123]

Sally Bin Demin's experiences, described in her autobiography *Once in Broome*, are similar. Sally, who is a descendant of the East Kimberley's Jaru people and whose husband is Malay, grew up in the immediate post-war period where there were 'many ... languages heard' and 'a great mix of religions'. According to Sally, 'there were Buddhists, Muslims, Shintoists, Christians, Hindus and Jews. We generally respected and accepted each other's religion and culture, and it was really only the Europeans who tried to change us.'[124]

Cultural merging

Particular family dynamics also had a significant influence on religious formations and sensibilities. In some cases Muslim Malay fathers, particularly those who practised their religion devoutly, avoided pork and alcohol. They gave their children Muslim names, instructed them (particularly the boys) how to pray and recite Qur'anic verses, and made sure their daughters were escorted when out of the house. In other cases, due to the Malay fathers' long periods of absence working the pearling grounds, their children received little Islamic religious instruction. Instead, they tended to identify with the religion of their Indigenous mothers. The women were usually mission-raised, which meant that their children often became Christians as well.

In one family's case Islamic influence came not from the father but through the Malay–Islander mother and her parents. Shnukal and Ramsay's research reveals that in 1930 Kyûkichi (Kyu) Shibasaki, a Japanese pearl-shell diver who was a Buddhist, married

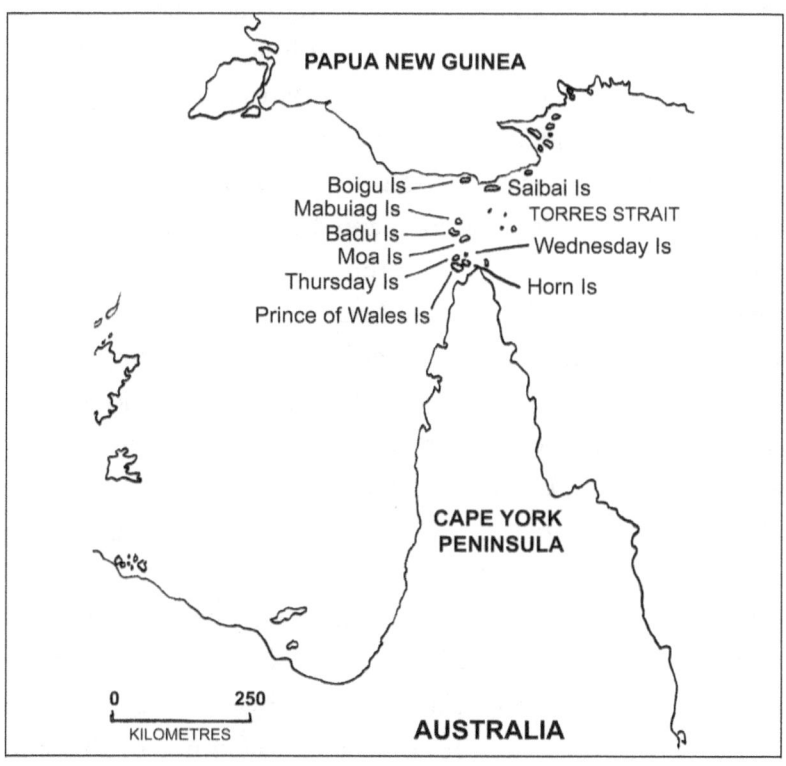

Cape York Peninsula and Torres Strait

Jean Ah Boo, a Muslim Malay–Islander.[125] Born on Thursday Island in 1940, Billy Shibasaki recounts that his father Kyu's absence while working out at sea for months at a time meant that he and his siblings 'grew up not knowing much about our Japanese heritage'. The Shibasaki family tended to identify more with their Muslim Malay heritage, religion and culture. This was, as Billy states, 'greatly influenced by the fact that my grandparents were living with us and practised their culture'.[126]

Billy's older brothers Jamel (born 1927) and Hismile (whose name is an Anglicised spelling of the Muslim boys' name 'Ishmael'; born 1929) also recalled the significant influence of their Muslim grandparents on their lives. The boys' Muslim grandfather Assan Ah Boo came to Torres Strait from Melaka (Malacca) and when he married his wife she, according to the late Hismile (or Izzie), 'turned herself into being a Muslim'.[127] Izzie clearly remembered his grandfather's recitation of the Qur'an and seeing him in prayer in the evenings. Each *malam juma'at* (Malay for 'Thursday night'),[128] Izzie accompanied his grandparents to the communal prayer sessions held, in the absence of a mosque, at the house of one of the senior Malays. Izzie never ate pork and always said *Bismillah* ('in the name of God') before embarking on any endeavour. This, he recounted, was also said by his grandfather as the throat of an animal was cut, ensuring that it was killed in the halal (lawful or permissible) manner.

This is not to imply that all of the members of a single family were equally influenced by the beliefs of their parents or grandparents. Jamel Shibasaki, while claiming in a 1993 interview with Joan Staples, 'I'm a Muslim, my whole family's Muslim … we always stayed with our grandparents' religion', changed his religion later in life. As he claims, 'I went from Muslim to Church of England, and then to Catholic.' When Jamel married his Catholic wife he said, 'OK, if they bury you, we die the same place. We [will] get buried the same place, so I been a Catholic ever since.'[129]

Many of the Muslim Malays who made the journey to mainland Australia and Torres Strait were very young. They might not have had extensive exposure to or schooling in Islamic doctrine, and they were often illiterate. Some of the men practised their own brand of Islam. In the wake of their contact with non-Muslim people it appears that Malay Muslims were willing to forgo certain practices. Over time they became less observant of the Islamic prohibition of the consumption of alcohol and pork. According to Halima: 'I think what happened here when my father left Indonesia, because of their young age and they were sort of searching for work in those days, I think they learned [about Islam] at home but, like Christianity, you sort of learn some and you leave out some … Some people, they kept some and left the other part out.'

The 'Muslim' mortuary rites practised on Thursday Island are a particularly fascinating example of the cultural and religious borrowings and adaptations that occurred in many multicultural communities across northern Australia. The death of a loved one is commemorated with the consumption of tea and cakes three days after death, and with feasts seven, forty and then a hundred days after their passing. The feasts honour various stages of the soul's journey to the after-life.[130] After seven days the soul of the dead is considered to be back in the house. Forty days after death the soul still lingers at the entrance to the house, or on the steps or in the garden, and after a hundred days it has left for the *akhirat* (Arabic and Malay for the hereafter).[131]

This, and the still common practice of leaving food and other offerings on the grave,[132] stem from Malay cultural traditions or *adat* – the customs and unwritten codes regulating social life

– rather than Islamic doctrine. Seriba Shibasaki (née Bin Garape), a Malay–Islander who was born on Thursday Island in 1941, acknowledges that the seven-, forty- and hundred-day feasts are 'just customs that came out, like with the Malays – come from their countries ... is not for all Muslims'.[133] In contradistinction to the hundred-day journey of the soul commemorated on Thursday Island, in Islamic belief the soul, immediately after death, resides in the grave until the Day of Judgment, wherein Allah reviews each individual's good and bad deeds to determine whether they will go to heaven or hell. According to the Prophet Muhammad a woman may mourn the death of a loved one for a period of three days[134] (which might explain the Islander custom of commemorating the third day after death), but after that Allah's will must be accepted.

Another widespread practice, tombstone unveilings or openings, suggests a further 'cultural merger between Islander and South-East Asian Muslim rites'.[135] The tombstone is wrapped in fabric and unveiled a year after burial. The religious and cultural origins of tombstone openings are unclear, but it is conceivable that they were inspired by Muslim families' practice of wrapping the body of the deceased in white cloth before burial (coffins are not traditionally used in Islamic burials). Kathleen Hirakawa (née Seden) recalls that when a Malay died, the relatives did not want others to touch the body. Malay family members prepared and buried the deceased themselves, with men preparing the male dead and women attending to the females. The body, in line with Islamic practice, was washed according to the rules of *wudu* (ritual ablutions, as before prayer) and wrapped in white fabric. The deceased, again according to Islamic practice, was buried as quickly as possible, preferably within twenty-four hours. In her recollections of her grandmother's death, Kathleen states:

> When Nene [grandma] died ... they'd [female relatives] wash the body down, wipe the body down, they'd dress her in white calico. No clothes, just the wrapping. Then they'd make like a [head] scarf out of the same material ... The feasting was after we buried the body ... The body had to be buried in 24 hours after death. We never put it in a morgue or anything like that. The body had to be buried 24 hours after the doctor proclaimed that person dead. The body would be all night at home ... everybody would be sitting around praying all night ... After the body was buried, three days [later] they'd have a cup of tea just among the men that prayed around the body, and then there was the seven-day feast – just a cup of tea and sandwiches and biscuits, and there was just a few [people], and then after 40 days, there'd be another feasting, and then there'd be 100 days when they'd say the body [spirit] had gone, reached its destination. That used to be a real big feast. They'd have rice, everything except pork.[136]

With the passing of time, the years of integration with the wider community and the death of the older Malays, younger generations of Malay descendants have become less committed to carrying on the religious ideals and traditions of their fathers and forefathers. The Malay community has also dwindled in size. The decline in the pearl-shelling industry and the advent of World War II were the most significant contributing factors. With the mobilisation of troops into the north, whites finally became numerically dominant. On the mainland the wartime evacuation of white and Asian women and children and the removal of Aborigines resulted in the decimation of the north and north-west's once strong multiethnic societies.[137]

The wartime evacuation of the European and 'Coloured' populations from Thursday Island also effectively destroyed its prewar Asian communities and their distinctive Indigenous–Asian culture.[138] In recalling the changes wrought by the advent of war for the Thursday Island Malay community, Jamel Shibasaki laments: 'They [used to] abide by all the right ways for funerals and other ceremonies. Then, as the old fellas died, there was nobody to carry on. Then the war broke out. That buggered everything. My [Muslim Malay] grandfather started to teach me and my brother how to say prayers. And we were just learning, then the war started and blew everything away.'[139]

Most remained on the mainland, and only a minority of the pre-war Asian families returned to Thursday Island. Without the constant infusion of newcomers from Asia, none of the previous 'Malaytown' communities in Torres Strait,[140] Broome or Darwin could be reconstituted – physically, ideologically or religiously. Notwithstanding the apparent decline in Muslim Malay practice in Australia's Top End, the next chapter takes a closer look at the religious legacy of these early Muslim sojourners and settlers on the lives of a number of families with Malay heritage. Despite the strong Japanese presence and influence before World War II, the result of Japanese wartime internment and repatriation has meant that the Malay Muslim influence is clearly the strongest Asian element still extant in Broome, Darwin and on Thursday Island.[141]

TWO

TELLING IT LIKE IT WAS

Chapter 1 provided a brief overview of pre-colonial and colonial connections between various Muslim and Indigenous communities across Australia. How were these broad patterns of human encounter experienced personally? How was their social influence registered in families, and what have been the long, intergenerational consequences of Indigenous and Muslim alliances? This chapter approaches these questions through the recollections of men and women who have married into or been born into Indigenous–Muslim families. Some are the descendants of the Afghan cameleers, others have Malay forebears. A number of interviewees are of Torres Strait Islander descent, the majority have Aboriginal ancestry. The narrators whose stories are told here have a keen eye for the external features of Islam. In later chapters, as we progressively approach the spiritual core of Islam's meaning to Indigenous people, it is the invisible rules and principles that come to the fore, but here family recollections focus on the more obvious external signs of Islamic influence: prayer, eating habits and prohibitions and, of course, high expectations of filial duty and respect. A feature of the lived reality of Islam then and now is the confirmation it provides of the centrality of community: Islam, at least in the stories related here, is a personal story of community survival.

The Makassan trepangers were seasonal visitors to Australia's north and north-western coastline. Their annual stopovers had a lasting influence on the Aboriginal people, culture and belief systems of the region, but the Muslim fishermen, unlike their Afghan and Malay counterparts, did not reside here permanently. As such there are perhaps no people living today who have had direct contact with these early Asian seafarers, yet there are many first- and second- (and subsequent) generation Indigenous–Malay and Aboriginal–Afghan descendants in Australia, and their recollections are the focus of this chapter. Rather than treat Malay and Afghan descendant families discretely, they are considered together as inheritors of Islamic religious and cultural traditions. Despite the spatial, temporal, legislative and industry-based differences between divergent Muslim communities in Australia, Indigenous–Muslim descendants articulate relative homogeneity in their experiences. Recent interviews with Aboriginal–Afghan descendants from the Akbar, Khan, Mahomed, Rind, Sahanna, Satour and Sultan families, and those conducted with Indigenous–Malays, including the Ahmat, Bin Awel, Bin Bakar, Bin Demin, Bin Juda, Bin Swani, Mokak, Nasir and Shibasaki families, reveal a considerable degree of overlap in their stories and identities.

Passages to Islam

The Afghan and Malay Muslims who came to Australia, whether as indentured labourers or 'free' immigrants, had usually left countries where Muslims were in the majority. Their religious practice in their homelands may have been 'automatic' or 'unreflective', but in Australia they were cultural, religious and social minorities and were thus liable to be drawn to reflect on their religious identity.[1] What had formerly been a conventional identification might assume a special personal significance in the new environment, a development that could have a significant influence on the way Muslim fathers and husbands interacted with their Australian-born families.

Nameth Khan, for example, who came to Australia in 1892 and died in Marree in 1950 at the age of eighty-two, was a devout Muslim and raised his children according to the Islamic religious and cultural traditions of his homeland. His granddaughter Marilyn Robertson (née Khan) believes that her grandfather's staunch adherence to his traditions was in part a reaction to the novelty of his situation and to the rapidly changing socio-economic environment: 'It would have been hard for everybody at that time, things were changing. Their lives were changing before their eyes and they really had no control over it.'[2] Experiencing the rise and demise of the Afghan camel-carting industry and the subsequent decline in the cameleer community, 'Grandfather must have been frightened too', reflects Marilyn's sister Beatrice Boerkamp (née Khan): 'like all the old Afghans that were up there [in Marree] that had created this new world for themselves, but [were] still really steeped in their own ways. It must have been so frightening that they lost their own country, and they were now ready to lose what they came here to make

… I guess that's why they hung on so much [to their Islamic traditions].'³

Beatrice (or Zanzibar) was, like her siblings, given both an English and an Afghan name as a child. Her mother Goolbegum Khan was the only child of Peshawar-born Nameth Khan and Afghan–Yankuntjatjara woman Galana Hackam. According to Beatrice, her Afghan 'grandfather was a very strict disciplinarian. He was a Muslim, and his family would live the life of a Muslim as long as he was alive. And we did, oh believe me.' Beatrice's sister Marilyn (whose Afghan name is Fatima) agrees, saying, 'We were brought up in the Muslim way … very strong Muslim ways, very strict.' Other Indigenous–Muslim descendants recount similar experiences. Mona Wilson (née Akbar) describes her Peshawar-born father as a devout follower of Islam who 'kept his faith till the day he died'.⁴ Similarly, the late Aboriginal–Malay Septu Brahim stressed that his father 'was a strict Moslem … [who] practised it very, very strongly'.⁵

In these and many other Indigenous–Muslim families, seeing their father at prayer was a common occurrence. As a young child Joanne Nasir remembers walking in on her Indonesian Muslim grandfather while in *sujud* (prostration to God). As noted in chapter 1, Muslims prostrate while facing Makkah (or Mecca), with the palms of both hands, their forehead, nose, knees and all toes touching the ground. Unaware that her grandfather was engaged in ritual prayer, Joanne assumed 'he [was] looking for something under the bed!'⁶ Some descendants recall their fathers and/or grandfathers donning Muslim prayer caps. The short, rounded prayer caps are not compulsory in Islam, but many men believe it is more respectful to cover one's head during salat or daily prayers. The Prophet Muhammad is also said to have worn a head covering, so some Muslims wear one to emulate him, as a way of obeying and following his traditions. Other descendants recollect their Muslim fathers using prayer mats. Prayer mats are designed to keep the worshipper clean and comfortable during the requisite prostrations. During prayer a niche or arch at the top of the mat is pointed in the direction of Makkah and, in particular, to the sacred cube-shaped shrine, the Kaaba, in the centre of Makkah.

Afghan and Malay descendants also recall the reverential way in which their fathers and grandfathers treated their holy book, the Qur'an (Koran). It was often carefully wrapped in layers of silk or other fabric, or in a sarong or pillow case, and some Muslims kept it high above the head as a mark of respect. Joanne Nasir's grandfather kept his Qur'an 'tied in his sarong type of handkerchief above his bed', warning the children, 'If you ever touch this, your hands will fall off.' Even after her grandfather died, no one in Joanne's family wanted to go near his Qur'an!

However, generalisation is difficult. Other descendants noted that their fathers were *less* committed to their religion than their Muslim peers. Born on Thursday Island in 1924, Eva Salam Peacock is the daughter of a Makassan father and Torres Strait Islander mother (of Islander, Danish and Sri Lankan descent).[7] According to Eva, her father 'wasn't a very religious man. I didn't see him do all the things that religious Muslims do.'[8] Speaking in our interview of her Muslim stepfather, who came to Broome from Singapore in the 1930s, Sally Bin Demin recalls, 'My stepfather never prayed that much.'[9] This apparent variety in religious devotion indicates that these religious minorities negotiated their relationship with the dominant society in a number of ways. Some sought to manage the transition to a new life and culture by abandoning their religious practices altogether; others practised their faith in private; some expected their wives and children to become Muslim, while others took a more ecumenical approach and lived happily in multicultural and polytheist households and communities.

Writing of contemporary Muslim immigrants to Australia, Gary Bouma, Joan Daw and Riffat Munawar suggest that some choose to withdraw by focusing on their own community and shunning relationships with the larger society. Muslims who fail to negotiate a place in their new homeland can look back nostalgically to the society they left behind. They may take exception to what they perceive to be the immorality, decadence or lack of religious commitment of members of the host society. Other Muslims take up the opportunity to participate actively in the community life of the larger society. In all likelihood Muslim immigrants to Australia, both historically and in the contemporary period, may engage in each option to varying degrees, either simultaneously or at different times.[10]

Notwithstanding this diversity, evidence of the strong desire of Afghan cameleers to maintain an Islamic identity in Australia is apparent in their early twentieth-century lobbying of the Australian Government to permit religious leaders to enter the country to serve the community's religious needs.[11] The building of mosques is another firm indication of their wish to preserve their religious practices and identities. In the early days resident Afghan and Malay Muslims either prayed alone in their houses or attended the congregational prayer sessions held in a room set aside in the house of one of the senior Muslim men. The Afghans built roughly hewn bush mosques in many remote locations, and in Adelaide (built 1888–89), Perth (1905) and Brisbane (1907), Muslim locals went to immense effort and expense to secure land and fund the building of permanent mosques.

Community spirit

People removed from familiar support networks and beset by cultural and socio-economic difficulties in a strange land tend 'to seek support among those with whom they share some commonality'.[12] In Australia, Afghan and Malay Muslims each created social and religious connections with compatriots and other Muslims. Chapter 1 illustrated the important role the various 'Ghantowns' or camps dotted throughout inland Australia played in the Afghan communities' negotiation of a new life in a new country. They were places of religious guidance, friendship and support and where recent arrivals could learn from the more established Afghans how to navigate an alien system and society.

The 'Malaytowns' or quarters in northern Australian coastal communities were also sites where ethnic and religious identities could be sustained and renewed. Mosques, including that built in Broome in the 1930s, strengthened community, cultural and religious bonds, too.[13] Broome resident Georgina Kaissis is the daughter of an Aboriginal mother (whose people are from Broome and Beagle Bay) and an Indonesian father who came to Broome to work in the pearl-shelling industry in 1936. She recalls Broome's close-knit Malay community in this way: 'I grew up knowing that my Dad came from Indonesia, and I was constantly surrounded by all the uncles – well, they had to be uncles because they were sort of like brothers to my father, because they were away from their families and their country, and here they were in this little community, so they got together. Their kids were kind of like my cousins – that's just the way that you grew up, because it's a connection.'[14]

Sally Bin Demin recalls seeing the Malay men in Broome's Malay quarters engaged in *silat*, a martial art form practised throughout the Malay Archipelago.[15] Others, including sisters Majunia and Rose Bin Swani (the daughters of an Aboriginal–Japanese mother and Singapore-born Muslim father), have very fond memories of the wonderful smells of the delicious food, including rice, curries and satays that the young Malay men shared with them and their siblings. Mark Bin Bakar was raised by his Kitja Aboriginal mother and Malay father (who is of Malay, Chinese and Arabic descent and who came to Australia from Singapore in 1950). He recalls his visits to the Malay lodgings on the foreshore when growing up in Broome in the 1960s:

> I felt very free when I went up to the Malay quarters … I could do what I liked up there and I used to run through the men's quarters that were laid out like an army camp with lines and lines of beds. I felt at home there. Dad used to take us to the Malay quarters prior to going down to the creek for fishing and crabbing. We'd drag all these Malay boys with us to the creek and would come back with all this fish … The kitchen there was a big communal one and … there were big pots of curries and chillies which gave off a beautiful aroma.[16]

Disagreements and in-fighting within Muslim communities in Australia occurred, of course, but Malays and Afghans also supported their compatriots in a variety of ways. Those who had been in Australia for many years, or were proficient in English, acted as interpreters for their less experienced counterparts in any dealings with police and other officials. Many Afghans and Malays offered financial support to newcomers, or a meal and a place to sleep for those who needed them. Majunia and Rose Bin Swani recall that when their Malay father died (in Broome in 1975), the younger itinerant Malay pearl-shell workers, who regarded him as a father, regularly came to their aid. The young Malay men helped the

Bin Swani family with odd jobs, brought them cooked meals and generally supported them in any way they could. Darwin-raised Joanne Nasir notes that her Muslim grandfather was 'very considerate to his fellow Indonesians and relations. He offered his family and his property and everything else, and if anybody was travelling through, [our family's twenty-acre property] was their meeting ground.' In the 1920s a number of Afghan men came to the aid and support of Peshawar-born Jack Akbar, who was fleeing Western Australia's Chief Protector of Aborigines for engaging in an 'illicit' affair with his Aboriginal partner Lallie (a story we return to in chapter 4). According to their daughter Mona Wilson (née Akbar), it was because of the help offered by her 'father's people', and a dear friend in Farina (in South Australia), that her parents made their way safely to Adelaide, where they were married.[17]

Afghan and Malay Muslims created their own ethnic and religious networks of support, but this did not preclude their engagement with the wider Australian community. Some Muslims, particularly in the early days, had limited contact with non-Muslim society, but over time the majority became active participants in their local communities. Christine Stevens notes that any Australian drovers, miners and bush people who happened to encounter a group of Afghans on their travels 'frequently found them welcoming and hospitable'.[18] They shared food, shelter and the warmth of their campfires with the visitors, placing an equal emphasis on hospitality back in the 'Ghantowns'. Some white Australian men worked side by side with the Afghans, while others worked closely with Malay men. In the event that an Afghan or Malay required a character reference, it was often white storekeepers and other influential townsfolk who did them this favour.[19] In Broome Anthea Demin, of Aboriginal–Malay heritage, notes that the local Muslim men have been long supporters of the town's church and school through their contributions to fundraising and other events.[20]

Festivals held at the end of the month-long fast of Ramadan were eagerly attended by Muslims and non-Muslims alike. The holy month of Ramadan is the ninth month of the Islamic lunar calendar, during which Muslims abstain from food, water and sexual relations each day from sunrise to sunset.[21] In the absence of food, drink and other pleasures Muslims can concentrate on prayer and worship without distraction. The festival marking the end of Ramadan is known in Arabic as Eid ul-Fitr. Europeans and others living near Afghan communities knew the huge communal feasts as 'Afghan Christmas'. Curries, rice, fruit and sweets were served, with dancing and singing, and gifts given to the Afghan, white Australian and Aboriginal children.[22] In Broome the Malay Muslims also invited non-Muslims to celebrate 'Malay Christmas' or Hari Raya, the Malay term for Eid ul-Fitr. The Malays not only fulfilled their religious obligations but also contributed to the town's social fabric. In Mark Bin Bakar's words: 'We used to have it at Malay quarters and everyone went to it, the whole town went to it. It didn't matter if you were white or black, everyone celebrated Hari Raya. For every one Malay there were probably two non-Muslims.'[23]

Today's Indigenous–Muslim descendants are woven into close-knit communities. Mark Bin Bakar maintains that he shares a special affinity with other Aboriginal–Malays in Broome: 'We're like kin to each other because we have a common background together, not only Aboriginality, but Malay or Muslim understanding.' As noted in the Introduction, Afghan descendant families organise and attend regular reunions, and when Mona Wilson went to a 2005 reunion of Afghan descendant families in Marree she was reminded again of the commonalities in their experiences: 'it was surprising how, even though we'd grown up miles apart, we all had the same upbringing' (see figure 7).

Routine, punctuality and cleanliness

Islam carries within it a set of laws and practices that guide and regulate every facet of one's life. A good example is Islamic prayers. Not only are they conducted at specific times of the day they also take a very particular and ritualised form. Each day practising Muslims bow down to Allah in prayer five times. The first prayer is offered up just before the sun rises, the second occurs at noon, the third is given in the afternoon, the fourth prayer is said at sunset and the fifth in the evening. Prayers take around ten to fifteen minutes to perform, and Muslims are expected to recite particular Arabic verses at specific stages while engaging in a ritualised series of movements that includes prostration and rising to sitting and standing positions.

It is little wonder that all Indigenous–Muslim interviewees, Afghan and Malay descendants alike, discussed the emphasis in their families on order, routine and punctuality. Born in the 1930s in regional South Australia, Shirley Wilson (née Akbar) is the daughter of a Peshawar-born Muslim father and an Aboriginal mother. She claims that her father adhered very strictly to his routines: 'Dad worked to a timetable. He did certain things on certain days, and he was always there at certain times. You could set your clock by him and that's what he did, and that's how we grew up.'[24]

Sally Bin Demin was raised in the post-World War II period in Broome. She described her upbringing with her Jaru Aboriginal mother and Muslim Malay stepfather as 'very disciplined'. She,

Telling it like it was   69

too, was expected to follow strict rules and to adhere to schedules. Like Majunia and Rose Bin Swani, members of another Broome Aboriginal–Malay family, Sally faced severe recriminations if she was not home from school by a certain time. As she says: 'If we weren't home by five o'clock, that was it. I'd be locked out sometimes. I was terrified of the dark so they'd make us sit in the dark, try to teach you a lesson ... I think that's where we got a lot of discipline from – everything on time.'

A strong emphasis on cleanliness was another significant feature of Indigenous–Muslim households. The children were expected regularly to clean the house and keep the yard neat and tidy. Born and raised in Darwin, Indigenous–Malay descendant 'Sarah' recalls, 'It was really strict, the whole household. We spring-cleaned on a Sunday, every Sunday – it was like a routine.'[25] Shirley Wilson notes that her Muslim father and Aboriginal mother were both tidy people, and they expected the same of their children: 'Well, Dad and Mum were both very clean. We only lived in a tin shanty, tin shed it was, with dirt floors and lino on the floor, but it had to be washed and polished all the time.' Later in our conversation Shirley summed up the abiding rules of her parents' household: 'Well, you had to be honest, you had to be hard-working, you had to be clean.' Sally Bin Demin's first husband was a Muslim from Malaysia (who came to Broome in 1955 to work in the pearl-shelling industry). The couple's son Johari noted, with regard to his upbringing, that 'you always had to be working and you always had to be busy and you always had to dress well'.[26]

Indigenous–Muslim descendants recall that they not only had to clean the house and yard, they also had to be clean and tidy themselves. Members of the Bin Swani and Bin Demin families noted that they had to bathe by sunset every afternoon – or else!

As children they accepted this requirement but did not always understand it. Upon reflection as adults they realised it was no doubt a legacy of their fathers' firm conviction that one must be clean before the *maghrib*, or sunset prayers. Sally Bin Demin's daughter Anthea recalled, 'As kids, if we didn't have a bath by five o'clock we were punished. And that's to do with prayer time – one of their evening prayers. But we didn't know that. We just knew we had to be bathed and clean by five o'clock as kids. But later on you work it out and it's right on their prayer time. It was a huge thing not to be clean by five o'clock.'

Even though the children were generally not engaged in performing prayers (a point we return to in chapter 3), this is an interesting example of the way Indigenous–Muslim households were organised around Islamic rituals. Before each of the five daily prayers Muslims perform *wudu*, or ritualised ablutions. They wash their faces, hands, arms (up to the elbows), heads and feet (up to the ankles) three times, commencing with the Arabic phrase *Bismillah* ('in the name of Allah').

For Shirley Wilson the directive to be clean and tidy came from both her parents. Other descendants stressed that it was not only their Muslim male forebears; their Indigenous female forebears also placed much emphasis on being clean. Darwin-raised Joanne Nasir, who had close contact during her upbringing with Abu Hassan Bin Nasir, her Indonesian Muslim grand-father (a former pearl-shell worker), and her Djugun Aboriginal grandmother Crescentia Carter, recalls that her grandmother also stressed the importance of being clean: 'My nanna used to run around and say cleanliness is next to godliness.' This was no doubt a legacy of her upbringing on a Christian mission. Almost all of the Aboriginal women who married or entered relationships with Afghan and Malay Muslim men were raised on religious missions or government reserves. Many had non-Indigenous (including white, Asian or Afghan) fathers and were members of the Stolen Generations. Their daily lives were characterised by strict routines, and they were obliged to observe the rules and regulations imposed on them. Punctuality, cleanliness and hard work were absolute requirements.

Growing up in such a regulated environment, it is little wonder that mission-raised Aboriginal women sometimes had similar expectations of their own children. The women's upbringing might also have contributed to the high incidence of Indigenous–Muslim intermarriage. Aboriginal women might have perceived Muslim men as suitable partners and husbands because they each came from environments where order, routine and structure were highly valued (this theme is explored further in chapter 4). Not all descendants commented on their mothers' and grandmothers' adherence to rules, but all of them noted that strictness was one of the defining features of their Muslim fathers and grandfathers. Was this borne of the men's Islamic cultural upbringing with its emphasis on accepted codes of conduct? Might the men have insisted on their Australian family's adherence to particular modes of behaviour because they were in a changing environment? Holding fast to the familiar practices of their homelands might have been one way in which they could reassert control over their lives.

High achievers

Muslim fathers and grandfathers expected their children to be punctual and clean, but they also expected them to work hard and do every job properly. Semah Mokak-Wischki's Muslim Malaysian father placed a very high emphasis on these qualities in his household. As she recalls: 'When we went fishing or when we went hunting or when we washed the car or when we cut the lawn, it had to be done properly. High standards were [set] in our family – hard working ethics.'[27] Semah's cousin Joanne Nasir's experiences were similar. Her Indonesian Muslim grandfather also stressed the importance of fully applying oneself to one's work or any other undertaking. In Joanne's words, her *Datu*'s[28] attitude was: 'If you can't do something really well, then don't bother doing it at all. So put your heart and soul in it. If you're not prepared to do that, don't start it. So I listened to that.' In Mark Bin Bakar's upbringing, 'You had to strive to achieve something with your life. You had to make a difference, and that's been the driving force of who I am.'

As children, the Malay and Afghan descendants I met often resented what Semah Mokak-Wischki described as the 'extremely controlling' environment in which they were raised. In recalling their family life their grand/fathers' authoritarian and uncompromising attitude was almost always a topic of discussion. On the whole Indigenous–Malays and Aboriginal–Afghans were raised by people who were extremely proud, principled and honest. Shirley Wilson stressed that she and her siblings were brought up 'to be respectful, and to have self-respect, because if you don't respect yourself, you don't respect other people … and [Father] always said you have to have principles. A lot of people used to call him "Jack Principle Akbar".' According to Mark Bin Bakar, his Malay father is 'pious and very honest and very real. Sometimes very frustrating to work with, too, 'cause he's so honest. So there's no bending of the rules. For example, if he gave you something, or if he says to you "I'll give you this", ten years later if you came back he'd say, "Well, that thing's still here for you." If he made a promise to give you something, he'll give it to you.'

The strict discipline and hard work ethic Indigenous–Muslim descendants had imposed on them were not appreciated in childhood, but as adults they all agreed they had derived immense benefit from them. This was because, to quote Mark Bin Bakar, the 'Muslim upbringing' these descendants had 'had a form of discipline as well as pride'. As Semah recounts: 'One of the most fantastic things that has come out of our upbringing is that … whatever we do, whether it's gardening or in the house, or studying, we've got from our father [to always] do your best.' The professional and personal success Indigenous–Muslims enjoy today is, they feel, directly attributable to the ethics and values that predominated in their households. Speaking of their Malaysian father, Semah's sister Halimah claims, 'I'm really thankful to him for that discipline now … because I don't think we would have ever, ever progressed or achieved what we have today. And even though they were hard times, I'm really thankful for that.'[29] This sentiment is echoed by Mark Bin Bakar, who asserts:

> I grew up with hard-core discipline. I was flogged in public as a child for misbehaving, and I'm not unique. We all were in one way or another, and there was no shame factor. If you stuffed up, you stuffed up, and it's moulded me to who I am today. And I've got no regrets at all and I went through a lot of pain with it, but it's made me what I am and it's taught me a lot of things about life, like discipline, focus, aspirations, dreams, and to follow your dreams.

Many Indigenous–Muslim descendants count themselves lucky, particularly in relation to other Indigenous people who have not had such an upbringing. Growing up around the Northern Territory's Adelaide and Daly Rivers, Halimah Mokak was aware of the 'big difference' between her upbringing and that of 'a lot of the Indigenous kids around us – you know, white father, Indigenous mother or both Indigenous parents'. Darwin-raised 'Sarah' is also conscious of the differences between her upbringing and 'some of the kids we see these days that never had that strictness on them'. As she says, 'They have no respect for anything in life, or for themselves.' Shirley Wilson agrees, claiming that 'that's what's lacking in the world today, a lot of the young ones don't have self-respect'. Mark Bin Bakar contends that the Muslim Asian influence has been a 'saviour for a lot of the Aboriginal people' in Broome and elsewhere in the Top End. It has helped them take control of their lives after years of institutionalised paternalism. Mark is speaking here of Indigenous–Malay descendants, but his sentiment applies equally to Aboriginal people with connections to Muslim Afghans. As he says: 'The Asian influence … taught us to be visionary, it taught us to aspire to something, to achieve something, to make something of yourself – a better way of managing money, get a job because if you get a job then you'll have money, and if you have money then you can buy this and this. Little basic things that taught a lot of children of Aboriginal–Malay heritage to be able to go to that next level.'

Pork

Differing levels of religious commitment among Afghan and Malay Muslims were also reflected in the observance (or otherwise) of Islamic dietary requirements. Muslims do not eat 'the flesh of swine' because the Qur'an prohibits its consumption. It is considered to be unclean and not fit for human use. An example of the Afghans' abhorrence of pigs is recounted by Pamela Rajkowski. Around 1900 some pigs belonging to the Marree butchers found their way into the ablution pool situated outside the mosque. The Afghans were so horrified by what they viewed as the defilement of their pool that they shot and killed every pig. In the fighting that ensued the local butchers retaliated by insulting the Afghans in a most injurious way – by throwing the dead pigs into the mosque.[30] This next story, told by Aboriginal–Afghan descendant Douglas Walker, is further testament of the revulsion pigs might inspire. As a child in the 1950s Douglas's father told him a story about an old Afghan in Farina (South Australia) who one day noticed, while working in his shop, that some pigs had wandered into his house and yard. The Afghan stopped what he was doing, left his shop unattended and upon reaching his weatherboard house proceeded to burn it down![31]

The Afghans' detestation of pork was well known among the wider non-Muslim population, and practical jokes were often played on them by white children and adults alike. Azeem (Johnny) Khan, the son of an Aboriginal mother and Aboriginal–Afghan father, recalls that his father once ordered a leg of lamb from the butcher in Salisbury (South Australia), only to find when unwrapping it at home that it was in fact pork. According to Johnny: 'Dad took it back to the butcher and threw it at the bloke and jumped over the counter and bang, he gave him a good hiding. He said, "I thought you were my mate. You're not a mate of mine if you're going to treat me like this." I don't think the butcher played any jokes with anyone like that again!'[32]

In her research on the Afghan camelmen, Rajkowski found that it was well known among the wider community that one way to prevent the Afghans and their camels from drinking from unguarded waterbags was to hang a rasher of bacon nearby.[33] Dean Gool Mahomed, born in Marree in 1941, whose parents were both of Aboriginal–Afghan descent, recalls that local whites pulled a similar stunt when he was growing up. In leaving the

Marree railway station one had to pass through a set of double gates. One day a 'white lad put a pig's head on the gate'.[34] The Afghans, unamused by the 'joke', forwent their usual route through the gate and proceeded through the turnstiles instead.

Fatima (Marilyn) Robertson's Aboriginal–Afghan mother had such a strong aversion to pork that she even found the distant sight of pigs highly unpleasant. In our conversation Marilyn related an incident that occurred on the famous 'Ghan' train (named in honour of the Afghan cameleers). She and her mother were travelling down from Marree to Adelaide when 'next minute we were going past a yard, and it was a pig pen and poor Mum – I'm sorry we ever sat her near the window! She spat [in contempt] all over the window. She just kept spitting all the way, over the whole window!'.

The Muslim Malays also ate strictly in accordance with their faith, and on the luggers they avoided tinned food if the label had been washed off in case it contained pork products.[35] Carol Tang Wei's Aboriginal mother and Chinese father (who arrived in Broome to work in the pearl-shelling industry in 1928) ran a successful noodle and long soup restaurant until the early 1980s. It was a meeting place for the Broome Asian community and, as Carol recounts, was especially busy during the 'lay-up season when the Japanese divers used to come in, and all the people who used to crew on the boats used to come in and they just used to sit here and have long soup'. She continues: 'And they had their various preferences, which sort of reflected their ethnic background. For instance, some of the Japanese liked their long soup with raw eggs, and of course the Malays, who are of Islamic background, used to order their long soup with no ham.'[36]

Pork was almost entirely absent from the vast majority of Indigenous–Muslim households. Virtually every descendant I spoke to commented on their families' avoidance of ham, bacon and other pork products. Halima Binti Hassan Awal grew up on Thursday Island just after World War II. She is the daughter of an Indonesian Muslim father and a Malaysian–Torres Strait Islander mother. When I asked her if she understood as a child why she, unlike her friends, was not permitted to eat pork, she replied: 'Oh, we were Muslims. We weren't allowed to eat pork. That was it. So we just accepted it. That was the law.'[37] The late Indigenous–Malay Septu Brahim recalled that under no circumstances did he or his Aboriginal mother ever eat pork,[38] while 'Sarah' maintains, 'Pig was a dirty animal … we weren't allowed to have bacon, you know, bacon and eggs – like normal people!' By distinction, Eva Salam Peacock's Muslim Malay father 'wouldn't eat pork', but he 'loved camp pie'. The irony was not lost on Eva: 'Everybody would look at him and say, "You're Muslim, eh? You don't eat pig, eh?" I'd say, "Well, what are you eating there?" He'd say, "Meat".'[39]

Not only did Indigenous–Muslim descendants avoid eating pork, the majority could not even say the word 'pig' without being severely reprimanded. As Shirley Wilson recalls: 'I got into trouble for coming home one day when I was learning to read, singing out "pig", and I got a whack for that. And [Father] said, "Don't ever say that dirty word in this house ever again." And I said, "What dirty word?" He replied, "*That* dirty word." There was never an explanation, it was just "Do it", or "Don't do it". You just didn't do it again.'

Zanzibar (Beatrice) Boerkamp was told the following story by her Aboriginal–Afghan mother. One day her mother's two brothers had been drinking alcohol, a major source of disquiet for their devoutly Muslim, Peshawar-born father. He expressed his disapproval, claiming:

'Oh, you drink like white men, you make yourself silly in the head, and people laugh at you', and because they'd had a drink, they started laughing at him. And he was getting riled up and puffing out his cheeks, and then they swore at him. One of them turned around and said, 'You silly old pig.' Well, that was it. All you could see was his pantaloons, he was moving so fast his pantaloons were flapping in the wind like sheets, and he ran and got his swords off the wall. He ran towards [his sons] with the swords and Mum shot through and got the sergeant and they took Uncle Rocky and Uncle Akbar and they locked them up, they locked them up to save them!

Many Indigenous–Muslim descendants still avoid eating pork today. Others eat it occasionally, but niggling pangs of guilt always attend its consumption. Esther Kite is a descendant of the Arabana (near Lake Eyre in South Australia) and Arrernte people (near Alice Springs in the Northern Territory). She was married for twenty-two years to the late Rameth Nameth (Rocky) Khan, of Afghan and Aboriginal descent. As she recalls, '[Rocky] was against anything that had ham in it, so we would never have ham. Even now I feel guilty – sometimes I'll have a bit of ham or bacon, and at the same time I feel so guilty.'[40] Semah Mokak-Wischki is the daughter of an Aboriginal–Indonesian mother and Malaysian Muslim father (who came to Australia in the 1950s from a small village near Kuala Lumpur). For Semah, her father's insistence that she and her siblings avoid pork has had a lasting influence. She recalls eating pork as an adult in this way:

When I went to Europe for the first time and ate salami I had so much guilt about it because of what I had absorbed as a child about how wrong it was to be eating it. Even though I was enjoying it, it still took me a while to say, 'Hey, it's OK, it's just something about the mind. I'm not going to drop dead. I'm not going to be struck by God.' But those things are real when you've been brought up [with them], they're quite real.

It is not only Indigenous–Muslim descendants who avoid or eat little pork. Philip Jones, senior curator at the South Australian Museum's Department of Anthropology, has had extensive contact with Aboriginal people in north-eastern South Australia. He has a keen interest in the history of the Birdsville Track and, in several oral history interviews with elderly Aborigines from that area, noticed their 'seeming aversion towards pork'.[41] This avoidance of pork, he claims, was not so much 'a personal aversion … but a cultural one':

> I believe it probably comes from a sort of shared world view that perhaps the cameleers put across to the Aboriginal people. Bearing in mind that some of these Aboriginal women had relationships with the cameleers and then maybe moved back into their own society, it is certainly feasible that this basic refusal to eat certain sorts of meat, and the idea that it was somehow unclean – and this was the basis of their dislike of pork – is something which must have come from the Afghans.

Halal food

Goatherds were raised on pastoral stations, in towns and by Afghan families in the Marree 'Ghantown'. The Afghans would have been familiar with goats from their homelands, and here, as there, they and their families commonly ate goat meat. Goats were relatively inexpensive to buy, and selling the milk, or the butter made from it, provided families with a livelihood as well as food.[42] Mona Wilson commented that she and her siblings were 'reared on goats'. They ate so much of it, she claimed, that they were akin to 'walking goats!' In addition to goats the Akbar family kept chickens, ducks and turkeys. Mona states that 'they [Muslims] don't have those infidels touching their meat or anything'. For this reason her Peshawar-born father killed and prepared their meat himself. Provided that the animal was killed in the correct Islamic manner, it was deemed halal. 'Halal' is an Arabic term used to describe any object or action that is deemed permissible or acceptable under Islamic law. It can encompass an individual's behaviour, speech, clothing, manner or dietary intake, but is customarily used in 'the West' with reference to Muslim dietary requirements.

Dhabiha is the Arabic name of the prescribed method of ritual slaughter in Islam (based not on Qur'anic mandate but Islamic tradition). It must be carried out with the animal facing Makkah and involves the use of a very sharp knife to cut the major arteries in the animal's neck with one swipe of the blade. This, it is claimed, provides a relatively painless death for the animal and allows for the draining of its blood. This is very important because the Qur'an forbids the consumption of blood. All this must be done while acknowledging God's creation and thanking God for providing sustenance by saying a prayer. During the ritualised slaughter of meat and poultry (excluding fish and most sea-life), the following phrase must be said: '*Bismillah* ["in the name of Allah"] *Allahu Akbar* ["Allah is the greatest"].'

Fish and other sea creatures need not be ritually slaughtered.[43] In a conversation recorded by linguist Luise Hercus in the late 1970s or early '80s, Arabana siblings Mona Merrick and Arthur Warrren commented: 'They [Afghans] cut the throats of goats, bullocks, rabbits, rock pigeons and even waterhens: they didn't worry about cutting the throat of fish, because they've had their throats cut anyhow, ha!'[44] As a child the late Aboriginal–Afghan descendant Miriam Dadleh recalled that her Peshawar-born father taught her why this was the case:

> My brother caught a fish down in the creek and we run back with it – jumpin' you know and cuttin' our hand and we was running back with the fish. 'What you got there, my kid, my children?' We said, 'We brought this fish here for you to cut the throat for us.' He said, 'It's already cut, you see, Lord cut it, angels cut it.' He explained it to us. He said, 'When Abraham had a holy place, it wouldn't stand when he built it up – falls down – built it up – falls down – something or someone come and push it over unless he killed one of his sons … father took this little boy and put him down and blindfolded him and got this knife. Angel replaced boy with lamb, cut with the knife and threw the knife up in the air … and it landed in the sea – that's how that fish is cut.'[45]

The older generation of Afghans, in particular, adhered very strictly to *dhabiha* and halal requirements and would not accept meat killed by other people.[46] Speaking of her father and her siblings, Miriam Dadleh recalled: 'We wasn't allowed to eat meat from the butcher – Afghan slaughtered them themselves – they had to cut the throat. We was that way, too. We couldn't eat meat without the Afghan killed it – cut its throat.'[47] According to Arabana siblings Mona Merrick and Arthur Warren: 'They [the Afghans] always killed their own meat; they cut the animal's throat. If you killed meat for them they wouldn't eat it.'[48]

In another conversation recorded by Luise Hercus the late Aboriginal–Afghan Ben Murray narrated the following story of one Afghan's unwavering commitment to eating only halal food.

In the early 1930s Ben came across an elderly Afghan camping alone near Murnpeowie station (north of the Flinders Ranges in South Australia). The old man was too sick to travel to the station where he regularly obtained food and killed his own meat. When Ben encountered him he was close to starvation, waiting for a Syrian hawker who periodically passed by and killed meat for him 'Afghan way'. Ben offered to kill a sheep for the old man, but he would only accept the offer on the condition that Ben called out the appropriate prayer as he cut its throat. Ben performed the requisite rites before reporting the old man's poor condition to the station manager. Shortly after this the elderly Afghan was taken to a hospital in Adelaide where he subsequently died.[49]

Of course there were exceptions to this Afghan's uncompromising attitude. In *Tin Mosques and Ghantowns*, Christine Stevens relates the following story about prominent Afghan camel merchant and businessman Abdul Wade. He was, it seems, 'reasonably comfortable about distorting the Halal principle when it suited'. Before visiting the Gumbalie Hotel, which was situated close to his station (near Bourke in New South Wales), he would call ahead to announce his intention of taking lunch there. Upon arrival he would alight from his coach and be presented with a live chicken to kill and bleed in the halal manner. He would then enter the dining room and immediately sit down to a lunch of poultry. Afterwards, 'with a twinkle in his eye', he would compliment the hotel owner on 'the efficiency and expediency of her culinary skills'![50]

Afghan and Malay descendants have vivid memories of their fathers and/or grandfathers killing goats, chickens and other livestock in the prescribed Islamic way. Broome-raised Johari Bin Demin recalls that 'it was always an exciting time' when his Muslim Malay father was going to prepare some halal food. As he says: 'The other thing I can remember [about] being a Muslim, growing up in a Muslim family, was halal meat. All the animals, all the chicken you ate they'd slaughter them in the backyard, do halal style, and the goats and the sheep. I always remember that and it always fascinated us as little kids to watch them slit the throats of the chicken and watch them jump around, and hear [the Malay fathers] say their prayers and all that.'

Born in Renmark, South Australia, in 1939, Aboriginal–Afghan Johnny Akbar also has clear memories, though perhaps less fond, of seeing his father kill animals in the Islamic way (see figure 8). Speaking of his Peshawar-born father, Johnny recalls:

> When he was killing a goat he used to face him in the proper way, where he reckoned Mecca was, and the poor old goat, he used to cut the goat's throat. I never used to hang around for that because the goat used to be my pet. And even with a chook, when he cut the chook's throat he'd let it go and the chook used to jump around this way and that. The poor old chook, he'd be lying there and we'd have to go and get him ready to pluck him.[51]

The Afghans and their descendants commonly ate various kinds of curry. From all accounts they were delicious, but extremely hot. Almost everyone I spoke to recalled the burning sensation they felt when they first tried their male forebears' curries. They were, it seems, an acquired taste. Arabana siblings Mona Merrick and Arthur Warren recall trying the Afghans' curries (perhaps in the 1920s or '30s): 'They [the Afghans] used to cook curry. In the olden days that curry was horrible, it burnt like fire, it cut into your throat and it bit your tongue!'[52] Eaten out of bowls with the hands, the curries were usually accompanied by rice and chapattis or other flat breads. Johnny Akbar fondly recalls his father's preparation of what he called 'Indian bread' when he was a child in the 1940s: 'Dad could make beautiful bread. Big, flat, round bread on the tray ... He'd be rolling it over and over, and putting more butter in it, more butter in it.'

In another sign of the extensive trade in ideas and commodities between Aboriginal and Afghan people, some Aborigines recall being taught how to make flat bread by the Afghans. Jimmy Pike, the late Walmajarri artist (from the Great Sandy Desert, south of the Kimberleys; see figure 10), told the following story about his countrymen's instruction in the ways of what he called damper:

> The Afghans were heading west and they gave food to some people – black people – flour and raisins. When they put the flour on the fire, it just burnt ... they put the flour in the fire, dry. They didn't put any water with it. 'You have to mix it with water,' one of the Afghans told them. He'd been watching them, and he showed them how to mix the flour with water. 'That's how you make damper.' The Afghans showed them how to make damper.[53]

The Malays also had a considerable influence on the eating habits of the Indigenous people they encountered. Almost all of the Indigenous–Malay descendants I met spoke of the significance of introduced foods such as rice, chilli, curry, satay and belachan (dried prawn paste) in their daily diets. Halimah Mokak grew up in the 1960s with her Aboriginal–Indonesian mother and Malaysian Muslim father in Adelaide River in the Northern Territory (about a hundred kilometres south of Darwin). She recalls that her family's diet was a product of both Aboriginal and South-East Asian culinary influences. Chilli kangaroo and curried kangaroo were family favourites, and for a recent dinner party Halimah prepared dugong rendang (a spice and coconut milk-based dish usually made with beef). A number of Broome residents stressed that it was the Malays, in particular, who had the most significant and enduring influence on the food eaten by local Aboriginal people. In her memoir *Once in Broome* Sally Bin Demin attributes Aboriginal families' predilection for rice, ginger, curry and chilli to the influence of the Malays:

> The Malay culture has influenced cooking in Broome more than any other. Lemongrass, garlic, ginger, chilli, tamarind, coconut, coriander, turmeric and other curry spices – all these flavours are found in the dishes made in our homes … Rice came in from Singapore and we would eat it every day, sometimes more than once, and we would often have nasi bubor (rice porridge) for breakfast … Our parents would call out, 'Makan dulu', and we knew it was time to come in, for a feed. The food we shared was mainly Malay food, like hot curry, chilli fish, chilli crab, mussels and pearl meat. There was no mercy. If you didn't eat curry, you starved.[54]

Alcohol and gambling

Muslims hold that alcohol and other intoxicants are haram, or forbidden in Islam.[55] They are prohibited because they render one forgetful of God and prayer. The Qur'an (5:93) orders worshippers to abstain from them, describing intoxicants (and gambling) as an 'abomination – Satan's handiwork'. Some Afghan and Malay Muslims were just as strict in their avoidance of alcohol as they were of pork. Others shunned pork but overlooked the Islamic prohibition against the consumption of alcohol. Many Muslims in Australia, Afghans and Malays alike, commonly used intoxicants. While the Afghan camelmen customarily avoided alcohol (which perhaps contributed further to their marginalisation from the broader society), they imbibed a variety of narcotics, including hashish, marijuana and opium. Chlorodyne, an opium-based medicine that was widely available in Outback Australia, was the most easily and cheaply obtained source of opium, and many of the Afghans used it. In the 1980s, while undertaking research on the Afghan cameleers, Stevens recalls finding chips of the distinctive blue-glass chlorodyne bottles among the ruins of every Australian 'Ghantown'.[56]

In his memoir *Camels and the Outback*, H.M. Barker, who worked with his string of camels in north-west Western Australia in the 1910s, notes that while Afghans generally abstained from alcohol, the same could not be said of the Malays. As he claims, the Afghans' abstinence was more than 'made up for by other Asiatics such as Malays … and Japanese'.[57] Eva Salam Peacock recalls that her Muslim Malay father, unlike 'some of the other Muslims', avoided beer, but he did 'drink neat rum', a legacy of his time in the navy.[58] Broome's Malays are fondly remembered for their love of partying and drinking. Aboriginal–Malay descendant Majunia Bin Swani reassured me during our interview that even though they were Muslim, the Malays she knew still drank alcohol: 'They loved their partying, yes, so don't worry, they were drinking.'[59] Assan (Ken) O'Shea, who was brought up in the post-war period on Thursday Island by his adoptive Muslim Malay grandparents, recalls that while his grandfather drank alcohol, he would not do so in the house.[60] This might help explain the following comment made by Scottish-born, former long-term Thursday Island resident (and practising Muslim) Balfour Ross: 'Some of the main Muslims on Thursday Island, you find them in the pub!'[61]

'Games of chance' are also proscribed in Islam, but this did not stop the Afghans in Australia from gambling, as Stevens notes.

Card-playing and two-up were favoured pastimes of the camelmen upon their return to the 'Ghantowns' (following the completion of a carting job). Gambling was illegal in Australia, but the men often played on through the night, usually at one of the senior Afghans' houses. Relatively large sums of money were involved, and disputes were common occurrences. Skilled Afghan gamblers sometimes invited unsuspecting Aborigines to enter a card game, but the Aborigines often got more (or perhaps less) than they bargained for: 'At the German Lutheran mission on the Birdsville Track north of Marree, card playing and other forms of gambling were strictly forbidden to the Aborigines. The Lutheran pastors had noticed that the cameleers who passed through the area were well-practised gamblers. Aborigines who displayed a keen gambling interest would meet them in secret, but the shrewd Afghans would often quickly relieve them of everything they owned.'[62]

Gambling was also a popular pastime among the Malay pearl-shell workers, particularly when they were onshore during the lay-up season. Stephen (Baamba) Albert, a descendant of the Baniol people in north-west Western Australia, grew up in Broome in the 1950s. According to him, when the Asian and Aboriginal crewmen came into Broome during the wet or lay-up season, 'all they wanted to do was spend their time with people'. They were chiefly interested in what he labels the 'three Gs: gambling, grog and girls'![63] In *Once in Broome* Sally Bin Demin devotes a chapter to the gambling that went on, in gambling houses and in the houses of local residents, when the pearling luggers came ashore. Card games were popular, as was *katjakatja*, a game similar to dominoes. According to Sally, *katjakatja* was a Broome expression for *kachau kachau*, a Malay word meaning 'to stir' or 'mix up' (the local name for the Chinese game *bacau*).[64]

Afghan and Malay Muslims in Australia engaged in both halal (permitted) and haram (prohibited) activities. Muslims, in the past and today, must work out for themselves how to live in non-Muslim (and Muslim) countries. How best to fulfil the requirements of their religion while living in a largely secular society is a question all Muslims in Australia confront. The reality of living in a new land where alcohol is an important social lubricant, and what Stevens labels 'the one great unifier of men', saw some Muslims engage in behaviour deemed inappropriate in Islam.[65] This was particularly so among the younger generations of Australian-born Afghan and Malay descendants. According to Aboriginal–Afghan Miriam Dadleh, once the 'old people went they [second-generation Afghans] all went berserk, stopped doing it [practising Islam], just blooming drinking. They all have taste of grog and they forget everything.'[66] Alice Springs resident Eric Sultan is the son of an Aboriginal mother and Afghan–Irish father. A former president of the Alice Springs Islamic Society, he suggests: 'The religion was lost with assimilation with the wider community. Once the camel industry had died down, the sons of the cameleers then had to go and find work with European men, and the religion was very strict, so they didn't follow it. They had to more or less fall in line with the assimilation process.'[67]

These external pressures and constraints have influenced the Indigenous–Malay and Aboriginal–Afghan descendants' adoption of Islamic practices and traditions. Chapter 3 shows that for many people of Indigenous–Muslim heritage their sense of Islam is closely bound up with their immediate families and extended kin. Their religious identity is derived from their familial associations, not their spiritual convictions, and many consider their Muslim heritage as another cultural or ethnic attribute.

THREE

KEEPING IT IN THE FAMILY

In chapters 1 and 2 we looked at the history of Islam in Indigenous Australia first from the outside, as it were, then from the inside. From the outside, which is the perspective historians mainly adopt, the focus tends to be on broad cultural patterns. History deals in generalisations, and the subjects of historical studies rarely possess much in the way of individual personality. But *Islam Dreaming* is a book of stories. This is why, in Chapter 2, we retraversed parts of the historical information previously provided, exploring its themes from the point of view of those who were directly involved in the myriad of cross-cultural negotiations that have characterised around three centuries of Indigenous–Islamic contact, exchange and accommodation. When you do this, you do not simply swap the impersonal standpoint of history for the engaged and participatory voices of those inside history: you enter a new, reflective space in which the storytellers are not only recounting events in the past but also, in narrating them again, are actively reliving them. Oral histories are always double histories: of people and places in the past and of the meanings of these things to the storytellers themselves. In telling you what happened, storytellers, unlike historians, undisguisedly put themselves in the picture.

In this chapter, advancing further into the labyrinth of storytelling, we take in the contours of kinversion – a term I have coined to describe an Indigenous connection to Islam that is culturally – usually family – based. Recognising the difficulty of classifying the different expressions of Islam among contemporary Muslims, Abdullah Saeed proposes the term 'cultural nominalists'; that is, 'those who are usually born into Muslim families and are associated with Islam but are not interested in the beliefs or practices of Islam'.[1] The shortcoming of this term in our context is that it fails to take into account the familial piety at the heart of kinversion. Like the terms 'culturally Muslim'[2] and 'cultural Islam',[3] it does not capture the family focus of this attachment, one consistent with the emphasis on family and kin in Aboriginal culture. Kinversion manifests itself as a legacy of social rules and ethical guidelines that simultaneously honour an Islamic heritage and the family that has been drawn together and defined by it. A sign that the word fills a gap may be its adoption by more than one of my interviewees to describe their own relationship with Islam – a relationship that they feel does not have a name. No doubt *kinvert* and *kinversion* are temporary terms ahead of a better classification but, provided they are not granted a false authority, I hope they will be found useful.

Any cross-cultural accommodation can involve kinversion, and the term is not put forward here to suggest that my interviewees' experience is unique. However, it is the case that the double marginalisation Indigenous people and Muslims experience in Australia makes kinversion particularly significant. Kinversion is a powerful means of creating social cohesion, and particularly warrants recognition in a time when the rhetoric of the 'clash of civilisations' devalues ordinary sociability and the creative ways in which individuals negotiate their religious and cultural identities.

Born and raised in Darwin in the late 1960s, Indigenous–Malay descendant 'Sarah' describes her family's lineage in these terms: 'We've got Malay, Torres Strait, Mohammed and Aboriginal.' For Sarah, self-identification as a so-called 'Mohammedan' (or Muslim)[4] has very little, if anything, to do with religion. It is primarily an expression of kinship. Assan (Ken) O'Shea is another case in point. Growing up on post-war Thursday Island with his Muslim Malay (adoptive) grandparents, he notes that they were 'Mohammedans and that's the most important thing', explaining, 'For me, that's my Muslim religion, and that's my Muslim background.'[5] He elaborates: 'I know the Muslim religion by how [my grandparents] reacted and how they did things, so all [my knowledge] is from seeing and hearing; I knew nothing about the Qur'an or anything. All I know is that my grandparents were Muslims, and this is how they behaved and what their belief system was. [I learned about Islam] by going on my upbringing, and listening to and seeing what they did.'

Evidently, kin-based identification of this kind differs sharply from that associated with the formal embrace of the tenets of Islam. Based on cultural affiliation rather than a dramatic spiritual transformation, it represents a form of identification that sociological studies of conversion rarely recognise. In the context of the long, tangled history of Indigenous exposure to Islam this is particularly unfortunate as it has the effect of devaluing that historical association. In contrast with conversion – which at least in its classic formulation involves turning one's back on the past – kinversion is an act of turning towards the family history and respecting the memory of the ancestors. It is, among other things, the phenomenon widespread among people of Indigenous–Muslim descent of invoking Islam as a marker of family continuity and identity. An identification with Islamic values that is not formal but familial is the result of long-term and widespread contact between Muslims (almost invariably men) and those (almost entirely women) of Aboriginal and Torres Strait Islander background. To invoke the term is to resist the dehistoricisation of the Indigenous–Islamic experience and to remind ourselves of its persistence across generations, genders and state boundaries.

Indigenous–Malay kinverts

Balfour Ross was the president of the (now defunct) Society of Islam, operating out of Thursday Island (TI) until 2005, when he and his wife June left there to live in Malaysia. In a telephone interview just before their departure, Balfour noted that the TI Indigenous–Malay descendants 'call themselves Muslim, but they don't know much about the faith, or the holidays, or anything like that'.[6] He adds, 'It's just something their grandfathers preached [but] they had no knowledge of what it really was, and because of the Arabic scripture, they can't read [the Qur'an], so they just put it up on the shelf and forgot about it.'

Indigenous–Malay descendants, or kinverts, are extremely proud of their heritage, but for them the label 'Muslim' (or Mohammedan) is about ancestor worship, not religion. This pride is evident in the care Muslim descendant families take of the Muslim graves in the local TI cemetery. In Balfour's words: 'Although they don't practise Islam, they're very protective of the Muslim graves in the cemetery. There are over a hundred of them up there; some of them are quite elaborate – from the old days. They've all got the Arabic inscriptions on the stones. The [Malay descendant families] all got them cleaned, weeded around them and so on, repainted them. Even though the people looking after them might not be Muslim any more, they still honour their ancestors.'

Balfour, of Scottish descent, converted to Islam at the age of twenty-one (taking the Muslim name Bahauddin). He subsequently came to Australia and in the 1960s was a student at Adelaide University and the secretary of the Adelaide mosque on Little Gilbert Street (the building of which was funded by the Afghan cameleers in 1888–89). He met June's father Wahap Bin Tahal, a staunch Muslim who had been on the pilgrimage or haj and could read the Qur'an in Arabic, when Wahap was representing the Muslims of Thursday Island at an Islamic conference in Melbourne in 1963.

Wahap Bin Tahal, originally from a village outside Ambon in Indonesia, worked in the Torres Strait pearl-shelling industry (see figure 9). He met his Malaysian–Torres Strait Islander wife on Thursday Island before World War II and after returning there, following the cessation of the war, set aside a room in his house where resident Muslims could come and pray. Wahap also acted as the local imam, leading the prayers for the important Eid festivals (Eid ul-Fitr, marking the end of Ramadan, and Eid al-Adha or the 'Festival of Sacrifice', held at the end of haj). Even though Wahap came to Thursday Island as a young man and was illiterate, he, unlike many of his Malay peers, was able to deepen his knowledge of Islam. Wahap worked as a pearl-shell diver, the most highly paid and esteemed occupation among the indentured labourers. He later bought and operated a successful taxi business on TI, and was able to afford multiple return journeys to Indonesia. He also went to Makkah for haj and, as Balfour recalls, made contact with 'the religious people in those countries and got a lot of teaching he could bring back'.

After Wahap's passing in 1984, Balfour and June established a prayer room in their house. They sent letters and other literature to TI's Malay descendants, as well as copies of the Qur'an and the prayer timetable for Ramadan. They also invited the Malay descendant families to join them in celebrating the two Eid festivals. Balfour and June, like Wahap before them, also sought to reinvigorate the Muslim community on TI by inviting Muslims from other parts of Australia to come to Torres Strait. Wahap had offered accommodation to Muslims who were willing to work as Islamic instructors, and in 1964 Balfour was one of those who answered his call. Balfour and June made similar entreaties, and in 1990 a congregation of six Muslims visited TI, 'opening up a World of Islam of which most [on TI] were unaware'. In 1992 Balfour and June founded the Society of Islam to 'promote propagation of the Faith, raise money for an eventual centre and put on displays of Malay Dances'.[7] They also conducted *da'wah* or missionary work by sending basic information on Islam to various Aboriginal communities in the north of Australia (they had contacted fourteen communities by 1992). In addition, the Society of Islam made the following plea in a 1992 edition of the *Australian Muslim Times*: 'I would appeal to young Muslims to consider settling in North Queensland, a beautiful area and climate, but with far too few Muslims ... So if, say, you are unemployed in NSW, or Victoria you may still be unemployed in North Queensland, but you will by your presence be helping Islam take root – so "Come North, Young Muslims".'[8]

Despite their attempts to revitalise the Muslim community and identity on TI, by 2005 Balfour and June were the only practising Muslims on the island. Their efforts to invite or call people to Islam were circumscribed by a number of different factors. First, of course, they were extremely mindful of the Qur'anic injunction prohibiting compulsion in religion. Second, their efforts were not always welcomed because their Islamic teachings sometimes differed from the practices of the descendants' Muslim Malay male forebears. According to Balfour, kinverts 'know about not eating pork and that sort of stuff'. But, he says, 'if you try and teach them anything [else], it's like, "Oh, that's not what my grandfather did" – like you're doing something wrong. We can't tell them because we would be insulting the memory of their grandfather.' Another difficulty the Society of Islam encountered is that many Indigenous–Muslim descendants, while extremely proud of their Muslim heritage, are not interested in taking on Islam. They are content to pay tribute to their ancestors by maintaining, where possible, their Islamic religio-cultural practices, but not their spiritual beliefs. In Balfour's experience: 'Yes, the [Indigenous–Malay descendants] call themselves Muslim. But if I say, "Karim, Karim, do you want any religious books?" They say, "No, no, I keep away from that … I am a Muslim," he says [laughter].'

The Muslim Malays who came to Torres Strait, Broome and Darwin were extremely young. Many were still in their teens when they arrived to work as indentured labourers in the northern Australian pearl-shelling industry. A high proportion was illiterate and, as such, their exposure to formal Islamic religious instruction was relatively limited. They practised, as Balfour remarked, their 'own version' of Islam. Their poor English language skills, at least initially, also made it difficult to pass on information about complex religious beliefs and practices. Child-rearing was largely the responsibility of the men's locally born wives, who were barely schooled in the ways of Islam. The children's exposure to their fathers' religious beliefs was further curtailed by the men's long periods of absence while out at sea on the pearling luggers. Added to this was the impact of World War II and the decline in pearl-shelling on the intergenerational transmission of Islamic values and customs. A thriving 'Malaytown' existed on TI before World War II, but a high proportion of Indigenous–Malay families who, among other residents, were sent to the mainland for the duration of the war, opted not to return to Torres Strait. While the number of Muslim immigrants in metropolitan Australia, particularly Sydney and Melbourne, has grown substantially since the post-war period, the reverse is true in Torres Strait. What Balfour refers to as the '"outflux" of Muslims on Thursday Island' meant that by 2005 there were only two practising Muslims on TI and, wanting to live in an Islamic environment, they have since relocated to Malaysia.[9]

Aboriginal–Afghan kinverts

Aboriginal–Afghan descendants, like their Indigenous–Malay counterparts, are tremendously proud of their heritage. They want their forebears' immense contribution to Australia's material wealth and cultural landscape to be acknowledged and appreciated. But, in common with Indigenous–Malay kinverts, honouring the memories of their forefathers does not necessarily extend to reclamation of their religious beliefs.

This distinction was brought into sharp relief when a mullah (a Muslim educated in Islamic theology and sacred law) based in Sydney visited the Broken Hill mosque. The mosque was constructed as a place of worship by the resident Afghan and Indian camelmen in 1891. In 1968 the so-called Afghan Mosque was restored by the Broken Hill Historical Society and is now a museum and tourist attraction. Philip Jones, historian and senior curator at the South Australian Museum, recalls that the (non-Indigenous) Afghan descendants he met in Broken Hill were unsettled by the mullah's assumption that their heritage necessarily meant they were religiously devout Muslims. His description of this misunderstanding, which illustrates that kinversion is not confined to Aboriginal people, is worth quoting at length:

> I know that a couple of the descendants, particularly in Broken Hill, that we had met, had had visits from a mullah in Sydney, who had come out there, and he wanted to pray at the mosque. Well, the mosque is now a National Trust building and it's essentially a secular building, and it's probably fifty years since it was used as a mosque. I know that the descendants and the sons of the last mullah, for example, were taken aback when these Sydney mullahs, who are not really of their group, came out in a sort of proselytising manner and said, 'Now we want to go to the mosque and pray, and you brothers should pray with us' and [the descendants replied], 'Oh no, we prefer – no, we don't want to do that'. There was this sense that, 'Hang on, this is not what we're on about, you know, we're honouring the memories and the traditions of our fathers and grandfathers, but that doesn't necessarily mean re-entering [Islam], or rewinding the clock to take up the religion.'

Philip Jones and Alice Springs-based anthropologist Anna Kenny co-curated a touring exhibition (which opened in 2007) called *Australia's Muslim Cameleers: Pioneers of the Inland 1860s-1930s*. The events of 9/11 in New York and Washington and the subsequent, and continuing, vilification of Islam and

Muslims in the mainstream media were important catalysts in Jones and Kenny's decision to use the word 'Muslim' in the title of the show. They felt it was important to demonstrate that Muslims have been in this country for generations and have contributed greatly to its cultural and religious diversity. In our interview Anna Kenny discussed the exhibition in these terms:

> The bad reactions in the media actually pushed me even more towards the subject, and for me it became completely clear that this really needs to be in the mainstream … that Muslims have been here for such a long time, and they have also contributed to our cultural fabric, Australian cultural fabric … And that was actually my motivation … an awareness that Muslims have been in Australia for 150 years … and they're not just asylum seekers or newcomers, and they didn't come as invaders, or terrorists.[10]

Yet a number of the Aboriginal and non-Aboriginal Afghan descendants objected to the label 'Muslim' in the title of the cameleer exhibition because they, like their Indigenous–Malay counterparts, do not generally use the word in relation to their ancestors. In our conversations some respondents variously called what we now know as a mosque a 'Mohammedan church' or 'Mohammedan chapel'. Another referred to the cameleers as 'Mohammedans', and yet another noted that they were followers of 'the Mohammedan religion'. Philip Jones understood that the appellation 'Muslim' was, as he says,

> probably seen as more of a modern term, that was not coming from their own past. I mean [many descendants] use the term 'Mohammedanism', and you see this 'Mohammedanism' term being used in the early literature. 'Muslim' isn't used so it's not a term that

they feel ownership of, and it's not even something to be defensive about, because they don't actually own it. So, it's a bit of a post-9/11 imposition on them, and I think they would prefer to be mis-labelled as Afghans than to be labelled as Muslim – or to have their ancestors labelled as Muslim.

Descendants might also object to this post-9/11 imposition because the images and news stories about Islam and Muslims that have dominated the airwaves and television and print media since the 2001 terrorist attacks bear little resemblance to their encounters with Muslim communities and traditions. Indigenous–Muslim descendants find nothing in their lived experience that even approaches the reportage they are confronted with, particularly the mainstream media's widespread conflation of Muslims/Arabs/Middle Easterners and fundamentalist terrorists.[11] They remember, instead, close-knit communities, hospitality and friendship. Growing up with her Aboriginal mother and Peshawar-born father, Mona Wilson recalls that 'our house was always full of people of every denomination'.[12] Azeem (Johnny) Khan recollects that his Aboriginal–Afghan father's many friends regularly visited their family home: 'White fellas, Italian fellas, and they were all our uncles, and they all respected us and we respected them, and they respected Dad. So they were all our uncles and aunties, and never mind they're no relation.'[13]

Indigenous–Malay kinverts also recount the strong community bonds that their Muslim parents and forebears brokered with non-Muslims. Mark Bin Bakar recalls that his Aboriginal mother and Muslim Malay father often welcomed people of varying racial, ethnic and religious backgrounds into their house 'to be looked after and fed'.[14] Speaking of the Broome Muslim Malay community in general, he notes:

As much as they practice and are passionate about their religion, their culture, they also see themselves as Australians. I mean, they take a lot of pride in their country, their motherland. They take a lot of pride in their religion, they've got family back home, but they also take a lot of pride in that they're Australians ... and it's interesting with what's happening now internationally, with the whole fear and phobias of Islam and terrorism ... I get a bit confused about the attitude of Australia – internationally and locally – of its view on Islam now, because a lot of them never grew up with it. We grew up with it in Broome. I mean, we were practising multiculturalism before the word was even invented in Australia. Before it became a word that was used politically, we lived it and breathed it.[15]

Religious differences

Family anecdotes indicate that most Afghan and Malay fathers were accepting of their wives' and children's adoption of a non-Muslim faith. The majority of Indigenous–Muslim families emphasised the way they mutually accommodated and valued each other's religious and cultural attitudes. Eva Salam Peacock's experiences are typical: 'Dad was a Muslim but he didn't mind if we were Catholic. He didn't mind us going to a Catholic school.'[16] As mentioned, this attitude might be partly due to the Qur'anic injunction, 'Let there be no compulsion in religion' (2:256). 'Ali', a Singapore-born Muslim Malay who came to Broome to work in the pearl-shelling industry in 1950, had this to say: 'No, that fella want to go Catholic, that's his business, his life. He want to go Muslim, his life ... According to my religion, wrong thing to push people ... I respect the other people.'[17] Ali's Aboriginal Catholic wife 'Patricia' agrees, commenting: 'Yeah, well he's got his – I don't interfere with his religion or when he goes out and pray or whatever. He doesn't interfere with mine so, just leave it at that and everyone's happy that way. No forcing business, you know.'[18]

The Aboriginal wives of Afghan men had similar experiences. Esther Kite was married to her late Aboriginal–Afghan husband for more than twenty years. In our conversation she described her husband as a 'strict' Muslim who always 'kept his religion'.[19] He avoided pork, prayed regularly at home, treated his Peshawar-born father's Qur'an reverentially and instructed their children how to say 'the Afghan prayer'. Notwithstanding this he was very accepting of his family's Methodism. As Esther recalls, 'In those days [late 1950s–early '60s] we didn't have anywhere to go, like Mohammadan church, but the kids used to go to a Methodist church. All the children were baptised in the Methodist church.' Other oral testimony suggests that a number of non-Indigenous wives of Afghan men had analogous experiences. Nazmeena Cumming's father Fiad Mulladad came to Australia in 1899. His Australian wife was of English descent, and Nazmeena recalls that each accommodated the other's religious and cultural beliefs: 'My mother all the time, I might add, that she was with my Dad, she still remained a Christian, and he never ever instigated [her becoming] a Muslim. They didn't do that. That was something that you made your own mind to be. And even though Mum made all the Afghan shrouds and helped them in any way that she could, she still remained a Christian.'[20]

Muslim husbands were perhaps also disposed to recognise their wives' and children's religious beliefs because they were in the minority. In the early twentieth century when there were relatively strong Afghan and Malay communities in Australia, the men held firmly to their Islamic customs and traditions. Over time, with a decline in the numbers of Muslim arrivals in Australia, and an increase in the rate of intermarriage between Muslims and non-Muslims, the men's Islamic beliefs tended to become more of a private affair. Joanne Nasir recalls that her Indonesian Muslim grandfather, or *Datu*, 'was of the belief that you're in somebody else's country, and he married into a different culture, so he was willing for his children to make their own decision … he allowed the children to make the choice, whether they became Catholic, the Uniting Church, Muslim, Hindu – but at the same time he followed his religion very much within himself.'[21]

Not all Muslim fathers and grandfathers tolerated their families' religious beliefs. Those who had to, as Aboriginal–Malay descendant Johari Bin Demin claims, 'swallow the bitter pill that their kids were going to be Catholics rather than Muslims', at least preferred them to have *some* religious instruction.[22] In many cases the Indigenous–Muslim children's attendance at church or Sunday school was at the behest of their mothers *and* fathers. Mark Bin Bakar recalls, 'My [Muslim Malay] father never said "You kids can't go to church". In fact it was the opposite. He said, "You've got to go – if your mother says you've got to go to church, then you've got to go to church."' Aboriginal–Afghan descendant Mona Wilson, who defines herself as a 'Muslim … although I'm Church of England as well', recalls that her devout Muslim father sent her and her siblings to the local Congregational Church, 'because we had to grow up to believe in a God instead of growing up to be free thinkers'. Muslim fathers might also have been willing to accede to their children's adoption of Christianity because in Islamic belief Christians, Muslims and Jews are all 'people of the book'; that is, those who have received scriptures revealed to them by God.[23]

Other Muslim fathers expected their Catholic Aboriginal wives and their children to accommodate Islam, if not fully embrace it. Aboriginal–Malay Septu Brahim recalled that during his upbringing his father's Muslim religion predominated:

> My [Catholic] mother was brought up with Irish and Germans [at Beagle Bay mission, 120 kilometres from Broome] and then she had the Aboriginal culture too. She had two cultures. But my father … he only had the one culture … and my mother had to fit in. Yes, we never ate pork or bacon and every Thursday night after he finished work at 9.00 pm we'd be served up drinks – tea, coffee, cocoa and scones my mother'd have to make specially – and he'd read the Koran and we'd get into it. If any visitors came, he'd make them sit there and listen to him praying.[24]

Septu's father was profoundly opposed to his son's christening as a Catholic, particularly when it occurred without his knowledge or consent. According to Septu he was a toddler (in the early 1930s in Port Hedland) when a visiting Catholic priest was conducting christenings at the local church. He and some other neighbourhood children were christened, an event that was casually communicated to Septu's father by an unwitting co-worker. According to Septu, his father 'just dropped everything and blew his top and went out the back door, came racing home and went berserk'. He ran straight to his toolshed where he kept a revolver and bullets. When Septu's mother saw him approaching the shed she took Septu and ran away. They stayed together for months, as Septu recalled, 'at an old Greek lady's place, old Mrs Constantine's. Oh, it took him months and months to get over that. My mother was too scared to go back. Half a dozen people had to negotiate a deal, you know? He was a Moslem and I'd become a Catholic and that was it. That's why I say I'm a Catholic Moslem!'[25]

Semah and Halimah Mokak's baptisms were also carried out in secret. Semah recalls that her Aboriginal mother took her and her sister to be baptised while their Malaysian Muslim father was out at sea. He was working out of Darwin as a pearl-shell diver, and during one of his long absences their mother took the opportunity, as Semah recalls, 'for us to be baptised as Catholics'.[26] Semah remembers that her mother randomly approached two young girls ahead of them in the queue to be the sisters' godmothers. In Semah's words: 'Mum takes us off to get baptised, Dad's off at sea, she grabs the first person [to be our godmother] and then they turned out to be only a few years older and happened to be schoolgirls that later wanted to beat me and my sister up!'

Semah's mother was obliged to have her daughters' baptisms performed in a clandestine fashion because, according to Semah, her Muslim 'father had this really strong hand on all of us about being Muslims and we were Muslims and that was it'. Notwithstanding her father's strong conviction that his children would be Muslim, Semah's father was not opposed to them attending Sunday school. When I asked Semah about this seeming incongruity she replied:

> I think it was probably respite from having eight kids at home. And also I don't think he saw it as Sunday School, as such. I think it was more of a social thing rather than religious instruction. So we'd all be there singing 'Jesus Loves the Little Children' and especially the little Aboriginal kids would be belting that out while we were over at Sunday School having fun and it was just a great, feel-good thing. No one was absorbing religion or anything like that. But when we went home we would know we could never, never sing that. No one even had to tell us that. We just knew that we could not sing 'Jesus Loves the Little Children' at home. And we loved that song. We would sing it all the way home, walking home, but we stopped as soon as we got home!

Indigenous–Muslim kinverts combined Islamic and Christian practices and traditions in their daily lives. They celebrated the end of Ramadan and Christmas. They were instructed to recite passages from the Qur'an and the Bible, how to perform salat (the daily prayers of Islam) and sing 'Jesus Loves the Little Children'. In an interview with Dilara Reznikas, Halimah Mokak described how she and her siblings combined their Muslim and Catholic identities: 'We ... used to practice Islam, but ... we still used to go to church when we went to my grandmother's place. People used to laugh at us because, you know, we would be practising our Five Pillars of Islam and then we [would] go to Sunday school [laughter].'[27]

Many kinverts absorbed Islamic religio-cultural beliefs and practices as a natural part of their upbringing in a Muslim household. Others were given more formal religious instruction. Several Aboriginal–Afghan descendants recall being taught how to conduct Islamic prayers, perform *wudu* or ablutions and recite the *shahada* (declaration of faith), and other Arabic phrases. Born in Marree in 1941, Dean Gool Mahomed was instructed in the ways of Islam by his great-uncle Mullah Assam Khan. Dean recalls that he and the other Marree 'Ghantown' boys prayed 'twice a day, morning and before sun-down'.[28] He continues:

> When we was kids we had to go there, you had to wash – the bore drain went through the chapel [mosque], and on the duckboard you had to wash your hands and wash your feet before you went in there ... You had to go in barefoot and you went in there and you said [the *shahada*] *'La illaha ill Allah, Mohammed rasul Allah'* ['There is no god but Allah, and Muhammad is the Messenger of Allah']. Mullah Assam Khan was in charge of all of us as we prayed ... and he said, 'My boy you've got to wash your feet and wash your hands before we go in that mosque.'

Semah, Halimah and the other Mokak children's Islamic religious instruction took an extraordinary form. The sisters have vivid memories of their school holiday visits in the 1960s to the Daly River (about 140 kilometres south of Darwin). A white South African imam who was a friend of the family resided there. Each day the Mokak children were instructed in how to conduct their prayers, given passages from the Qur'an to recite (in Arabic) and taught about the basic tenets of Islam. The children had their own prayer mats, which they placed on a specially laid tarpaulin, and, when they heard the next call to prayer, would run back to camp to pray. The girls wore very modest clothing and covered their hair when engaged in salat (ritual prayer). Halimah's fascinating (and entertaining) recollection of proceedings deserves repeating in full:

> Well [the imam], I think he was a bit of a shady sort of a character, but I don't know – he was a friend of a very dear old lady friend of ours, who used to look after this community with the Malak Malak people on the Daly River. So we used to go on holiday there every school holidays, and so that's where Dad met him. So he was then appointed our religious instruction imam, and so we would have to – in the bush, with all the local kids all peering through the grass – we'd have to put down our little mats, and what I strongly remember, we used to laugh so much because the imam had his two big toes missing, so he didn't have balance. When he used to go down to initiate his prayer, we were all behind him, so we would just start laughing, we just couldn't stop laughing, you know – we had to try and be serious. So, we were learning all this, and we'd do the Islamic chant, *La illaha ill Allah* ['There is no god but Allah'] and then, you know, you'd look around and you'd see all these little eyes in the bush, doing the same thing, all the local Malak Malak kids, and it was just

so funny. When I talk about it today, you sort of think, did this sort of stuff really happen – is this for real [laughter]?[29]

In light of this testimony the question of whether Indigenous–Muslim descendants are *Muslim* seems a little simplistic. To answer in the negative is to disregard the immensely significant role that Islamic beliefs and practices have played in their daily lives. But nor do the vast majority of Indigenous–Muslim descendants I have met necessarily consider themselves members of the *umma*, or international community of believers. Whether or not they are Muslim is a question that only individual descendants can answer. To judge from the evidence presented here, responses will be highly personal. When I asked Halimah Mokak if she would call herself a Muslim she replied: 'Well no, but I would say I was brought up a Muslim because it's just been involved in all of my daily life.' Growing up with what he described as 'a very strict Catholic upbringing, but also the disciplines of the Islam faith', Aboriginal–Malay Mark Bin Bakar stresses that 'the convergence of the two religions' made him who he is today. Another Aboriginal–Malay, Johari Bin Demin, also possesses this doubled cultural and religious identity: 'I've had, I suppose, a Catholic influence throughout my life, but I do feel some affinity with Muslims and I can understand [them], I can connect with them and I'm aware of what their issues are.'

Aboriginal–Afghan descendants espouse a similar view. Rosie Sahanna suggests that even though her father Jack (who was nicknamed 'the Ghan' in Broome) was baptised at Beagle Bay mission as a Catholic, 'he never forgot who he was … He always knew his father was a Muslim and he remembered himself being part of that, but that never clashed with having to become a Catholic.'[30] Shirley Wilson's stance is comparable: 'We were brought up with a Christian upbringing, plus the Muslim thing at home, part and part.' This dual identity is eloquently summed up by her sister Mona: 'I sit on two chairs, you know. I sit on the Christian chair sometimes and on the Muslim chair sometimes. I sit on the Afghan chair sometimes and I sit on the Aboriginal chair sometimes. All this I do in memory of our parents.' This is a statement of considerable wisdom and wit. It captures the formidable resourcefulness that informs the everyday lives of kinverts. Kinverts belong neither to the past nor to the present. They insist on the kinship of past *and* present, on the value of a continual accommodation of different histories in building a sense of self in the present. And this attentiveness to the way identities are negotiated when there is goodwill and commitment to human values is not only a personal legacy; it also defines an attitude to the world that translates into principled action designed to communicate the exceptional contribution kinversion can make to the larger projects of thinking who we are, how we narrate ourselves, and where we propose to 'sit'.

Practising kinverts

Among the nearly fifty kinvert and convert Indigenous Muslims I have interviewed, four men and one woman are descendants *and* practising Muslims.[31] Their unique spiritual journeys are testament to the facts that conversion encounters are manifold and that social *and* personal dynamics both inform and affect the outcome.

The heritage of one of my interviewees illustrates the long history of association between Indigenous communities in Torres Strait and Muslim Malays. Halima Binti Hassan Awal, who is in her late sixties and was raised on Thursday Island but who now resides in Brisbane, is a third-generation Indigenous Muslim. Her heritage exemplifies the way ethnic, religious and cultural identities are intertwined cross-generationally through family ties. In 1891 Halima's maternal grandmother Annie Ahwang (née Savage) married Ahwang, a Muslim bêche-de-mer fisherman from Singapore.[32] Halima's mother Saia (born in 1909) was raised as a Muslim, and she later married her Muslim husband Omar (or Hassan) Bin Awel, a pearl-shell diver who arrived in 1914 from Ambon in the Dutch East Indies (now Indonesia) (see figure 11). Halima met Mohammed Wajih Zahab, her late Lebanese-born Muslim husband, on Thursday Island in the 1960s.[33] He answered Wahap Bin Tahal's call inviting mainland Australian Muslims to come and live on the Island and give talks on Islam to interested locals. The Islamic classes, conducted in the prayer room in Wahap's house, included instruction on salat, or daily prayers, and the Islamic *deen* or way of life.

In contrast with the steady decline in Indigenous–Malay identifications with Islam noted elsewhere, here ties to the faith are being reaffirmed. As Halima puts it, 'I lost my religion and then went back and explored it all again.'[34] In this trend, migration to Australia of new waves of Muslim communities has, of course, been an enabling factor. In Halima's case, meeting her Lebanese-born Muslim husband was an important catalyst in her desire to learn more about Islam. Their association not only contributed to a deepening of her understanding of Islamic concepts and practices but also offered her a way of developing a richer and fuller understanding of her heritage, to 'find out why [her] father was a Muslim'. In Halima's words: 'I married my husband and we moved to Sydney, and then they started classes and I said, "I want to know more", because when I was born, I was a Muslim and I married my husband who was a Muslim, but I wanted to go in depth and find out, do research, what is Islam really about?'

The Islamic classes Halima attended in Sydney helped her, as she says, 'rediscover myself'. In recovering the beliefs held by her Muslim forebears, but which had been 'lost along the way', Halima's renewed and strengthened identification with Islam produced a much stronger sense of who she was as a person. A symbol of Halima's reconnection with her cultural, ethnic and religious identity was her decision to change her name. Muslim converts often change their names to a recognisably Islamic one, but Halima's decision was motivated by a desire to recuperate a family name that had been recorded incorrectly by local administrators. On his pearl-shell diver's certificate Halima's father's name had been recorded as Hassan Binawel. According to Halima 'Binawel' should have been spelled 'Bin Awal'. When she learned more about Islam, Halima discovered that the patronymic 'Bin' is Arabic for 'son of' (also written as 'ibn'). The name Hassan Bin Awal denotes that Hassan is the son of Awal. Australian authorities had recorded Halima's surname as 'Binawel', implying that she was the 'son of' Awel, when she was the 'daughter of' ('Binti' or 'Bint' in Arabic) of Hassan. Changing her name through deed poll to Halima Binti Hassan Awal, she followed a naming pattern used in many parts of the Arab world (and by Malays) as well as formalising her family connection to her Muslim forebears.

In our first interview in 2005 Halima often referred to herself as having 'reverted back to Islam'. At the time I mistakenly assumed that she meant to say 'converted' but had made an error of nomenclature. Our conversation occurred early in my journey of learning about Islam, and I had not encountered the Islamic notion of 'reversion' before. Later I understood her to use the word 'revert' in the same manner as convert Muslims who wish to make a (political or symbolic) statement about always having *felt* Muslim (a point we return to in chapters 5 and 6). According to Islamic theology, each human being is born with an innate belief in the Oneness of God. This natural inclination to worship God alone is known in Arabic as *fitrah*. Left to their own devices, all children would grow up being aware of God in His Oneness, but external pressures from one's parents or societies can mean that they choose a faith other than Islam. Thus when individuals accept Islam, they are not turning their backs on any prior revelation but, rather, returning to the original and true knowledge of Allah. This is why people who adopt Islam are said to 'revert' rather than 'convert' – they are going back to their original nature. In Halima's case, however, her spiritual journey was also bound up with a process of reverting to the ways of her Muslim father and forebears.

Unlike Halima, who was born into the Muslim faith, another practising Muslim interviewee, Justin Agale, came to it in adulthood – yet each was descended from Muslim men who arrived in Torres Strait in the late nineteenth century. Justin's story confirms the complex ways in which the Islamic faith resonates in Indigenous families across generations. In the late 1800s Justin's great-grandfather Pablo Ahmat, a Muslim Malay pearl-shell worker, arrived in Broome. He moved some years later to Torres Strait, where he met and married Justin's great-grandmother. Like Halima's grandmother, Justin's great-grandmother also embraced Islam after marrying her Muslim husband. Just before his death, Justin's great-grandfather prophesied that his family would leave Islam, but that one member would adopt the faith in time. His prediction came true. Justin is the first in his family in generations to return to Islam and become a practising Muslim.

According to Justin, the long history of Muslim migration to Torres Strait was one reason his family was completely at ease with his decision to embrace Islam. As he says: 'When I became Muslim it was more of "Oh, he's just going back to what his forebears were doing." It wasn't a big jump for them, you know, it was merely just embracing the past.'[35] For both Justin and Halima, embracing the past by reconnecting with their Muslim ancestral roots was a process, not of conversion, but *reversion*. Their personal testimonies ably illustrate the fact that for Indigenous Muslims the issue of reversion has a double significance because a number of those who identify with Islam today have Muslim forebears. In reaffirming their connections to their Muslim ancestors they are actively reclaiming a spiritual identity lost through the external factors of war, displacement, family break-ups and the vicissitudes of international trade. Their vision is both retrospective and forward-looking. The important family histories they are recovering do not remain in the past. Rather, they transform the way these Indigenous Muslims conduct their lives in the present and future.

The family story of another interviewee, Shahzad (Shaz) Rind, marks a radical point of departure from Halima's and Justin's. For a start, Shaz is a descendant of the 'Afghan' cameleers. In the mid-1870s Shaz's great-grandfather Goolam Badoola came to Port Augusta from Baluchistan, the largest of four provinces in modern-day Pakistan. With a string of camels he ran supplies to and from the Western Australian goldfields until he was given a government citation that allowed him to own his own sheep station (Bulgabardoo Station, near Mount Magnet).[36] It was here that he met his future wife, Marium Martin, whose father (who worked on the station) was a Muslim Malay and whose mother was from the Badimaya clan of the Yamatji tribe.[37]

Their marriage was an imposing affair, as 'Miss Martin now Mrs Badoola' wrote in a letter dated 22 March 1918: 'We went to Perth to the Mohommedaan Church,[38] in present of forty Mohommedean religion men & all Indian people, & all under the British subject, And then gave them a great feast. Most of them spoke on my behalf on my married night 12 Dec 1917.'[39] The same letter emphasises that, in accordance with Islamic custom, the groom had given his bride the mandatory gift known in Arabic as *mahr*. According to the Prophet Muhammad, the dowry or *mahr* is an essential condition of the legality of a marriage: 'every marriage without *mahr* is null and void'. The reason for this emphasis is that the Aborigines Department deemed Shaz's great-grandparents' Muslim marriage illegal. The Chief Protector of Aborigines, A.O. Neville, wrote at the time: 'If the ceremony was performed in the mosque by a Mohammadan, it would not be a legal marriage', and the department immediately began taking steps to remove Marium from her husband to what Neville called 'one of our settlements'.[40]

Marium Badoola's letter is, in fact, a poignant plea for recognition and respect, and besides stressing the legality of their marriage she goes to great lengths to assure the authorities that every aspect of the arrangements leading up to the 'Mohammadan' marriage were also entirely in accordance with Islamic custom. The context of her writing is explained starkly in the first sentences: 'I am writing to you a few lines and I hope that you will take a great interest … as I am a poor unfortunate girl. And the Aboriginal Department is trying to put me away from my good home.' In explaining that she 'married Mr Badoola with my own liking', Mrs Badoola gives the background to their marriage. She and her father had come to work on Mr Badoola's station:

> After some time I got to like Mr Badoola and then asked my father can I marry Mr Badoola, & my father himself asked Mr Badoola

two or three time, can you marry my daughter. At first he did not care much & at last he said "if your daughter marry me under the Mohommdean church law", & my father told him the same that I am Mohommedaan & I don't want my daughter to marry in English church law, & my father ask me are you satisfied to marry Mr Badoola in Mohommedan church law, I was very please to hear that & I am quite satisfied to marry Mr Badoola in the Mohommdean church law.

As Marium emphasises, this arrangement was quite satisfactory to her and followed naturally from her upbringing and education: 'My father was Mohommedean & I like to follow my father religion, & when we was going to school at Magnet he told the school master, that when he took Scripture, to tell my children to go outside, so we dont no nothing about English religion, our father is always teaching us about Mohommedan religion. So I am quite satisfied in my father religion.' Mrs Badoola expressed the hope that because 'I have got good home, & a good hus-band & he looks after me well' the Aborigines Department 'will leave me alone, my father is not a Aboriginal he is a Malay man, & under the British subject & also my mother is a good & sensible women, our father brought us up to be respectable & honese.'

When Shaz's great-grandmother died prematurely in 1930, however, the Aboriginal Protection bureaucracy threatened to take the four Badoola children away. Shaz's great-grandfather sent them back to Baluchistan with his nephew before returning himself at a later date. In having to flee government control, Shaz's forebears were, as he says, rendered 'refugees in their own country'.[41] Shaz describes his family's predicament here:

When my great-grandmother passed away the Chief Protector [was] going to take the kids away, so my great-grandfather, knowing the struggle that he had to just marry an Aboriginal woman, [knew] that this was going to happen to the kids. So he put them on a ship and sent them back to Baluchistan. So [from the age of twelve] my grandfather got brought up in Baluchistan but luckily [in that way] we maintained one strong culture – you know, being brought up over there, and people are Muslims, so ... that's how [Islam's] come to me.[42]

'Ramiz' has been a practising Muslim for more than two years. His Muslim grandfather came to Australia in the 1920s from near the Afghan border, in what is now Pakistan. Unlike the earlier generation of indentured Afghan camelmen, he arrived independently. Jumping ship in Queensland, he worked for some time in the sugarcane fields before moving south. He later found himself near the Aboriginal mission in Angledool, close to the Queensland–New South Wales border. It was here that he met his future wife. It is not clear how or whether Ramiz's grandfather gained permission from the authorities, or her mother, to remove the fourteen-year-old from the mission, but that is what he did. As she has frequently said to Ramiz, 'I grew up behind barbed wire and I had to marry an illegal immigrant to get off the mish [sic] ... In those days you were lucky if they gave you a blanket.'[43] Initially the pair led an itinerant lifestyle, selling goods from a horse-drawn sulky. They later settled in Auburn, in Sydney's western suburbs, where they had five children. Ramiz's grandfather, a devout Muslim who worked as a butcher, supplied the Indians and Afghans who arrived by ship in Sydney with halal meat. He was also responsible for preparing the bodies for Islamic burials.

According to Ramiz, his Yuwalalraay grandmother became a Muslim after her marriage. As he recalls, 'Nan was practising, you know, as well. Like, she had to, so she adopted all those things and was always cooking curries.'[44] Whether or not the Aboriginal wives of Muslim men generally adopted their husbands' religio-cultural attitudes and behaviour is a question we return to in the next chapter. But in Ramiz's family, at least, it appears that his grandmother's identification with Islam 'just faded away' after her (much older) Muslim husband died. According to Ramiz, his father, who was the youngest child of the marriage, 'never practised Islam'. Despite the fact that Ramiz's grandfather was 'very strict in his faith himself', he did not impose his religious beliefs on his Australian-born son, saying instead, 'As long as you believe in something I'm happy. It doesn't matter if you [don't embrace Islam].' As we have seen, Aboriginal–Afghan descendant Mona Wilson's Muslim father adopted a similar stance. His preference was also for Mona and her siblings to identify with a non-Muslim religion if the alternative was, as she put it, 'growing up to be free thinkers'.

It seems that Ramiz's father, in turn, adopted a similar approach. 'Religion and politics were always discussed in the household', Ramiz recalls, but no 'belief systems were ever enforced'. In Ramiz's words, he has 'always been interested in the spiritual side of things'. 'Growing up', as he says, 'with the spirituality of Aboriginality', he later identified for more than ten years with Rastafarianism before embracing Islam. Like Justin Agale above, Ramiz's Muslim family heritage had no *direct* influence on his decision to become a practising Muslim. However, he does recall how, as a child, his Aboriginal grandmother showed him how to clear his nostrils with water and wash his face and head as in *wudu* (Islamic ablutions), remarking, 'I remembered this when I started practising Islam and from all those years ago remembered it was her who showed me first.'[45] Even so, like Justin, Ramiz came to Islam primarily as a result of independent study and reflection. But their experiences suggest that in a number of cases, recent Indigenous Muslim converts are not necessarily the first in their families to be exposed to Islam. Rather, we are witnessing the *reintroduction* of Islam into particular Indigenous families that had lost contact with it for a number of generations.

In common with the other interviewees discussed in this section, Tuguy Esgin is both a kinvert and a practising Muslim. But, unlike his Indigenous–Malay and Aboriginal–Afghan counterparts, he is the descendant of a more recent Muslim arrival. Tuguy's Muslim father came to Australia from Turkey in 1971. Gary Bouma indicates that Islam in Australia grew particularly from the early 1970s with the admittance of large numbers of Turks and Lebanese refugees who, together, make up about a third of all Muslim immigrants to Australia.[46] On his arrival here Tuguy's father ran a fruit and vegetable shop in Fremantle, where he subsequently met Tuguy's mother, a Nyoongar from Perth who is part of the Stolen Generations. Tuguy has vivid memories of praying alongside his father from an early age. He recalls his father's Qur'an, the religious tapes and videos that were a regular feature of his household, his family's strict avoidance of pork and, later, visits to the Turkish mosque. Tuguy's Aboriginal mother, although a Catholic, took on her Muslim husband's religio-cultural practices during their marriage (again, a theme we return to in chapter 4), but the couple divorced when Tuguy was around eleven and, after spending a year with his brother and mother, Tuguy moved to Shepparton in Victoria to live with his father.

In our conversation Tuguy recalled the close-knit Turkish–Australian community in Shepparton as being relatively conservative and quite insular. Through his engagement with it he developed both a deeper level of religious knowledge and commitment and his primary source of self-identification. As he says, 'In Shepparton you're either a Wog or a Turk or an Aussie, so you sort of had your own little groups. I grew up within the Turkish community so I was more of a Turk than anything else.'[47] Until he returned to live with his mother in Perth at the age of sixteen, Tuguy was unaware of his Aboriginal heritage. Before, as he says, he had 'always been Muslim'. At first he rejected his Aboriginality: '[For] the first three years I sort of denied being Aboriginal because of all the stereotyping.' Later, when he began to learn about Aboriginal culture and identity from his uncles and other elders and mentors, he 'started to embrace it'. His knowledge of Aboriginal people and history was considerably widened after completing a masters degree in Indigenous community health. As a first aid instructor at a Perth-based Indigenous organisation Tuguy had further opportunities to engage 'not only [with] the Nyoongar community but also up north in the remote communities'. He found it, he says, 'fascinating to learn about the smoking ceremonies and funerals and all those types of things'. Wary of rejection because of a lack of cultural knowledge, Tuguy was instead embraced – largely because many of the people he met had suffered a similar fate. As he puts it: 'When I first got my job I didn't really know much about my Aboriginality and I felt a bit awkward working in an Indigenous organisation. It wasn't until I realised that a lot of people are part of the Stolen Generation and they don't have that knowledge [themselves], so they were accepting and I had no problems fitting in.'

Tuguy's sense of identity has shifted considerably over the years. Initially, he says, he identified as Turkish. Later he embraced his Aboriginality. These days he self-identifies differently again. He describes his journey of self-discovery in these terms:

> I say I'm Aboriginal and Turkish, I don't say I'm Australian. I guess … because of the Stolen Generation and what's happened to my Mum, there's a bit of anger there still, so I never used to say I was Australian. But [recently] my perceptions have changed. I mean, I grew up being Turkish, then I grew up being Aboriginal, then sort of Turkish Aboriginal. It's sort of changing to Aboriginal Turkish now and the Australian [part of my identity] is slowing starting to creep in.

As a young man Tuguy's struggle to find a sense of identity was profoundly unsettling. What got him through, he says, was his faith in Islam. Without it he might easily have succumbed to a sense of loss and despair and the attendant alcoholism that afflicts many Indigenous people. In Tuguy's words: 'If I didn't have my religion then I don't know what I'd be doing. It's given me a framework, a set of rules to follow, a roadmap, if you like.' He adds, 'If I wasn't a Muslim I'd probably be drinking, you know, almost compelled to do it, but as a Muslim I show a bit of self-restraint.' Throughout the 'hardest times [he has] gone through', Tuguy says he has always 'thought of God and spoken to God or Allah and I think I've been carried through the hard times'. Tuguy's main concern now is that his children do not experience the identity crisis he went through. He and his Turkish–Australian wife have enrolled their son and daughter in a Turkish Islamic school 'so they can learn about Islam and learn Turkish'. Tuguy is equally keen to 'try to make them proud of [being] Aboriginal'. He hopes that in his children's generation these identities can mutually coexist.

Figure 1: Members of the Aboriginal–Afghan Khan family, 1969 (L–R): Marilyn with baby Robert, Nameth (Donald), Esther with Akbar, Amy, Rameth (Rocky) holding Abdul and Azeem (Johnny).

> Figure 2: Torres Strait–Malay siblings Halima and Karim at Thursday Island cemetery, 2007. Note their father Hassan Bin Awel's headstone in the foreground.

Figure 3: An Aboriginal woman at Oodnadatta with a camel.

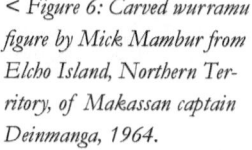

Figure 4: Malay pearl-shell workers on Thursday Island in the 1920s. Halima Binti Hassan Awal's father Omar (or Hassan) Bin Awel is second from left in the front row

> Figure 5: 'Unknown Man New South Wales', Julie Dowling, 2003, acrylic, red ochre and plastic on canvas, 80 cm × 50 cm. The Arabic-looking script in the background of the painting repeats, in English, the word 'Aboriginal'. According to the artist, it symbolises how 'Afghans became part of our families'.

< Figure 6: Carved *wurramu* figure by Mick Mambur from Elcho Island, Northern Territory, of Makassan captain Deinmanga, 1964.

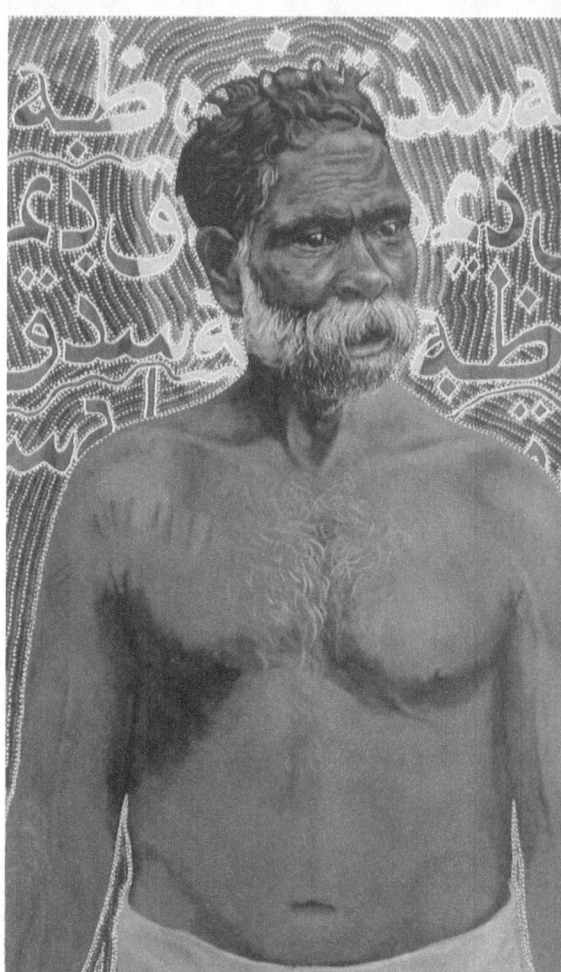

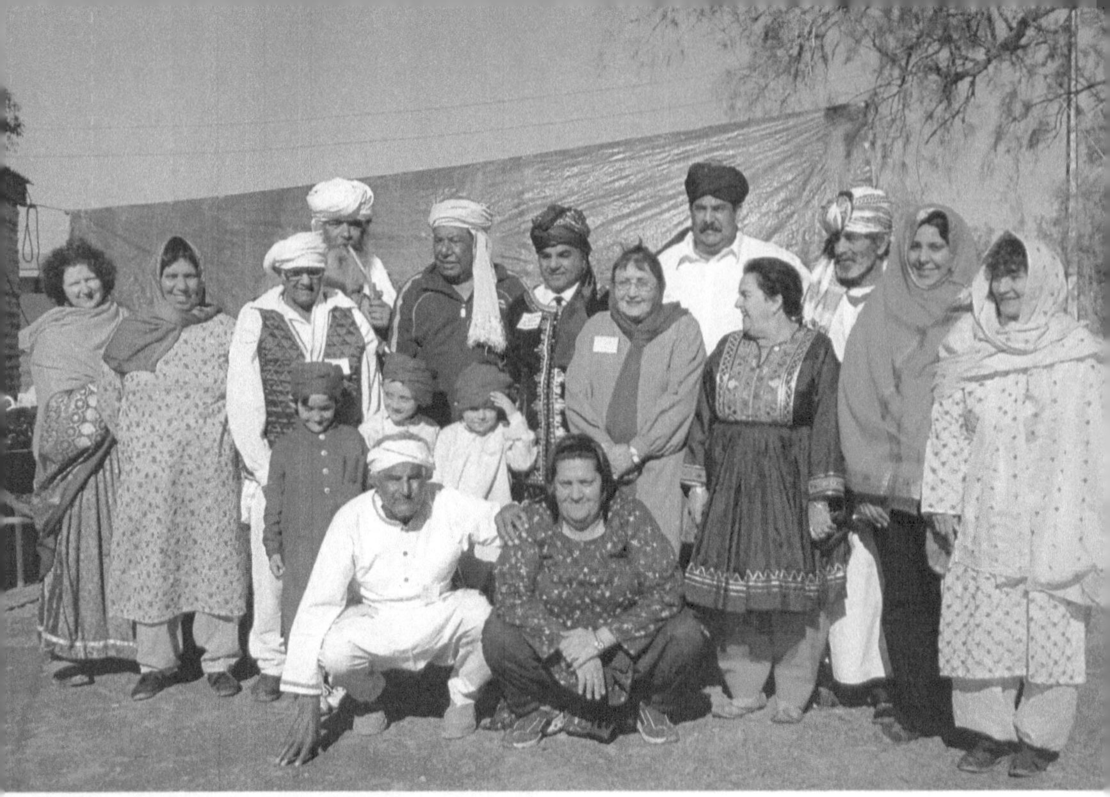

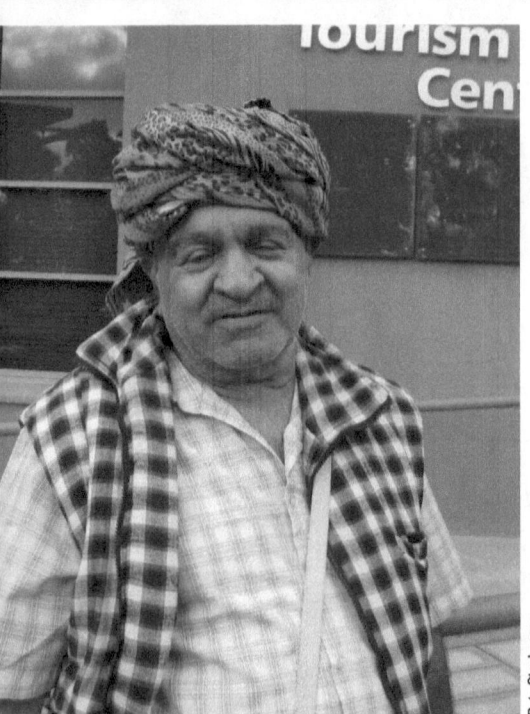

Figure 7: A gathering of Aboriginal and non-Aboriginal descendants of Afghan cameleers in Marree, South Australia, 2005. Interviewee Eric Sultan, whose grandfather came to Australia from Kandahar in the late 1860s, is in the back row with a pipe.

Peta Stephenson

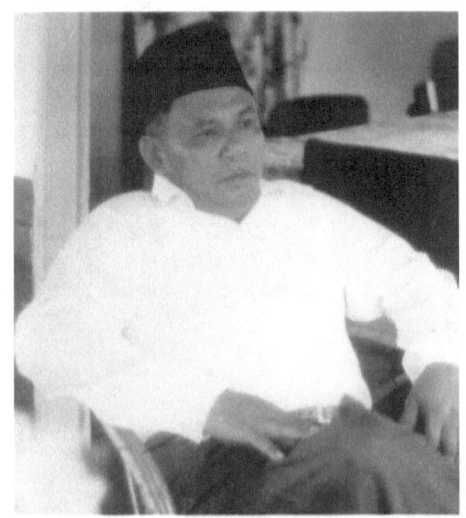

Figure 8: Aboriginal–Afghan descendant Johnny Akbar, Port Pirie, South Australia, 2009.

Balfour Ross

Figure 9: Wahap Bin Tahal, c. 1977. Wahap was the imam of Thursday Island from 1960 to 1984.

< *Figure 10: Camels at Udialla', Jimmy Pike, c. 1998. Felt-tip pen on paper.*

Figure 11: Members of the Ahwang family, c. 1915. Seated are L-R Ahwang and his wife Annie (née Savage); seated between them is their young daughter Saia, Halima Binti Hassan Awal's mother.

Figure 12: Peshawar-born Jack Akbar as a young man, c. 1900s.

Figure 13: Lallie Akbar (née Matbar) c. 1940s, Renmark, South Australia.

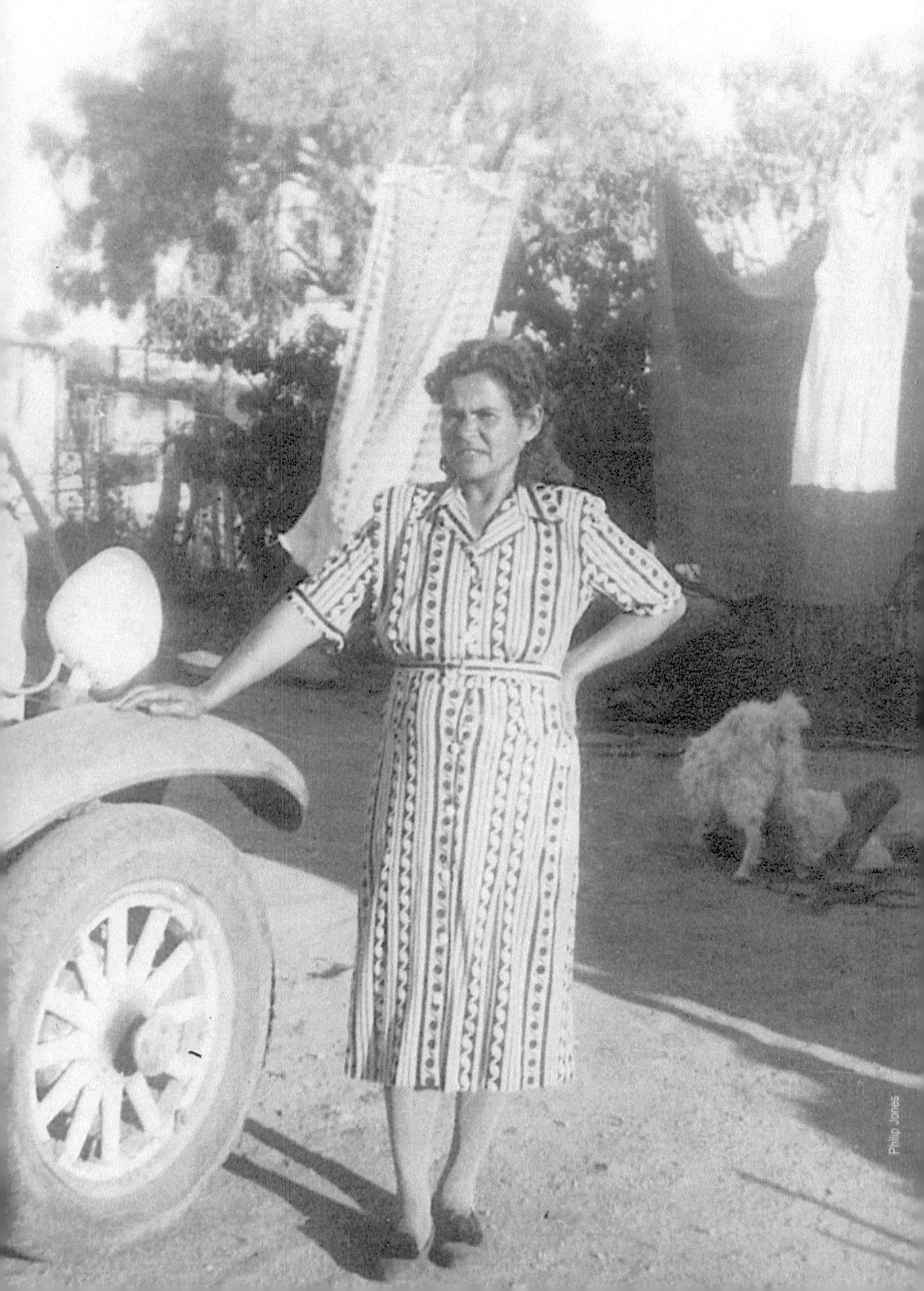

Philip Jones

Figure 14: Peshawar-born Nameth Khan and three of his children, c. 1920s L–R: *Miriam, Rameth (Rocky), Nameth and Akbar.*

< *Figure 15: Indigenous Muslim Eugenia Flynn, Al-Khalil Mosque, Adelaide, 2009.*

Figure 16: Aboriginal–Afghan sisters Mona Wilson (née Akbar) and Shirley Wilson (née Akbar), Port Pirie, South Australia, 2009.

Australian, 17 August 2006/Newspix/Renée Nowytarger

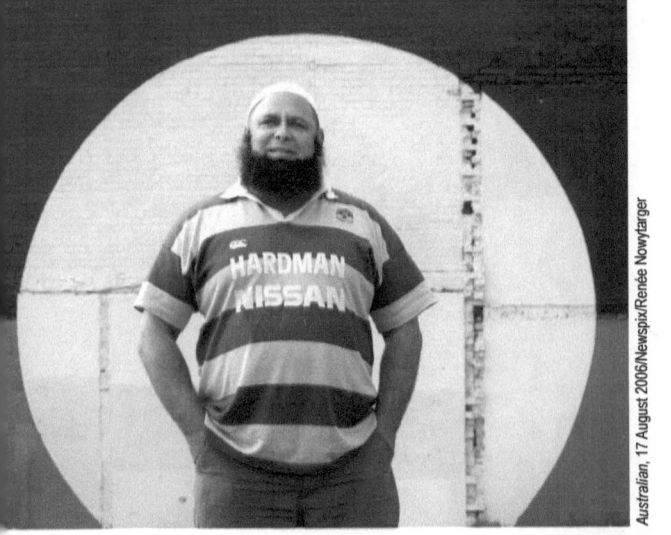

< *Figure 17: Rocky Davis (aka Shaheed Malik) of the Koori Muslim Association.*

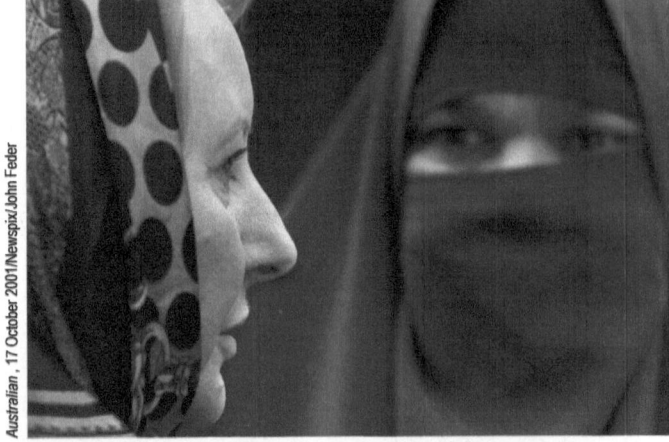

> *Figure 18: Janette Howard chats to Indigenous Muslim Nazra Ibrahim (now Nazra Wali) during Prime Minister Howard's visit to a mosque in Preston, Victoria.*

Australian, 17 October 2001/Newspix/John Feder

Figure 19: Indigenous Muslim Anthony Mundine holding a book about Malcolm X.

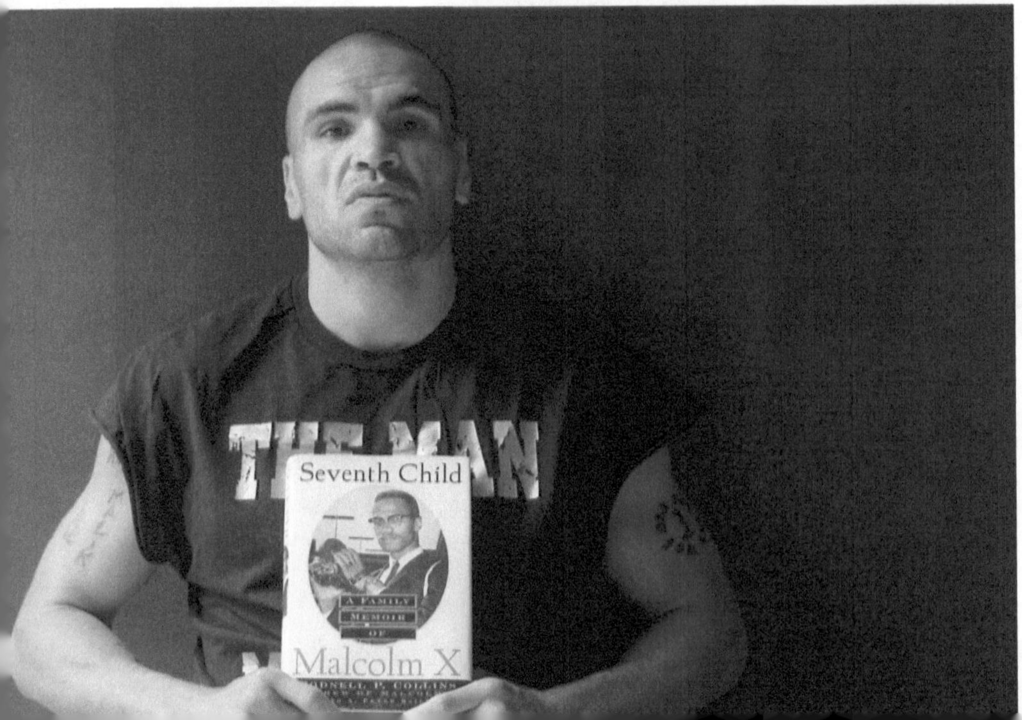

Sydney Morning Herald, 4 May 2007/Fairfax Photos/Wade Laube

FOUR

MARRIAGE MATTERS

Historically, Islam in Indigenous Australia is less a story of conversion than kinversion. The primary and culminating expression of this willingness to engage with Islam is marriage. Historically, Aboriginal women have married Muslim men, rather than the other way around. These facts play out in a number of ways. First, they naturally focus attention on the mindset of the women who were willing to take this step and, second, they remind us that Islam, far from being a stable, fixed and clearly bounded state, was, in the lives of these women, a dynamic, challenging and often changing environment. Marrying, these women also married together two or even three sets of beliefs: besides reaching agreements with their husbands over matters of daily routine and organisation, they were also having to weigh up in their minds often conflicting loyalties, responsibilities and emotions. Reconciling different trainings and affiliations in this situation was rather like parenting, the management of different temperaments and personalities. This chapter explores this working out of these complex human, ethical and cultural permutations.

The stories told here touch on intergenerational family life-cycles as well as illustrating the dynamics of individual marriages. Here, as elsewhere in *Islam Dreaming*, one is highly conscious that the accounts of key moments in these women's lives – upbringing, courtship, marriage and parenting – are also disguised dialogues between mothers and daughters. Although they show the gender dynamics at play in Indigenous–Muslim families and analyse how Indigenous women have responded to their husbands' and fathers' insistence on modesty and chastity, they also display women's solidarity in the face of patriarchal attitudes, which, however unfairly associated with Islam, played an enormous role in their experiences of marriage to Muslim men. Their personal and family anecdotes reveal an extensive range of accommodations of Islam in a wide variety of situations, but one thing these women's stories have in common is that they do not involve an adoption of Islamic theology but, rather, an incorporation of its everyday prohibitions and observances. Another interesting facet common to these stories is the strong independence of spirit the women exhibit. The very act of narrating their life stories is a vital way in which they take agency over their lives and identities.

A further point to make, one that underlines the relationship between these historical narratives and the contemporary experience of Islam, is that the Aboriginal and Torres Strait Islander women whose lives are recalled here grew up as colonised subjects. They mainly had mission-based Christian educations, and even if they retained links to Indigenous families and communities, they were witness to their disintegration. These experiences of fragmentation and disenfranchisement resonate down to the present generations, who are not only heirs to that dispossession but also may experience its recapitulation in the continuing disadvantage of Aboriginal people in Australia.[1] In this sense, respectable marriage into the Islamic fold was a survival strategy, both for sometimes beleaguered individuals and for families and ways of life that were otherwise under threat of disappearance.

Kinvert families: security or isolation?

Great emphasis is placed in Islam on the primacy of marriage and family. The Prophet Muhammad is reported to have said that when a man marries, he has fulfilled half his religion. As well as being understood as a religious duty, marriage also helps to regulate and safeguard one's morality. In Islam marriage represents the only legitimate or halal way of engaging in intimacy with the opposite sex. Sexual relations outside marriage (whether pre- or extra-marital), known in Arabic as *zina*, are totally unacceptable according to Islamic teachings.[2] In this context, there is no better place to begin than with a story previously recounted by Pamela Rajkowski in *Linden Girl*.[3] The marriage of Aboriginal woman Lallie Matbar (the Linden girl) to a Muslim man is a rich and moving story that touches on many of the key moments in a female kinvert's lifecycle. It is also a story about a particularly orthodox, and persistent, Muslim named Jack Akbar (see figure 12). In interviews I conducted with Jack and Lallie's two daughters Mona and Shirley, it also became apparent that the Akbar family's story is interesting in another way, for it is as much a story told by women about women as it is about Jack Akbar himself.

Jack Akbar's strict adherence to Islamic teachings helps explain his prolonged quest to marry Lallie Matbar, an Aboriginal woman he met some years after arriving in Australia (see figure 13).[4] Jack came to Australia in 1894. Born in Peshawar, he was of Afghani descent but lived in Punjab in the north of India before his arrival. Working at various hawking and carting jobs in the Mount Morgans area (a former goldfields townsite about 900 kilometres north-east of Perth), Jack came across different Aboriginal groups. During the 1910s and '20s he came to know Lallie, a so-called half-caste who lived with her Wongai people in the bush (and at other times at the Mount Margaret Mission).[5] Around 1925 Jack approached Lallie's elders, requesting that they consider him as a marriage partner for Lallie. Selling foodstuffs in and camping at Aboriginal camps in Linden (southern Western Australia), Jack learned much about Aboriginal customs and laws. He appreciated that he required the permission of the elders of the Linden mob to have Lallie as his wife. In his homeland, too, it was customary for marriages to be arranged with the parents or family of a prospective bride.

The decision did not rest with Lallie's elders alone. Western Australia's 1905 Aborigines Act made it illegal for an Afghan or other non-Aboriginal man to marry an Aboriginal woman without first gaining the permission of the Chief Protector of Aborigines. For two long years, from 1926 to 1928, with the support of a solicitor and numerous character references from local townspeople, Jack repeatedly petitioned the Western Australian Government for permission to marry Lallie. Each of his three petitions was denied. While his requests were turned down, his persistence meant that the Akbar–Matbar couple became well known to the Aborigines Department. A.O. Neville, in his capacity as Chief Protector, sought to separate the pair by removing Lallie to Moore River Native Settlement. Although police raids on the Linden mob's camp failed to find Lallie, they so upset her elders that they withdrew their consent for the couple to marry.[6]

Unable to secure the elders' or the state's permission to formalise their relationship, the couple took matters into their own hands. They secretly fled Western Australia and crossed the state border into South Australia. They were finally married in the registry office in Adelaide in 1928. As Rajkowski puts it, from Jack's perspective:

> There was only one option left for him to take. If Lallie and he were to be free to marry, to be liberated from being pursued by the government's authorities, free of the police net, free of injuries or lethal punishment by her people, they would have to find a set of laws elsewhere that would give them permission to be husband and wife and permit them to feel safe. They would have to leave the State of Western Australia entirely, telling no one of their departure, and find more sympathetic authorities and more tolerant laws regarding Aborigines and Asiatics.[7]

Respecting the dictates of his religion, Jack was determined to marry Lallie and to establish with her a loving and secure family environment (even if he took the somewhat unorthodox approach of contravening the wishes of her elders). The same respect for religious and cultural convention determined his understanding of marriage and parenting. According to Jack and Lallie's younger daughter Shirley, her father 'controlled the household'.[8] Her older sister Mona noted that their father was 'the boss' and 'the head of the family'.[9] However, he also placed great importance on Lallie's role as wife and mother. The Muslim community believes that while roles differ between the sexes, a difference often interpreted by outsiders to imply man's superiority, both genders are accorded rights and responsibilities and an equal measure of accountability in the hereafter.[10] According to Mona, Jack described his vision of the complementary roles of men and women in these terms: 'Daddy used to explain it like this. We're talking about an umbrella now. The father is the umbrella, the top. But the umbrella cannot do its job if it doesn't have a handle, and the handle is the thing that keeps it all together, the mother. That's how he explained it to us ... The man, he protects the family, and the mother she holds the family up.'

Mark Bin Bakar, the son of an Aboriginal–Malay couple in Broome, suggests that local Aboriginal women often entered into long-term relationships with Muslim Malays because they had a reputation as hard workers and were seen as good providers for their wives and families. They may also have been attracted to the Malays because of the great emphasis the men placed on the importance of marriage and family. As Mark says, 'The Muslims were an escape for a lot of the Aboriginal women ... [who] got provided security as well as removed from a lot of the chaos.'[11] Mark refers here to the chaos that followed the near-disintegration of traditional Aboriginal societies produced by colonialist government policies, and the high levels of alcohol abuse, domestic violence and unemployment associated with it. As his mother 'Patricia' asserts: 'So instead of going with their own colour, [Aboriginal women] would go with an Asian man to support and feed their children, because things were very hard.'[12]

Mark feels that the fact that his mother was a member of the Stolen Generations 'contributed to the whole sanctuary of closing the world out and living in that castle with her husband'. While he appreciates that his Muslim Malay father provided his mother with the sense of security she yearned for, at times Malay husbands, who were 'chauvinistic by culture and by religion ... also ostracised the wife and kids from everybody else. Their world was home and that was it.' Security, it seems, could become isolation.

Mark recalls the pain of being, as he put it, 'removed from our community': 'A lot of the Malays, because they didn't indulge in alcohol, when we bumped into a drunken Aboriginal family or friends, they were shunned. Partly because of the Muslim culture, partly because they saw themselves as protecting their kids and their families, and at times it hurt a lot of us too, because we wanted to connect with our Aboriginal families as well.'

In some instances the children of Indigenous–Muslim couples were cut off from their Aboriginal families for many years. In one family's case the isolation they experienced from their Aboriginal relatives came as a result of the intrusion of the Aboriginal Protection bureaucracy into their affairs. In the previous chapter we saw that after the death of his Yammatji–Malay wife, Shaz Rind's great-grandfather sent their four children to Baluchistan to circumvent the Protector's removal order. Taking his children from their home country and extended Aboriginal kin was, ironically, the only way they could remain together as a family. It was only years later that Shaz's grandfather was able to return to Australia and be reunited with his Aboriginal relatives.

Authorities also sought to break up the Khan family, but they were able to stay together, maintaining a connection with their Aboriginal kin. In the 1940s Aboriginal–Afghan Goolbegum Khan gave birth to her first son in an Adelaide hospital. He was promptly taken from her and when she returned home without him, Goolbegum's father Nameth Khan hurried to the hospital, intent on retrieving his grandson. Zanzibar (Beatrice), one of Goolbegum's daughters, recalls her family's moving story here:

> Every time one of us was born, the white man would come and take it from her – as the baby was screaming from her stomach. They'd take us away because our eyes were different [we were of mixed

descent]. They took my brother, our oldest brother first and when our mother went home and she had no son, our grandfather, he saddled up his camels and took his two Afghan swords. They're long and curved. He had two of them and he come down here to Adelaide and he was twirling them high in the air. He walked through the halls of the Adelaide hospital slashing his swords, for his grandson. They couldn't stop him. He got his grandson, packed him in the camel sack and home he went. Bloody oath. They wasn't going to touch his grandson.[13]

This was not the first time Nameth Khan had fought to keep his family intact. The Aboriginal Protection bureaucracy had tried to take his own children away years earlier. Happily for the late Miriam Dadleh (née Khan) and her siblings, they were able to stay with their father and thereby associate with their Aboriginal kin as well. When Miriam's Arrernte mother died in 1919 the Protector threatened Nameth Khan with the removal of their three children (see figure 14). In a published interview Miriam recounted: 'Afghan people never let their kids go. The police used to come to take us away and my father said, "No. They're my kids and I'm going to rear them."' She continues, 'They said, "You're a man, you're travelling [with a string of camels]." He said "I can look after them. I can take time off to cook their tucker." He used to sew our clothes and all.'[14]

Travelling around with her younger brothers and hawker father, Miriam claimed: 'I was never brought up in the mission home or with the Aboriginals. I was with my father.'[15] In a mid-1980s interview with Pamela Rajkowski, Miriam noted that even though her mother's sister offered to look after her and her brothers, 'The old fella said, "No, I want to grow my kids up myself." He said, "They're my children, I want to rear them up how I want to rear them.'"[16] But the Khan children were certainly not isolated from their immediate Arrernte family or other Aboriginal people. Hawking various groceries, clothing, tinned foodstuffs and other provisions along the Oodnadatta track, Nameth Khan employed two of his late wife's brothers and his sister-in-law's son. During her time with them Miriam learned to speak Arrernte. She also had the opportunity to associate with many other Aboriginal communities during their long journeys. The Khan children regularly accompanied their father as he sold his wares from Oodnadatta in South Australia to as far as Katherine in the Northern Territory. As Miriam says: 'I'm proud of my black people. I go back to Hermannsberg [her mother's place of birth] and talk to people – stay there couple of weeks or two or three months. I can talk [Arrernte]. I can talk Luritja, understand Pitjantjatjara, bit of Dieri, bit of Arabana.'[17]

Semah Mokak-Wischki, who is the daughter of an Aboriginal–Indonesian mother and Muslim Malaysian father, also experienced varying degrees of security and isolation in her upbringing. She wonders whether some Muslim men felt comfortable with Aboriginal women (particularly those brought up in missions) because the 'women's gentle nature and subservience was something that could work really well with the Muslim discipline'.[18] Unlike Aboriginal women of her generation (the 1960s), Semah notes that women who grew up in the mission era 'didn't speak back. Not to their husbands, or even their GPs. I know with my mother when any authority figure, a doctor, asked her a question, it would be, you know, "Fine, thank you."' Some Muslim men feel that their designated role as head of the family entitles them to control and dominate their wives (and children), even though the Qur'an depicts men and women as having inherently equal value.[19] The Qur'an stipulates that men and women were created from one soul to be mates to each other and that woman was made to be in the service not of her husband but of Allah.[20] Even so, while Semah finds 'lots of things that I am really happy and proud and privileged to have had with my Muslim connection', other aspects are difficult to reconcile. As she claims, 'I think it's the woman's place, from my experience anyway … it wasn't suitable for me … it was too controlling for me.'

The four surviving Akbar children, who grew up in the 1940s in Renmark, South Australia, were raised according to the rules of their devoutly Muslim father, but Mona and her sister Shirley, unlike their brothers, were not permitted to leave the house alone (see figure 16). If they were not together one of their parents, brothers or a trusted family friend had to chaperone them. They were obliged to wear very modest clothing, which was, according to Shirley, 'like they're wearing today, like the [Muslim] women are wearing today'. Rather than permit his daughters to go shopping to buy their clothes, Jack Akbar asked the local store owners to bring a range of garment samples to the house for them to choose from.[21] Male callers were not allowed to enter the Akbar family home in Jack's absence. As Mona recalls: 'You don't have any men about in the yard or anywhere when the man [of the house] is not about. And if a visitor did come, like an old [Afghan] man came from Farina one time and Daddy wasn't home, so he sat in the yard. He didn't have to be told. He sat out in the yard until father came home, and then he was welcome to come into the house.'

Arranged marriages

In the mid-1940s Jack set about arranging the marriage of his older daughter Mona.[22] Arranged marriages were the norm in

Jack's homeland and are still common in many traditional Muslim societies. Children are expected to obey their parents in this, as in all other matters, but the prospective bride and groom do have the option of declining a suitor chosen by their parents.[23] Mona's husband was to be one of the sons of her father's close cameleer friend and countryman Gool Mohamed. From Jack's perspective he represented an ideal choice. In deciding on a match, the parents of daughters look for particular traits in a prospective bridegroom, including 'compatibility in nationality and social background, a good education, a sound occupation and earnings and religious devotion'.[24] Gool Mohamed's son had all of these. Mona recalls seeing him for the first time at Adelaide's Little Gilbert Street mosque, which she and her siblings visited with their father during school holidays: 'Well, I met him. I met him when I was about twelve. We were at the mosque and these two boys were coming in as we were going out, and Mum said, "That's your husband." And I thought, "Husband? What do I want a husband for?" And this old man … must have been in his twenties I suppose, but to a twelve-year-old, it's a grown man, he's a grown-up old man. Yeah [laughter]. One of Gool Mohamed's boys it was.'

A few years later, before the proposed marriage could go ahead, Mona fell pregnant to another young man. The news of Mona's pregnancy shattered her father. Within the framework of his religion and culture he felt Mona's actions disgraced him and his family.[25] We have seen that *zina*, sex outside the sanctity of marriage, is totally unacceptable in Islam. In most Muslim societies illegitimacy thus carries great stigma, and a Muslim woman who is pregnant outside wedlock risks being condemned by her community. Tainted herself, she is thought to have stained the honour of her parents and extended family as well.[26] According to Mona:

'Yes, I was supposed to marry one of Gool Mohamed's sons, I was promised to him, but then I went and got pregnant, and that was the biggest shame of all ... I was soiled goods then, couldn't pass me off on to anyone. That's how they [Muslim Afghans] are.'

Jack forced Mona to give up the baby for adoption.[27] Mona remained close to her father but, she recalls, the pregnancy and baby remained 'a closed subject, it wasn't talked about. And he never broached it again, you know, the job had been done. The shame job had been done, finished.' It was another forty-three years before Mona was reunited with her daughter. Today they share a very close relationship.

Halimah Mokak's arranged marriage did not come about either – but for completely different reasons. She was fourteen years old (in the early 1970s) when her father invited a compatriot to come and stay with their family. He had met the then 27-year-old Romly Yusuf when they were both working in the pearl-shelling industry in Broome. The men came from the same village in Malaysia, and Romly was invited to stay with the Mokaks following the end of his period of indenture. Shortly thereafter, Halimah's father suggested that Romly might make her a good husband. It was then that Halimah understood why Romly had been invited to stay. Halimah, as she recalls, 'was horrified, so I told my Nan, my [Aboriginal] mum's mum – who had a love/hate relationship with my father. And she told my dad that she was going to tell on him, tell the Welfare on him.'[28] In the event, Romly decided not to pursue Halimah. Realising that Halimah was, in her words, 'a bit too rough for him', he returned to Malaysia alone. Halimah told me with much amusement how, growing up in the Northern Territory, she and her sisters learned to shoot, skin and gut animals. Her older sister Semah also spoke of this in our interview:

We used to fish a lot and we used to hunt and we used to get all of our own food, and kill a cow to provide for the family, and all the girls were expected to know how to skin and cut. That was a very, very large part of our life. I mean, he was such a good fisherman, my father, and all the girls became the fish gutters and scalers [laughter]. In terms of skills, I think if we ever went out there on [reality TV show] *Survivor*, we'd do very, very well [laughter]!

Growing up in a small kampong (village) in Seremban, Malaysia, Romly came from a world in which men and women observed strict gender roles. Halimah's father knew this world too, but in Australia he learned to make certain adjustments. Living in remote Adelaide River in the Northern Territory, with eight mouths to feed, all of his children, male and female, helped kill and prepare the family's meals. In Halimah's words: 'Being young girls brought up in the Northern Territory and knowing how to shoot and drive a bull-catching Land Rover, we just took him [Romly] out for a few days, we took him out scrub-bashing with us. But he didn't like that at all, so he went back to Malaysia [laughter] … So, no, it was never going to work.'

Modesty and gender segregation

The Aboriginal Protection bureaucracy was not the only patriarchal agency keen on controlling Aboriginal women's sexuality. Many Muslim men sought to manage and restrict their wives' and daughters' interactions with other men. Sally Bin Demin grew up in post-war Broome. Raised by her Jaru Aboriginal mother and Muslim Malay stepfather, she shared very close ties with the other Aboriginal-Malay families in Broome and recalls how the Malay fathers she knew 'were more strict with the girls … A boy's allowed to do a little bit more than the girls, stay out a bit later. They could get away with a bit more than the girls.'[29] Sally's first husband was a Muslim from Malaysia (who came to Broome in 1955 to work in the pearl-shelling industry). Comparing the way he and his sister were disciplined, the couple's son Johari recalls, 'Dad was always a little harder on the girls ... he was very strict with [my sister], whereas he wasn't as strict with me, and it's a girl thing, it's a Muslim thing.'[30] Halimah Mokak, referred to above, had a similar experience. Her father was, she says, 'mainly [strict with] the girls' in her family. 'When the boys came along I think they got away with a bit more.'

Jack Akbar regularly travelled to Adelaide to purchase fresh fruit, vegetables and other supplies, which he later sold to the locals back in Renmark. While in Adelaide he stayed at the mosque on Little Gilbert Street. Financed by donations from the cameleers and built between 1888 and the early 1890s, it was the earliest Australian city mosque and 'a place of pilgrimage for camelmen from all over the country'.[31] Jack and Lallie's children accompanied Jack there during school holidays. Before they reached puberty, sisters Mona and Shirley were permitted to stay overnight at the mosque when they visited with their father. But once the girls reached about twelve years of age it was no longer deemed appropriate for them to stay overnight in the mosque itself. From then on they had to sleep in the back of their father's truck in a neighbour's yard across the road. This sort of gender segregation was commonplace among the Afghans. Mona recalls that once they got older the daughters of her father's compatriot Gool Mohamed stayed in a hotel up the street from the mosque.

Mona and Shirley also remember that they and their siblings ate separately with their mother when a male caller visited their home. Usually the whole family ate their meal, often curry and chapattis, together. They ate from a communal bowl and, although spoons or forks were sometimes used, the family generally ate with their fingers. Shirley notes that she 'never learned to eat with a knife and fork until [she] was about ten years old'. However, when one of their father's Afghan friends visited, she says, 'the men ate together and the children and the wife ate together'. This practice was also observed when they visited the mosque in Adelaide. At home the Akbar family sat at a table to eat but, Shirley recounts, at the mosque people sat in a circle on the floor and 'the men used to eat together and they would put out separate food for Mona and me because we weren't allowed to eat with them'. Mona feels she is fortunate to 'have had two brothers' because, she says: 'I've come across families that were all sisters, and to them, men are a foreign entity. They don't understand them at all. And I've met fellas that have been all brothers. They don't understand females because they haven't had that mixing.'

The late Aboriginal–Afghan Miriam Dadleh recalled seeing an Afghan wedding when she was young. A mullah (who might well have been her Afghan father's brother Mullah Assam Khan) officiated at the ceremony. The service was followed by much festivity. Large tarpaulins were laid down on the ground, upon which platters of food were placed. The men and women sat separately while they ate their rice and curries, after which there was singing, dancing and music playing. Miriam recollected that various instruments, including accordions, mouth organs, tin whistles and flutes, were played. The men and women also danced separately. In an interview with Pamela Rajkowski, Miriam recounted: 'The women would be in another dance together ... And the men used to dance by themselves, and all the women on their own, because they never allow another man to put an arm around his wife or things like that. They reckon that too close. No good.'

In an interview with Joan Staples, Thursday Islander Kathleen Hirakawa (née Seden) recalls that whenever she and her girlfriends went to a dance they had to be escorted by their Aunty May. This did not always sit well with the youngsters, with Kathleen thinking, 'Oh, what do you want to come with us for?'³² At other times the girls were escorted by their Uncle Sandy. Kathleen laments that 'it got that bad that [Uncle Sandy] used to sit outside while we were at the dance hall, and then … he'd come upstairs and he'd say, "Come on, girls. It's time to go home."' May's son Assan (Ken) O'Shea recounts an amusing anecdote about Sandy's chaperoning of a young couple when they were on a date. In his words:

> I think it was Mary and Georgie, they were courting. Georgie would come to take Mary to the pictures and Sandy would be all dressed up, with his tie and everything on and Georgie would say, 'We better go before the picture starts', and Sandy would get up as well, and he'd say 'Well OK, let's go.' And the three of them would all sit there, side by side … They were at least twenty years old, at least. And then they'd be coming back and Sandy would make them walk in front, and he'd walk behind so he could see [what they were doing]. As they were coming down the road they sort of tried to drag their feet to slow up the pace and Sandy would keep saying, 'Come on, hurry up, don't drag your feet, move it! The picture's over now, we can go home.'³³

Halimah Mokak recalls that if a boy wanted to take her or one of her sisters out on a date, all of the Mokak children would accompany them. As she says: 'There was one boy in Adelaide River [in the Northern Territory] who was allowed to take us to the movies, but he had to take five of us.' Halimah continues: 'He liked one of my sisters, but all the younger ones had to come too. So whenever we went out with a boy, the whole family came – except Mum and Dad.' After the movie Halimah's Muslim Malaysian father quizzed his children to make sure nothing untoward had occurred. As Halimah recounts: 'And then we'd come home, and then Dad would question the younger two and say, "Where did you sit at the movie? Did your sister go out and have some ice-cream?"'

According to Halimah, her father Mohammad Nor Bin Mokak (known by locals as Manu Mokak) was well known in Adelaide River for closely guarding the chastity of his daughters. After finishing school in the early 1970s Halimah lived for nearly two years in the Malaysian village of Seremban (her father's home village). After returning to Australia she worked briefly on a prawn trawler. Here she recounts the time when her father visited her on deck before she and the rest of the (male) crew went out to sea:

> Again, my dad was stamping his toughness. He came down to the trawler, and because I was going out on this trawler for six weeks and my dad knew the owner of the trawler, he met the skipper and the crew and basically, got on there, and I was so embarrassed. He lined them all up and he said that if anybody touches his daughter – he even told them he'd drunk human blood before! I'm just thinking, 'Why is he threatening people like this? Why is he like this?'

In some families Muslim grand/fathers not only sought to control their grand/daughters' interactions with the opposite sex. They also tried to prevent their daughters from wearing make-up. While there are no Qur'anic injunctions or Hadith (sayings and deeds of the Prophet Muhammad) against the wearing of cosmetics, many Muslims believe that women should not wear make-up when outdoors or in the presence of men to whom they are not married or related. Aboriginal–Afghan Zanzibar (Beatrice) Boerkamp notes that her Peshawar-born grandfather was vehemently opposed to his daughter's use of make-up. Beatrice's story, reproduced here at length, provides insight into the way some Afghan men tried (not always successfully) to control their Australian-born daughters:

> In town, my mother had her long hair, and she'd walk out, and she used to put lipstick on. She had lipstick on going to the shop, the old shop in Beltana [South Australia]. Grandfather caught her, in front of the whole town. They used to have water troughs for the bullocks. See you must remember, when the railway started to get built and the camels were no longer used, they used bullocks and Grandfather used to cart water and he had the water troughs. And he found my mother with lipstick on. You know when women started doing their lips red? He grabbed her in front of the whole town, dragged her to the water trough – and have you ever seen the brushes they used, the old wire brush they used on camel coats? He used that on her face! With her head dipped in the water, to wash that lipstick off, because women were not allowed to wear make-up or anything like that. She was crying, she ran home, and came out ten minutes later – lipstick on again [laughter]!

Female agency

In this instance Beatrice's mother Goolbegum – from all accounts a particularly strong-willed character – defied her Muslim father openly. At other times Goolbegum and her Aboriginal mother Galana opposed him in subtler ways:

> This old man, he used to load up his camels in Beltana. My grandmother, our grandmother Galana Hackam, she was a

traditional Yankuntjatjara woman. When he used to load up his camels she and my mum would be standing at the door, real sad, because he was heading out. But the minute he was gone, they used to run. Because an Afghan was not allowed to eat camp pie, corn beef, or any food product that man has packed, he had to kill his own food. So the minute he's turned his back, Nana and Mum used to go down and buy corn beef and camp pie and all that, and when they knew he was on his way home they used to run out, dig a big hole and throw all the tins in and cover them up [laughter]!

Numerous kinvert interviewees told how Aboriginal women suspended conformity to their Muslim husbands' or fathers' religious and cultural traditions when their men were away. In chapter 3 we saw how, in the Aboriginal–Malay Brahim and Mokak families, the mothers secretly took their children to be baptised without their Muslim husbands' knowledge or consent. Semah Mokak-Wischki's mother and grandmother both had Muslim husbands, and each, according to her, 'very quietly and sneakily practiced whatever they wanted [laughter]. Mum and Nana, they just ignored their husbands. They were strong Catholic women who just thought, "Well OK, yes you're right, but I'll still do what I want to do!"' Semah observed that her mother resisted her father's strict and uncompromising attitudes, not by directly opposing him but 'in a very quiet way … it was almost like she'd just duck and avoid.' She further explained, 'I mean, my mother was subservient to my father, and he was the boss. But she was smarter [laughter].'

Afghan and Malay descendants alike also spoke of the way their Indigenous mothers became Muslim after marrying their husbands. It is true that the women took on many Islamic cultural traditions, but few identified with Islam spiritually and theologically. The mission-raised women often tended to identify with various Christian denominations and, while they adopted particular Islamic rituals or behavioural norms during their married life, this was perhaps more an indication of their preparedness to accommodate their husbands' beliefs and practices than of any desire to become practising Muslims. Adoption of Islam helped Indigenous wives to create a sense of unity within their racially, culturally and religiously diverse families. In the words of Semah Mokak-Wischki, 'I think Mum just, you know, she was a Muslim to please Dad really.' Semah's sister Halimah Mokak (in an interview with Dilara Reznikas) characterised their mother's (cultural) acceptance of Islam in these terms: 'My mother was a Catholic woman and she converted to Islam, but she didn't practice Islam as such ... We [children] were the ones that used to practice Islam, but she still used to go to church with her mother.'[34]

Historian Christine Stevens, in her work on the Afghan cameleers, has suggested that when an Anglo-Australian or Aboriginal woman married a Muslim man 'she became irrevocably immersed in his Muslim code and lifestyle'.[35] This coincides, at least to a point, with my findings. When I inquired whether or not Mona Wilson's Aboriginal mother took on her Muslim husband's beliefs when they married she replied, 'Oh well, she sort of had to, really.' Similarly, the late Aboriginal–Malay descendant Septu Brahim commented that his Aboriginal mother 'had to fit in' with his Muslim father's 'very, very strong' Muslim beliefs.[36] But obeying the new religious and ideological codes of their husbands did not mean abandoning previously held beliefs and commitments. Converting to a (new) religion often entails a complete change of allegiance from one source of authority to another.[37] In this sense these Indigenous wives of Muslim men were not 'converts'. Although Aboriginal and Torres Strait Islander women adhered to many Islamic religious and cultural practices during their married lives (at least in the presence of their husbands), they maintained cultural and social practices from their pre-marriage milieu. Their identity formation might be more appropriately described as one of 'alternation'. According to Richard Travisano, unlike conversion, alternation refers to a less radical form of religious and ideological change, one that is much more inclusive of former commitments.[38] Rather than *replacing* the old with the new, both are *combined*.[39]

Indigenous women who entered partnerships with Afghan and Malay Muslim men may have accommodated at least three religio-cultural systems. Unless completely cut off from their country and kinfolk at a very early age, the women were familiar with the beliefs and practices of their local tribe or language group. These were usually overlaid with the stories, routines and rules acquired on Christian reserves and missions. Both layers of belief were, in turn, further sifted and reorganised when they came into contact with their Muslim husbands' religious and ideological practices. In another permutation, many Aboriginal and Islander women who married Muslim men had themselves been raised by Muslim fathers or stepfathers. These women also negotiated different ethnically or doctrinally based interpretations of the Qur'an. In any case, these contextually defined rules of behaviour raise the question of whether we might more accurately characterise these women as kinverts or as *alternators*, individuals engaged in an ongoing process of 'alternation'.

Indigenous wives exercised agency in deploying particular world views and identities in particular contexts. In some environments it was appropriate to utilise a specific set of beliefs and practices, while in other situations an alternative set of religious and cultural traditions was foregrounded. Adherence to particular religious principles could also change over time. Halimah Mokak recalls that as a child she ate pork at a friend's house and, upon returning home, asked her mother why their family did not eat it. Halimah recalls the incident in this way: 'Mum said, "Don't say that. I'll put chilli in your mouth. Why are you talking like that [using the word 'pork'], Halimah?" She said, "You must not tell your [Muslim Malaysian] father."' But as Halimah grew older she and her mother would sometimes go into Darwin for lunch, and her mother would order a ham sandwich! She also allowed Halimah to do so, if she wanted. In Halimah's words: 'It was lovely, because she used to say to us, "It's up to you, what you feel, what you want to do." It was really nice because [unlike my father] we had the choice with her. Mum had a really nice, gentle way of accepting both sides.' Halimah's older sister Semah agreed, claiming that, while her mother 'would talk [to us] about Christianity, Dad would impose all this other stuff on us, and really impose … [From his perspective] we were Muslims and that was it.'

Certain religious customs practised by their husbands were not acceptable to some Aboriginal and Islander women. Eva Salam Peacock, who was born on Thursday Island in the early 1920s, is the daughter of a Makassan father and a mother of Torres Strait Islander, Danish and Sri Lankan descent. Before her parents met and married, Eva's Catholic mother was married to her second husband, indentured pearl-shell worker Haji Salam, a Muslim Malay from Singapore ('Haji' is an honorific title given to a Muslim who has successfully completed the haj or pilgrimage to Makkah). Eva's mother had five children with her late Filipino husband before Haji Salam 'came to her rescue and married her'.[40] They had three children together (one of whom, sadly, died as a child) before Haji Salam's ten-year period of indenture ended and he was obliged to return to Singapore. According to Eva, Haji

Salam said, 'Oh well, you can come with me, I'll send your fares. You'll be all right in Singapore.' She continues, 'So Mum was quite happy about that. She loved him. Anyway, he went home and he sent her the money, also a letter explaining that he already had two wives over there.'[41]

In Islam polygyny is permitted on condition that the husband takes no more than four wives and that he treats his wives equally. If he is unable to deal justly with more than one wife, then he should only marry one.[42] Haji Salam might have considered that he could treat his wives equitably, but his Australian-born wife obviously doubted it, and in any case, in the words of her daughter Eva, '[Haji Salam] didn't let [Mum] know in the first place. And she didn't know how to take it. She was really upset and she said, "No." She said she couldn't share him. She said, "I'll stay here and starve", because there was no pension or anything like that in those days … She wrote and told him that she [couldn't] go, she couldn't live that way. So that was the end of that.'[43]

After years of marriage, Jack Akbar's Aboriginal wife Lallie also found that she could no longer submit to her Afghan husband's strict religious views and cultural inflexibility. She had been perturbed by the way Jack dealt with their teenage daughter Mona's out-of-wedlock pregnancy. When Jack insisted that the baby be given up for adoption, Lallie finally left the marriage. Lallie could not accept this because, as Rajkowski argues, 'it was the belief of her people that mothers especially should look after their children', providing them with love and support.[44] It is likely that Lallie was also distressed by Jack's handling of the situation because it recalled the widespread practice of Aboriginal child removal that many Indigenous families suffered. After years of living in exile in South Australia, Lallie was also keen to be reunited with her Wongai people in Western Australia. Her feelings of homesickness were perhaps exacerbated by Jack's inflexibility. Rajkowski suggests that it is highly likely that Lallie 'felt that if Jack insisted on sending Mona away from home to relinquish her baby then she would have to leave his home also'.[45]

Return journeys

At the age of twenty-four 'Afghan' cameleer and hawker Nameth Khan came to Australia from Peshawar in 1892. He remained in Australia for the next fifty-eight years, dying in Marree at the age of eighty-two in 1950. He had a daughter and two sons with his wife Alice (or Alison) Mabunka, a Western Arrernte woman who was the Sunday School teacher at Hermannsburg Mission. A couple of years after her death in 1919 (she was a victim of the Spanish influenza epidemic), Nameth remarried and had another daughter by his Afghan–Yankuntjatjara wife Galana Hackam. Today, his locally born grandchildren are themselves grandparents. It is more than 118 years since Nameth Khan put down roots in this country but, amazingly, the Australian branch of his family is still in contact with their extended kin in Peshawar.

Nameth already had a wife and three children when he came to Australia. He continued to support them, sending back food parcels, fabrics, clothing and other goods. He told his Australian wife and children about his other family, and Miriam Dadleh (née Khan) and her siblings corresponded with them, over the years sending many letters and photographs. Nameth never saw his original family again but, following his death, his locally born children stood to inherit his Peshawar property. Instead, Miriam, her two brothers and sister signed over the estate to their relatives. In an interview with Bruce Shaw, Miriam explained:

[My father] had a family over there too. He had two daughters and a son, I think. And two passed away. One was still living. That's the other family. And the will over there was made out to me. And I said, 'Well, I'm not going to get over there' ... So ... me and my [siblings] we signed it for that sister of ours over there, to pass it on to that family. She got a grown-up family and grandchildren and that. [We would have inherited] everything that was there: farm ... some homes and camels and that. I said, 'It's not good for us. We here and that's there.'[46]

Some years after this the family lost contact with their relatives in Peshawar. In my interview with Nameth's grandson Azeem (Johnny) Khan, he mentioned that he had 'been wondering for a long time what had become of our family in Peshawar'.[47] Then, happily, their connection was re-established through a fortuitous encounter. Rochelle Fielding, Nameth Khan's great-great-grand-daughter, happens to have an Afghani–Australian colleague. Rochelle told him of her Afghan cameleer heritage and her long lost family in Peshawar, and having a few days to spare during a recent visit to Afghanistan, her colleague decided to see if he could find her relatives. He travelled to Peshawar and, amazingly, tracked them down. They still had the letters they had received over the years from their Australian relatives, including some going back to the 1930s. Rochelle's colleague brought back video footage of them holding up the many letters and photographs they had in their possession. Azeem (Johnny) became very emotional as he described seeing his Peshawar relatives on film, and he and his family have since recommenced the written communication that was interrupted so many years ago.

To my knowledge this story of reunion is unique among the Afghan cameleer descendants in Australia. Around four generations have passed since camel strings made their way along the inland tracks, and it has been more than fifty years since the 'mosques of Coolgardie, Cloncurry, Marree and Broken Hill fell silent'.[48] Beyond retaining their families' oral testimony or lore, many descendants have carefully preserved their forebears' clothes, camel-riding equipment and other artefacts. But very few Afghan kinvert families in Australia have been able to maintain a connection with their relatives living overseas.

In this regard the Malay descendants have been more fortunate. Unlike their Afghan counterparts the Malays, like all other Asian indentured pearl-shell labourers, were exempted from the provisions of the 1901 White Australia policy, and demand (albeit greatly reduced) for their labour continued until the late 1960s. Many first generation Indigenous–Malays still reside in Broome, Darwin and Torres Strait and, of these, some have been fortunate enough to meet their fathers' extended families in various parts of Asia. Some Malay descendants, including Halimah Mokak, have spent considerable periods of time in their fathers' home countries. As a fourteen-year-old, Halimah lived for nearly two years with her father's siblings and other relatives in his home village of Seremban. There she attended a local school, learned to speak Malay, wore an Islamic headscarf or hijab, observed the month-long fast of Ramadan and prayed in congregational prayer sessions with the other women. After her arrival one thing immediately apparent to Halimah was her family's expectation that she dress and behave modestly. She very soon discovered that the sort of behaviour she took for granted as a young girl growing up in the Australian bush was highly inappropriate in her new setting.

In Seremban, Halimah and the other locals bathed in a nearby spring. She recalls that 'being brought up in Australia, you know, I'd just strip all my clothes off and go to jump in the water'.

Halimah was roundly scolded and given a lesson in the proper etiquette: women wear sarongs when bathing. Even accepting a lift on her brother's motorcycle was fraught with difficulties. Halimah's father was married to a Malaysian woman before meeting and marrying his Aboriginal–Indonesian wife in Australia. To this day Halimah and her Australian-born siblings are very close to their half-brothers and sisters. Here Halimah recounts riding with her Malaysian brother on his motorbike to nearby Kuala Lumpur: '[Until you go there] you just don't realise just how strict it can be on women, and of course, as a young girl when I was there my brother would come and pick me up to go to Kuala Lumpur, and automatically, I'd just pull my skirt up to jump on the motorbike. Well, you can't do that. You've got to sit side-saddle, and you might look elegant but you end up with such a sore back and neck by the time you get to KL!'

On a subsequent visit, after the death of Halimah's father, she recalls the scolding she received for pulling her skirt up and climbing a coconut tree. Halimah's anecdote reminds us of the difficulties kinverts could experience in their attempts to reconcile the different cultural worlds they inhabited:

> When my Dad passed away and we arrived back at the kampong [village], all the women were cooking, and all the men were in the lounge room praying. My stepmother said that we'd run out of coconuts, and asked if one of the girls could go up to the markets – and I said, 'No, no, no, I'll go and get them', because I knew Dad had lots of coconut trees out the back, and he had the little footholds on them. So I just rolled up my dress and tucked it in my pants and started climbing up the coconut tree, and my great aunty screamed out, 'Haram!' Haram means forbidden – and then I suddenly realised that Muslim girls don't do that. So I sort of came down the tree. But

that's where it's been a mixture of being brought up as a Muslim by my Dad in Australia, but also learning how to fish, gut fish, skin a bullock, learning halal, like cutting the bullock's throat and bleeding it, and yet women don't do that – you know, the flip side of it – in the village you just don't do it. So it was a bit of a shock to the system.

Members of the Bin Demin, Bin Swani and Nasir families have also spent time with their extended families in Asia. In many respects these Australian-born kinverts feel very comfortable with their extended Muslim relations because they were raised by their fathers and grandfathers to observe and respect Malay and Islamic religious practices and cultural conventions. Johari Bin Demin has visited his Muslim Malay relatives on a number of occasions. When he was young he stayed with his father's mother in Malaysia for a month, during which time he learned some Malay and taught his grandmother 'a little bit of Aboriginal–Broome language'. He felt very comfortable in his ancestral home. As he states: 'The thing is we grew up eating the food and aware of their culture so it wasn't like we were strangers. It was like I knew what to expect.' Majunia Bin Swani's Malay father never returned to his native Singapore after coming to Broome as a young man in the early 1950s, but she has visited her father's brothers, mother and other family there on several occasions since her initial visit in the early 1980s. She, too, feels very at ease with her Malay relatives, stating, 'There's no problems there, to go and stay with them. They eat the same food that we're taught to eat and we know their customs and everything like that, what to do and what not to do.'[49]

Majunia's experiences have much in common with those of Aboriginal–Malay descendant Joanne Nasir. Joanne's Muslim grandfather Abu Hassan Bin Nasir came from Madura in

Indonesia to Broome where he worked as a pearl-shell diver and later met and married Joanne's Aboriginal Catholic grandmother before moving with her to Darwin. Joanne's aunt married a Malaysian man, and when they were about eighteen years old (in the early 1980s), Joanne and her sister Tanyah travelled through Asia, stopping to visit Samsuding, their uncle's brother, in Malaysia. As Joanne says, 'It was quite easy for us to slip into the [local scene].'[50] The Nasir sisters felt completely at ease with the Malaysian cuisine, eating with their hands, and seeing their Muslim relatives at prayer. Even so, they were Australian enough to be surprised at some of the limits placed on them as young women. As Joanne recalls, 'When my uncle actually found out that we were planning on travelling through Thailand, he said, "No way. You cannot travel because you are young women", so we ended up staying with them for [the whole] two months.' She continues, 'You know, we just thought no worries backpacking around, thinking that we're the same as other Australians, but forgetting that that this is our upbringing as well.'

FIVE

HAVING FAITH

I [was] ... involved in other things like sports, academic pursuits, relationships, but inside [was] a bit of an emptiness, a bit of a hunger. It was almost like there was a jigsaw puzzle with one piece missing ... [Once] I knew that I had a relationship with God through Jesus that revolutionised everything. There was a real sense of peace, a real sense of joy and a real sense of satisfaction and completeness ... I found all the things that I was searching for.[1]

Since 1997 I became more involved with Tibetan Buddhism. It came at a time in my life when it was right, when there was a void in my life, where there were all sorts of things going on in my life and Tibetan Buddhism had all the answers for me ... I was on a search for myself and Buddhism helped me do that.[2]

I was a staunch black nationalist and [Malcolm X] is basically the black nationalist hero. After I read his autobiography I realised that he wasn't a black nationalist, he was actually on about Islam. And so I started investigating Islam and what it was about, and realised that it actually had a lot of the answers that I was looking for.[3]

The first of the conversion stories above is narrated by a non-Indigenous Australian man who embraced Christianity. The second is told by an Aboriginal woman who identified with Tibetan Buddhism, and the third is the story of an Indigenous Australian man who found Islam. These quotations describe the experiences of religious converts of different racial and cultural backgrounds, genders and ages. The religious beliefs these individuals adopted are also widely divergent. Despite this variation, there are some striking similarities in their stories. Whether consciously or subconsciously, each convert was on a quest. They were acutely aware that something was missing in their lives and, after a period of research and reflection, came, by various routes, into contact with religious ideas that appeared to provide the answers they were seeking. Finding the missing piece of the 'jigsaw' filled the 'void', providing them with a profound sense of inner peace and fulfilment.

Religious conversion is a process, and often a lengthy one. Of course conversion *can* involve a sudden and radical alteration in one's beliefs. The Christian conversion of Paul – formerly Saul, a well-known prosecutor of Christians – on the road to Damascus is perhaps the most famous example of a sudden and wholesale shift in one's religious beliefs and affiliations. Generally, though, conversion takes place over a period of time. It can entail *affiliation*, the movement of a person from no or minimal religious commitment to full involvement with a religious institution or community; *tradition transition*, involving the conversion of an individual from one religion to another; *institutional transition*, where a person changes from one group to another within a particular tradition; or *intensification*, the revitalisation of one's lapsed religious beliefs and practices.[4]

Regardless of these different types of conversion, it is not a process that ends when the individual decides to adopt a (new) faith. Religious converts characteristically undergo a second process of conversion, in which former patterns and behaviour are increasingly replaced with more orthodox beliefs and practices. Given that it involves an ongoing process of transformation, Lewis Rambo and Charles Farhadian suggest that *converting* is the more appropriate term.[5] Etymologically the word *conversion* is derived from the Latin *convertere*, which means 'to revolve, turn around' or 'head in a different direction'.[6] Conversion, then, involves two processes, a turning away from the past and a heading towards the future. As Rambo states, at the heart of conversion 'is the difficult combination of saying no and saying yes'.[7]

This chapter considers the complex experiences of Indigenous men and women who say 'yes' to Islam. After all, finding an answer to life's meaning is not simply about finding the missing

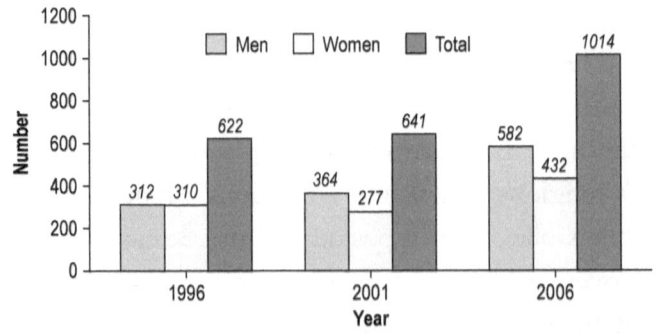

Indigenous Muslims in Australia 1996–2006

SOURCE ABS 2008 and 2010

piece in the jigsaw; before conversion, life may be experienced as a void, where no pieces fit, where nothing seems made to fit. One of the great revelations of conversion is a sense of connectedness: converts feel connected to a world in which they formerly felt they had no place – and they can now make sense of the seeming disorder. Conversion is complex because it provides both a new identity for oneself and a new identification with others.

In both the 1996 and 2001 censuses, more than 600 Indigenous Australians nominated Islam as their religion. By the 2006 national census, however, the number had risen by more than 60 per cent to 1014 people.[8] Statistical data from the 2006 census indicates that most Indigenous Muslims (more than 63 per cent) reside in metropolitan areas.[9] Reflecting this demographic distribution, the practising Indigenous Muslims I met live in major cities (and, in conformity with census figures, the majority in Sydney). The following draws on in-depth interviews undertaken in Brisbane, Sydney, Melbourne, Adelaide and Canberra as well as one published account from an Indigenous Muslim based in Perth. The Indigenous Muslims discussed in this and the remaining chapters mirror the 2006 census figures in other ways as well. Australian Bureau of Statistics data indicates that more Indigenous men (58 per cent) than women are Muslim.[10] In the interviews I conducted with almost twenty practising Indigenous Muslims more than half were men. In terms of age, my findings reflect recent statistical evidence, which suggests that, while Indigenous Muslims of all ages find Islam attractive, most (60 per cent) are younger than thirty.[11]

The individuals I met differ in age, gender, marital status, occupation, place of birth and residence, and Indigenous language or cultural group and, not surprisingly, each interviewee has their own unique trajectory in coming to Islam. This diversity represents the many ways Islam has been transmitted, received and interpreted in Indigenous Australia. Despite these differences, Indigenous Muslim converts on a journey to Islam share not only surprisingly similar experiences with one another but also with non-Indigenous converts in Australia and beyond. The subjective experiences of converts in New Zealand, Great Britain, North America, Sweden and Denmark are, for example, remarkably similar. In this sense, the growing Indigenous spiritual encounter with Islam reflects a global trend. There are, though, some significant differences and nuances, as we shall see in succeeding chapters.

Stage model

In an attempt to organise and understand the dynamic matrix of factors that affect individuals across space and time, and within which conversion occurs, a stage model is presented here. Borrowed from Lewis R. Rambo, a leading US theorist of conversion, this model should not be seen as universally valid but as a useful way of integrating and elucidating the complex processes involved in conversion.[12] The seven stages in this model – crisis, quest, encounter, interaction, commitment, consequences and context – are not sequential but make up the overall environment in which religious change takes place. Unlike the other six stages, 'context' is not passed through; rather, its influence resonates throughout the entire process, affecting all other conversion stages.[13] Context is the total environment, the 'big picture' in which conversion takes place. According to Rambo, what he calls the micro- and macro-contexts both need to be taken into account.[14] A good part of what we describe in this chapter considers the microcontext of conversion. It refers to the immediate world of one's family, ethnic and language group, religious community and neighbourhood.[15] We save our discussion of the macrocontext of Indigenous conversion for chapter 6.

Crisis

Spiritual quests are often precipitated by a particular event. It might be a traumatic experience, a personal or family crisis, or some other existential concern that leads one to question the meaning and purpose of life.[16] In our conversations several interviewees recalled the particular event that led them to embark on their spiritual journey. Sydney-based Alinta Smith, a young Indigenous woman who, at the time of our first interview in 2005, had converted to Islam only recently, began to ponder the meaning of life after a number of unhappy events in her life, including breaking up with her partner. As she states:

> I think also it was the time in my life, I was going through a lot of stuff, I'd just broken up from a relationship that I was in for four years ... So I had a lot of spare time and I just felt maybe a bit depressed about all this time I had by myself, and I started to wonder what's the meaning of life? Why are we here? I don't want to just work all my life. What is our purpose here?[17]

Another experience that prompted Alinta to question the meaning of existence was a sudden death in the family:

> Just before October [2005] my aunty passed away, and she'd just had a baby four days before she passed away, and that really had an impact on me. She was only thirty-three ... So it was probably a number of events that have happened in my life over the past two

years that have led me to – first, looking for God, and then actually taking action on looking for God – and it led me to Islam. It wasn't just one thing that happened to me; there were a number of things that contributed to the path that I fell upon.

The death or illness of a close friend or relative has been a significant turning point for other respondents. Troy Meston, a Brisbane-based Indigenous Muslim in his early thirties, became preoccupied with existential questions following the death of a friend from a drug overdose, as he stated in our 2005 interview: 'I think it was 2000. One of our close friends, a fellow we went to school with, he overdosed on heroin and he was only twenty-one. That really brought death home to me ... It wasn't until I stood at his grave, I actually saw the earth and really started to visualise myself being there, that it started – that was the window that was opened to me, that was the opportunity that I got to see.'[18]

Eugenia Flynn, a young Aboriginal–Chinese woman who embraced Islam in her early twenties, was also moved by painful personal and family experiences. When I asked why she turned towards Islam, she responded:

> I think it was because I had a lot of problems with my sister, we weren't the best of friends and we used to fight a lot, and my Dad got pretty sick ... and I guess for me it was also about the fact that I had thought about how I wanted to live my life. Because I was going through all of this change, and nearing the end of high school ... you know, what am I going to do with my life and that kind of stuff.[19]

Many non-Indigenous Muslim converts in Australia and beyond also experience trauma and emotional distress before converting. Australian convert Asiya Mahmoud recalls that 'to reach the day' when she felt ready to become a Muslim, she 'had first to reach a crisis point'.[20] Another non-Indigenous Australian convert, Catholic-raised Jan Jackson, began to consider alternative religious options when her 'personal circumstances changed drastically'. She continues, 'My beloved father died tragically; my marriage broke up painfully ... and I was living alone. I was forced to take stock, reflect, and reassess my life. And I found myself in a thoroughly meaningless void.'[21] Nearly half of the seventy men and women who participated in Ali Köse's research on British converts to Islam also began 'to look for something new' following a period of emotional turmoil.[22]

Quest

Those on a spiritual quest are, as we have seen, on a search for meaning. Human beings need frameworks within which they can understand, direct and interpret their lives.[23] If a crisis throws their previous beliefs into disarray, the need for a new and meaningful system of thought can intensify. The search for meaning can take one down a number of paths, and for some respondents their identification with Islam was far from being a foregone conclusion. Many investigated the teachings of several alternative religious systems before adopting Islam.[24]

The 'sampling' of a range of religions is certainly not unique to Indigenous Muslims in Australia. Local and international research on the experiences of Muslim converts reveals that they typically study many religious traditions in their quest for truth and knowledge. In her analysis of Muslim conversion in New Zealand, Ruqayya Sulaiman-Hill's findings have much in common with those of Larry Poston, who examined the experiences of Muslim converts in North America.[25] These, in turn, reflect the experiences of many non-Indigenous Australian converts recorded in Islam Australia's *My Path to Islam*.[26] In the words of Hanan Conroy, a 'fifth-generation Australian with mostly English and Irish heritage': 'I wanted to look into every religion that I could ... I decided, after a while, to become a Buddhist. I was attracted to the ideas of tolerance, compassion, defeating ego and non-attachment to worldly things. Then spiritual hunger led me to search for God in Buddhism, Taoism, Confucianism, Astrology, New Age, Pop Psychology, Shamanism and witchcraft.'[27]

Sulaiman-Hill and Poston note that the majority of their, respectively, New Zealand and North American interviewees examined a number of religious systems before deciding that Islam was qualitatively superior. The non-Christian alternatives most often mentioned were Hinduism, Buddhism and the Hare Krishna movement, while several '"Christian" cults' such as Mormonism, Jehovah's Witnesses and the like were also sampled.[28] My findings largely conform to these international studies. Many Indigenous Muslim respondents compared and contrasted a range of religious faiths and ideologies before embracing Islam. Alinta, for example, spent more than six months looking into various religious alternatives. As she recalls: 'I really just started wondering about God as a whole, and just thinking about my future and I just thought having a religion was something I wanted ... so I looked at all different types of religions ... Christianity, Jehovah's Witness, Judaism.'

Justin Agale, a thirty-something, Sydney-based Muslim of Aboriginal and Torres Strait Islander descent, had a similar experience. His spiritual quest led him to explore different political philosophies as well as a number of Christian and non-Christian religious traditions: 'Since I was about fifteen I started getting heavily involved in politics and I was always looking for a solution for my people, so I checked out Communism, Socialism, and at the same time I was also going through a spiritual journey of my own, so I went through doing meditations, I checked out Buddhism and really looked at Catholicism.'[29]

On their spiritual journeys a number of Indigenous Muslim converts noted that it only occurred to them to investigate Islam after weighing up a number of different religious claims. Alinta's progress illustrates this. To begin with, she 'didn't really consider looking at Islam'. Her disinclination to consider Islam as a likely vehicle of salvation reflected numerous 'issues' she had with the faith. Before examining the teachings of Islam Alinta thought of it as a religion that oppressed women. She was particularly opposed to the headscarf or hijab, viewing it as a symbol of gender inequality. After familiarising herself with the main tenets of Islam, though, she recognised that her prejudices were little more than the myths peddled in the mainstream media. Still, becoming a Muslim was not a decision reached easily: 'I thought, 'What are you doing? I can't believe this. Am I really considering becoming a Muslim?' Like, you know, a *Muslim*? We get this whole stereotype of what they are and who they are … [I was] believing the stereotypes, which is really sad.'

Interviews conducted by Tuba Boz with non-Indigenous Australian converts in Melbourne yielded similar findings. A number of Boz's respondents started out with negative views of Islam. As one woman remarked: 'Oh, the media has so much to answer for. I had [Muslims] pegged as people who are violent, extreme, limited and women were oppressed.'[30] A male respondent who during his religious quest investigated Christianity, Catholicism, Hinduism and Buddhism, initially excluded the idea of becoming a Muslim on the basis that 'they're terrorists'.[31] In her research on

British Muslim converts Kate Zebiri also found that her interviewees 'not infrequently describe[d] how they initially shared the "prejudices" of mainstream society, and how these had to be overcome before conversion could take place'.[32]

Conversely, in a number of cases it is precisely *because* of the negative stereotypes of Islam that people become interested in it. Recent events including the Salman Rushdie affair, the Gulf Wars, the Danish cartoon episode, and suicide bomb attacks in Madrid, London, Bali and particularly those in the United States on 11 September 2001 have, ironically, accelerated the pace of Muslim conversion in many countries in the West.[33] While it might be an exaggeration to say that more people have converted to Islam because of these events, it is nonetheless true that over the past decade we 'have seen a marked growth of interest in Islam, at the same time that anti-Islamic sentiment seems also to be on the rise'.[34]

The 9/11 terrorist attacks in New York and Washington inspired a number of Australians to seek further information about Islam. In the words of a non-Indigenous male convert, 'When the terrorist attacks on September 11 occurred I suddenly found myself going to the library looking for books on Islam. I was curious about this religion that everyone was talking about.'[35] A non-Indigenous woman, who also subsequently embraced Islam, was drawn to the religion for the same reasons. As she states: 'September 11th was to prove a turning point for me. I was totally shocked by these attacks, and I was further shocked to read some truly negative comments by Australians regarding Islam ... I was determined to learn as much as possible about Islam.'[36]

These potential converts were not on a *spiritual* quest as such but a search for knowledge. In her research with non-Indigenous Australian converts Boz found that many did not consider themselves spiritual pilgrims. Rather, she says, they '"bumped" into Islam, or were researching it, not with the intention of converting, but to gain information' out of curiosity's sake. In other cases the future converts' interest was piqued because 'they had some sort of interaction with a Muslim',[37] an event that Rambo describes as initiating the *encounter* stage in the converting process.

Encounter

A number of Indigenous Muslim respondents were not on a self-consciously religious quest but came upon Islam almost by chance, although, as it turned out, at a particularly propitious moment in their personal journeys. Sometimes it was a book that piqued their interest, sometimes an article or website. Alternatively, an encounter with a Muslim served to tip the balance of the interests and potential affiliations. Indigenous Muslim convert Justin Agale was inspired by a book but, as the quotation at the beginning of this chapter indicates, his initial interest in Malcolm X was politically, not spiritually, based. He revered Malcolm X not as a Muslim but as a symbol of the Black Power struggle. However, Justin read Malcolm X's autobiography at a time in his life when he was on a spiritual quest, but to that point he had not considered Islam, or realised that the black liberationist's message was based in Islam: 'When I started university I really got into Black Nationalism and, you know, chanting slogans of the Black Panthers and Malcolm X and all of that from the 1960s in America ... I came across the autobiography of Malcolm X and I realised that this man, who I had held up as my sort of personal hero ... wasn't about Black Nationalism. Black Nationalism was a tool to get people interested in Islam. He was all about Islam.'

Justin's first encounter with Islam came through reading about it. His interactions with Muslim individuals and communities followed. The initial encounter of practising Muslim 'John', a professional in his fifties, with Islam in the mid-1980s was also textual: 'I read about it.'[38] It was later, he notes, that 'by chance I met [a Muslim] and got involved that way'. In most cases potential converts interact with Muslims and come across Islamic texts simultaneously. It was champion boxer Anthony Mundine's Muslim manager who first gave him Malcolm X's autobiography, which, according to Anthony, 'really inspired me to look at Islam and get closer to God'.[39] Alinta Smith's interest in Islam grew steadily after reading about it, but she, like Anthony, also had Muslim friends who could answer questions she had. In her research on Muslim converts in New Zealand, Sulaiman-Hill similarly found that 'reading or study' was influential in a person's decision to embrace Islam. But her findings, like mine, suggest that an interest in Islam is itself often 'sparked by personal contacts'.[40]

Future converts encounter Muslims in different places and under varied circumstances. Some have Muslim friends and acquaintances they have met at work or school; others have Muslim neighbours or have come across Muslims during their travels. Much international research confirms the significant role that one's encounter with Muslim individuals plays in the conversion process. In a study of Swedish Muslim converts Madeleine Sultán found that many became increasingly curious about Islam after spending time with Muslims.[41] Writing of British converts, Köse notes that 'most come to know Islam through personal contact, which usually plays a great role in conversion'.[42] According to Tina Jensen, Danish converts' 'socialisation with people of Muslim immigrant background is one of the many motivations for converting to Islam',[43] while a number of Poston's North

American respondents 'mentioned [a] specific individual who had influenced them in their decision-making'.[44]

Converts, local and overseas, Indigenous and non-Indigenous, are often impressed and influenced by the social demeanour of the Muslims they encounter. Many observe and value the fellowship evident in the way Muslims interact with each other and with their non-Muslim counterparts. What Poston labels 'example and imitation' played a significant role in the conversion of his North American interviewees.[45] In our conversations numerous Indigenous Muslim respondents noted that they found the qualities of generosity, hospitality and piety they observed in the Muslims they encountered appealing. A considerable number of interviewees had the opportunity to observe and interact with Muslims on a daily basis. Long before she made the decision to convert, most of Alinta Smith's friends were Muslim. She was 'brought up around the Muslim community' in the Sydney suburbs of Bankstown and Greenacre, both of which have large Muslim populations and was, accordingly, 'exposed to Islam for a long time' before her conversion.

Australia's Muslim population has increased markedly since the 1970s, particularly following the rescinding of Australia's discriminatory immigration policy (commonly known as the White Australia policy), and the subsequent introduction of a policy of multiculturalism. While around two-thirds of the 340 000 Muslims in Australia were born overseas, almost 40 per cent have been born and raised in Australia.[46] As the numbers of Muslim immigrants and the second generation of locally born children continue to rise, the opportunities for meaningful encounters between Muslim and non-Muslim Australians naturally grow exponentially. This is especially the case for Australian youth. More than two-thirds of Muslim Australians are younger than thirty-five.

For many, particularly those born in Australia, English is their first and sometimes only language. They are fully immersed in Australian society and culture and may have little direct experience of their parents' country of origin. Non-Muslim Australians are increasingly encountering Muslims who not only speak English but also have a fair dinkum 'Strayn' accent. A shared linguistic and cultural frame of reference means that an encounter is more likely to lead to a mutually beneficial *interaction*.

Interaction

The interaction phase represents an intensification of the friendships and other relationships initiated during the encounter stage. It is also characterised by an intensification of the potential converts' reading and learning about the teachings, lifestyle, outlook and expectations of the religious group with which they are becoming increasingly aligned. At this stage a potential convert might begin to enact the rituals associated with their chosen religion. In the case of prospective Muslim converts they might take advantage of Islamic classes, attend Muslim-organised events, or frequent mosques. The interaction period is also often characterised by a process of comparing and contrasting previous religious attachments with potentially new ones.[47] For Muslim converts in Australia, and the West generally, this often involves comparing Islamic teachings, practices and values with their equivalent expressions in Christianity.

Alinta Smith initially took only a casual interest in Islam, regarding it as one of the many religious avenues open to her. In time, finding what Islam had to offer appealing, she gave up reading about the doctrines of other faiths: 'I stopped reading all these books about other religions, as I was very intrigued by

Islam. It made a lot of sense. That was the most surprising thing ... I got different sources, I got a copy of the Qur'an, I read about the Prophet Muhammad (peace be upon him),[48] and I just wanted more and more of it. I got immense satisfaction in reading about it.'

Years before converting, Eugenia Flynn was one of a growing number of young (Indigenous) Australians who shared a close friendship with a second-generation Muslim Australian. Eugenia's interest in Islam grew after years of observing and interacting with her and her family. She recalls:

> I learned a lot about Islam from [my friend]. Not really directly. Initially I never really asked her questions and she never really talked about it. But I learned a lot through her behaviour ... Because I was friends with her I went and slept over at her house and spent time with her family. They'd pray five times a day and everything – so [I was] learning about Islam through their mannerisms and seeing how it was in every part of their life. I suppose it was really subconscious for me for a really long time. We were friends since year 8 and it took me until the second year of university to finally say that I wanted to be a Muslim.

In our conversations Eugenia and several other respondents stressed that their Muslim friends never sought to convert them to Islam. In Islam, as we have seen, freedom of religion is ordained in the Qur'anic injunction 'Let there be no compulsion in religion' (2:256). Many interviewees welcomed the fact that Muslims, unlike the advocates of some other religious traditions, did not 'push' their religion. Non-Indigenous Australian converts have also appreciated this fact. In the words of Abdullah Islam, a former Christian 'Bible basher':

> As a Christian I was told to love, but yet in our actions – and that was how we were – the only time we entertained a Muslim, a Jew, a Buddhist, a Hindu was when we were trying to convert them. Now, a Muslim will not Bible bash you or should I say Qur'an bash ... If you wish to talk about it, they will talk about it, if you ask questions; they will answer you about it. We as Muslims believe that you will come into the realization yourself, by the guidance of Allah.[49]

Many Indigenous and non-Indigenous Muslim converts in Australia, in common with those from other Western countries, were practising or nominal Christians before converting to Islam. A number felt confused by aspects of Christian theology and consciously rejected their original faith. Although withdrawing from their parents' or culture's religion, most did not stop believing in the existence of God.[50] As their interest in Islam intensified they inevitably drew comparisons between Islam and Christianity. Some, like Indigenous Muslim Justin Agale, a former Catholic, appreciated the fact that in Islam one's relationship with Allah is not mediated by another human being. Roman Catholicism in particular grants the Church and its priesthood a central role in administering the grace of God. Justin was impressed by the fact that Islam allows for a direct approach to the Divine: '[In Islam] God can speak to you individually. You have a direct relationship with Him.' It is a sentiment echoed by Indigenous Muslim 'John', who finds attractive the fact that in Islam 'there is no priest, as such ... you're responsible [for religious observance] yourself.' In Anthony Mundine's words: 'It's a relationship between you and God; that's it.'

Muslim converts, in Australia and beyond, are almost uniformly impressed by the clarity and simplicity they perceive in Islam. It is widely believed that the Qur'an, unlike the Bible, has been preserved in its original form and is 'thus simple in the sense of being "pure and unadulterated" as well as "uncomplicated"'.[51] The idea that Islam is relatively simple and logical also stems from its monotheism, which contrasts strikingly with the Christian concept of the Trinity. In our conversations the majority of Indigenous Muslim converts emphasised the appeal of *tawheed*, an Arabic term meaning 'doctrine of Oneness (of God)'. Anthony Mundine explained it as follows: 'The belief in one God, with no partners and no associates, just the oneness in God. You know you see in other religions there are godheads, you know Christians, they're the closest to Islam, they believe in the Trinity, three is one and one is three. But in Islam there's just one, and the book's [Qur'an's] telling us there's only one God, no partners, no associates. That pretty much sealed it for me.'

A number of Indigenous Muslim converts have also struggled with the notion of the divinity of Jesus. Originally from Badu Island in Torres Strait, 'Jamila' felt that the Islamic characterisation of Jesus as a Messenger or Prophet, rather than as the son of God, made more sense. After all, she wondered, if God was not human, how could he have a son? 'I read the Bible as well as the Qur'an, and I compared the differences and I thought, in the Bible, when I read the Bible, I felt confused, so I'm not sure. In the Bible they're talking about Jesus being the son of God; in Islam it makes sense when I read about Jesus [as a prophet].'[52]

Closely connected to a rejection of the doctrine of the Trinity and the divinity of Jesus is the perception that Islam, unlike Christianity, is a supremely rational religion.[53] The Qur'an is said to accommodate and pre-date the findings of modern science. Islam, it is remarked, does not require one to suspend ordinary common sense in order to embrace it. International and Australian research indicates that this is an aspect of Islamic doctrine that would-be converts find immensely appealing, and Indigenous Muslims are no exception. Aboriginal convert Rocky Davis, whose Muslim name is Shaheed Malik, claims: 'As a person of logic and rationality, I cannot believe that God and the Son – the Father, the Son, the Holy Ghost – that these three are one. I cannot believe three Gods are one because it's not logical, and it's not rational.'[54]

Through an increasingly attentive and thoughtful reading of the Qur'an, and the expansion of their relationships with Muslims, subjects on a spiritual journey find not only answers to existential questions but also an alternative to the religion of their childhood. Encounter and interaction with a religious group are more likely to proceed to the *commitment* stage if potential coverts perceive continuity between their own forming world views – often based on disillusionment with inherited teachings – and the resolution of existential questions that the new religion proposes. In other words, a negative spiritual environment often works, paradoxically, to make potential converts more positive about their choice and new direction. Whether Islam would attract Indigenous Muslims if, for example, they were not dissatisfied with Christianity is a question taken up in the next chapter.

Commitment

At the threshold of commitment the convert has finally made the decision to renounce the old orientation and embrace the new. Converts often experience a great sense of relief and joy after what, for many, has been a long period of indecision and anguish. During the commitment phase the convert also becomes a full member of the new religious community. This is usually achieved through rituals of incorporation.[55] In Islam converts mark their formal entry into the Muslim community by performing the *shahada*. The Arabic word *shahada* is best translated as 'testimony' or 'bearing witness'. Converts testify in Arabic, in the presence of two witnesses, the following dual declaration of faith (reproduced here in English): 'There is none worthy of worship but Allah and Muhammad is his Messenger.'[56] There are seven critical conditions attached to the *shahada*, without which its declaration is meaningless. One must have full knowledge of the meaning of the *shahada*; complete certainty and surety of it; regard it with sincerity and exclusively worship Allah; truthfully believe what it signifies; have love for the *shahada*; submit to its requirements, which are obligatory duties; and acceptance, achieved by doing what is commanded and avoiding that which is prohibited.[57]

It is also recommended, although not obligatory, that after performing the *shahada* the new Muslim take a shower or bath. The full ritual washing of the body is known as *ghusl*, as opposed to *wudu*, a partial washing or ablution that Muslims perform before prayer or when handling and reading the Qur'an. If the *shahada* is performed at a mosque (*masjid* in Arabic), imam or prayer leaders usually issue the new Muslim with a certificate. Under the aegis of the Australian Federation of Islamic Councils, the Islamic Council of Victoria and those in other Australian states issue converts with a certificate confirming that the named individual has adopted Islam upon the deepest consideration and in the fullest liberty of choice. Muslim converts can produce these certificates, if required, when performing the pilgrimage or haj (non-Muslims are prohibited from Makkah, or Mecca, and the rites of pilgrimage).

For Alinta Smith, Eugenia Flynn and other Indigenous Muslims, declaring the *shahada* was a profoundly moving experience. Alinta describes the sense of elation she felt after making her public declaration of faith in 2005: 'After I did it I just thought, "This weight was lifted off my shoulders, and off my heart." I just felt like I could breathe and take a big breath, it was just great. I thought, "Oh, thank God I've done it. He's given me the strength to get here."'

Eugenia clearly remembers the day she declared the *shahada* in February 2002, recounting it in these words:

> I went to [my friend's] house and there's an imam called Brother Khalid in Adelaide, so he led me through my conversion and I did it at her house with her and her older sister, and her mum and her dad were there too. It was nice, it was really simple. We sat there and Brother Khalid made sure that this was what I wanted to do, and explained to me about Islam some more and made sure that it was definitely something that I agreed to 100 per cent and no one was forcing me. And then he led me through the *shahada*, the declaration of faith ... He did it in Arabic and in English and made me repeat after him and after that I was a Muslim ... Some people say you don't have to, but I went and had a shower afterwards, because it's like you've been reborn.

An 'authentic' or 'genuine' conversion to Islam means that the person is prepared to live by what God (or Allah in Arabic) and His Messenger have decreed in both the Qur'an and the Sunna. Together these form the basis of Islam and its law, known as Sharia.[58] Muslims believe that the holy book of Islam, the Qur'an (Arabic for 'recitation'), is the final revelation from God to humankind. The divine guidance found in the Qur'an was revealed to Muhammad by the archangel Jibril (known to Christians as Gabriel) over a period of twenty-three years, between 610 CE and the time of the Prophet's death in

632 CE. The recitations came to Muhammad at different periods in his life. Muhammad memorised God's words, which were then dictated to his companions and written down by scribes. All the recitations were fixed in writing after Muhammad's death. Muslims believe that the revelations contained in the Qur'an are literally the word of God, and since they were delivered in Arabic, translations of the Qur'an are viewed by some Muslims as sacrilegious (this is why, as we discuss later, converts often learn to read the Qur'an in Arabic, regardless of their original language).

The rule of Allah is given directly in the text of the Qur'an and indirectly through the Sunna, the exemplary conduct of Allah's Messenger, the Prophet Muhammad.[59] *Sunna* is an Arabic word meaning 'trodden path'. The Sunna of the Prophet, then, is the words, deeds, ways and manners of the Prophet Muhammad. The Sunna records how the Prophet put the Qur'anic message into practice in his everyday life, and Muslims today model their actions after the Prophet's customary practice. After Muhammad's death many scholars began collecting and compiling the known deeds and sayings of the Prophet. Each of these sayings or deeds is called a Hadith. The published compilation of these Ahadith (plural of Hadith) is the Sunna. Thus, although one becomes Muslim through recitation of the *shahada*, a convert's belief is not complete unless they follow the Qur'an (the word of God) and the Sunna (the example set by the Prophet Muhammad).

Having said the *shahada*, which is the First of the Five Pillars (or major requirements) of Islam, it is expected that the new Muslim will engage in ritual prayer (called salat) five times a day. Prayer is the Second Pillar of Islam and, although it is preferable to pray together at a mosque, a Muslim can pray almost anywhere. Muslims around the world, either together or alone, pray in the direction of the most sacred site in Islam, the Kaaba, a cube-shaped shrine in Makkah (Mecca), Saudi Arabia. The third religious duty for every Muslim is to give a portion (roughly 2.5 per cent) of their income to charity. The annual alms-tax or zakat (which means 'purification' in Arabic) helps purify the soul of the giver and reduce greed, while distributing wealth throughout society. The Fourth Pillar requires every Muslim to fast (through the avoidance of food, drink and sexual intercourse) from sunrise to sunset during the holy month of Ramadan, the ninth Islamic month of the year.[60] The pilgrimage to Makkah, known as the haj, is the Fifth Pillar of Islam. It is an obligation, at least once in a lifetime, for those who are financially and physically able to perform it.

In addition to learning and practising the Five Pillars of Islam it is also expected that anyone entering the faith will familiarise themselves with the five categories of rulings. Broadly speaking, there are five categories of 'do's and don'ts' in Islam. Practices deemed *fard* are compulsory or obligatory. The Five Pillars obviously fit into this category. *Mustahab* actions are recommended or encouraged, but not compulsory. An example of behaviour deemed *mustahab* is praying more than five times a day. Anything categorised as *mubah* is permissible or allowed. Actions in this category are neither encouraged nor discouraged and are left up to the individual's conscience. *Makruh* practices or actions are discouraged, but not forbidden. Divorce comes under this category. Eating pork, drinking alcohol, committing adultery and murder are all deemed haram; that is, prohibited or forbidden. Having introduced some of the main tenets of Islam, it is time now to explore the *consequences* of embracing them.

Consequences

Saying yes to Islam requires the new Muslim to create and consolidate alternative relationships, follow new and complex rituals, change their eating and drinking habits and perhaps even their line of work, and learn the language or rhetoric to express these experiences to oneself and others.[61] Islam is thus better described as *deen*, a way of life, rather than a religion, because it influences every part of a Muslim's existence.[62] The 'four Rs' that make up the 'matrix of transformation' converts experience include relationships, rituals, rhetoric and roles. In other words, with whom does the new Muslim now interact, what unique practices does the convert now engage in, how does she or he think and speak differently, and what does the convert believe they have newly become?[63]

Relationships

The close personal relationships that new Muslims discover provide an environment of security, belonging and acceptance. Interactions with other Muslims, 'born' Muslims and fellow converts help to nurture and sustain converts as they negotiate their new life. News of a conversion is greeted with great delight, and new Muslims are addressed as 'brother' or 'sister' and often given gifts, including prayer mats, a copy of the Qur'an or books on Islam.[64] In the words of Indigenous Muslim Stewart Humes (also known as Abdur Rahman Humes): 'When you are with the Muslim brothers you know where you are, you find a place where you belong.'[65] Following her conversion, Alinta Smith attended weekly classes at her local mosque where she established a strong rapport with the other 'Muslim sisters' she met. As she comments: 'They previously all had different religions, and we're all Muslim now. It's good to get their feedback and hear their experiences. Knowing that I'm not alone going through this has been good as well.'

Through conversion new Muslims become affiliated with a Muslim community that is not just locally based. They also join an extensive transnational network of Muslims, known in Arabic as the *umma*.[66] In submitting to the will of Allah new Muslims convey their willingness to join this global Muslim community. According to Indigenous Muslim 'John', one of the reasons Islam has been an overwhelmingly positive force in his life is because it gives him access to an international community: 'The first thing is that most people don't have any sense of internationalism, and Islam gives you that. You know, this is the first, and maybe the only international community that's ever existed.' Even if, in reality, the Muslim convert remains relatively cut off from other Muslims, they no longer *feel* isolated. In this sense there is a double movement – the Muslim community embraces the new Muslim, and the new Muslim feels she or he has entered the *umma*. Alinta sums up this twofold association well: 'I belong somewhere, not just to Australia or to the Indigenous community, I belong as a Muslim. When meeting a person, it's not their background or the language they speak, or where they come from. The number one is God. In Islam, we all unite no matter what. Your belief is beyond everything ... And having that, it's not just the community's reaction to me, but the feeling I had inside that I finally [became part of] it.'

This newfound sense of belonging can, at times, contrast sharply with the exclusion converts sometimes experience from their non-Muslim friends and families. In her interviews with Muslim converts in New Zealand, Sulaiman-Hill found that 'on a personal basis the impact of conversion can be mixed as relationships with friends and family are frequently placed under strain'. She continues, 'Interfamilial tensions, particularly if family members are themselves religious, can encompass feelings of betrayal through rejection of long-held beliefs'.[67] Estrangement from friends and family is an experience with which many Indigenous Muslims are also familiar. Some found that once they stopped drinking and going to pubs or nightclubs their non-Muslim friends drifted away and they found themselves spending more time with fellow Muslims. A number of respondents found that while family members often initially expressed disapproval of their decision to embrace Islam (sometimes stridently), they usually became more favourably disposed once they observed the positive change it had had on their lives.

Rituals

Acquainting themselves with the vast range of Islamic rites and rituals can be, at first, a daunting process for new Muslims. It is one rendered more difficult by the diversity of opinion that exists in the Muslim world. There are a multitude of different interpretations of what it means to submit to Allah's will. Some divergence of opinion arises from the cultural interpretations that different Islamic and non-Islamic nations, communities and ethnic traditions place on the Qur'an. There are also other well-established divisions, not least those between Sunni and Shi'a Muslims.[68] Even within Sunni Islam there are four main schools of Islamic law: Maliki, Hanafi, Hanbali and Shafi'i, and within these there may be further sects or subdivisions. As Nicole Bourque wryly notes, 'Needless to say, each of these groups claim[s] that they are the true servants of Islam.'[69]

New Muslims customarily ask their Muslim friends for advice on ritual, theological and other issues, but the information they receive will vary, reflecting their friends' background and affiliation.[70] Further confusion can result when the advice they are given does not correspond to what they have read in books or on the internet or been taught in Islamic classes. Some converts, in their desire to construct an identity that simultaneously affirms their new religious orientation and demarcates it from their former life and habits, can exhibit so-called convertitis.[71] According to Jensen, who has studied Danish converts to Islam, the newly converted often exhibit 'a so-called fanaticism with their new religion, which is expressed in very ritualised behaviour such as only wearing Islamic dress and a preoccupation with the Islamic rules of what is haram ('forbidden') and halal ('allowed') – of doing things "right"'.[72]

This can lead to a rather ironic situation in which new Muslims repudiate those born into the faith for not fulfilling their religious obligations or behaving in the 'correct', religiously sanctioned manner. When she first converted, Nazra Wali, an Indigenous Muslim of Aboriginal and Fijian–Indian descent, was confounded by the difference between the conduct of some of her Muslim friends and what she understood as appropriate Muslim behaviour. Nazra was first introduced to Islam by some Indonesian students when she was at university. When she subsequently met Muslims from Ethiopia she was confused, not only by the difference between the way the Indonesians and Ethiopians practised Islam but also by the divergence between their behaviour and what she had read. As she recalls:

> So I started to observe how [my Ethiopian friends] practised the religion and it was interesting in some ways, the things they did were different to the girls I knew and the Indonesian community which I came to know … It was just a different side of Islam, because these

young [Ethiopian] men went out and did everything else, some of them did pray five times a day, but they still drank alcohol and things like that, which really confused me at times. I'd say to them, 'How can you do that?' and they said, 'Oh that doesn't stop me from being Muslim', but when you are new [to a religion] and you're taught one way of doing things and you're convinced, and you read everything which proves to you that is the right way – and then when you see people do different things, it's confusing.[73]

Far from exhibiting signs of 'convertitis', other converts might engage with Islamic rituals or dress codes only after a period of years. They might view their religious identity as a highly personal affair, opting not to tell friends and family. Still others resent being labelled a 'convert', particularly when they have been Muslim for many years. When (non-Indigenous) Australian Muslim Bilal Cleland was asked to take part in a study of Melburnian converts by honours student Tuba Boz, the reply was an emphatic, 'No, I'm not going to do it. I am sick of being everybody's convert for the past twenty-five years. I have been Muslim longer than other Muslims.'[74]

Some who have been brought up as Muslim are impressed by the diligence with which new Muslims practice their faith. Others are reluctant to accept that a convert could possibly know more about Islam than they do.[75] Once an individual embraces Islam they become part of the *umma* or international Islamic community and, theoretically at least, there should be no differentiation between those born into Islam and those who come to it later in life.[76] In practice, marked internal divisions between new and born Muslims, between those of different doctrinal orientations and between Muslims of different national, cultural and racial backgrounds, coexist with the theory that all Muslims are members of the brotherhood (and sisterhood) of Islam. As Richard Reddie claims, it might be refreshing to believe that there is an international community of believers within Islam and 'that racism or skin colour do not figure, but this isn't always so in practice'.[77]

Rhetoric

Becoming Muslim also involves familiarising oneself with the language or rhetoric 'to express that experience to oneself and to others'.[78] Claiming that one has 'reverted' rather than 'converted' to Islam is an example of this. In identifying with Islam, new Muslims often stress that they are not converting but reverting to their original nature. Embracing Islam is regarded as 'coming back to the truth rather than finding it for the first time'.[79] Many Indigenous Muslims, in common with non-Indigenous Muslim converts in Australia, and those in Britain, the United States and elsewhere in the West, describe the feeling of having *always* been Muslim without knowing it.[80] Some respondents in my study commented that the precepts of Islam reconfirmed beliefs that they had always had and that, without knowing the name for it, they had been Muslim all along. Of course whether converts are retrospectively reading into their experience a doctrinal idea learned at a later time is difficult to determine.[81]

Another aspect of learning the language and rhetoric of Islam involves familiarising oneself with Arabic. New Muslims require a basic working knowledge of the Arabic language to conduct the five daily prayers, and Arabic phrases are used when Muslims greet one another. In Islam it is also customary to use Arabic salutations (known as *salawāt*) after saying (or hearing) the name of God, Muhammad and any other Prophets of Islam. The Arabic phrase *Subhana wa ta'ala* ('Glory to Him, the exalted') is said to glorify God when mentioning His name (the abbreviation 'swt' is used when writing the name of God or Allah). *Salla Allahu alaihi wa salam* ('May Allah bless Him and grant Him peace') is often said after hearing or saying the Prophet Muhammad's name, while *Alaihi al salaam* ('Peace be upon Him') is usually pronounced after the name of one of Allah's other prophets or messengers. Learning Arabic is not a requirement for practising Islam. Indonesia has the largest Muslim population in the world, but the majority of people speak languages other than Arabic. But as classical Arabic is the language of revelation, some Muslims choose to study it in order to read and understand the Qur'an in its original form.

It is common, although not obligatory, for people to take on an overtly 'Islamic' name on becoming Muslim.[82] Reverts often feel that their previous names are not compatible with their new identity. Changing one's name is a potent symbol of a desire both to leave their former identities in the past and to start afresh. New Muslims might also change their name as a way of being recognised by other Muslims. Not all Muslim reverts elect to change their names on official documents.[83] Some are content to use their Muslim names in their dealings with fellow Muslims and their given names when associating with the non-Muslim community. This is not to suggest that those who decide not to change their names are any more or less 'Muslim'.

Role

Role changes reflect the new Muslims' movement from mere personal conviction to 'a living out of conversion in the social world'.[84] As reverts construct a new identity for themselves at an individual and social level, they usually become keenly aware of, and committed to, the welfare of others.[85] This reorientation often results in new Muslims playing an active role in community service. As we have seen, Muslims should never force one to embrace Islam. But *da'wah*, an Arabic word meaning 'to invite (to Islam)' is an obligatory role for every Muslim according to their knowledge and ability. Some Muslims perform *da'wah* proactively, giving classes or lectures, disseminating written information about Islam, or through answering inquiries about the tenets of the faith. Others observe a less proactive form of *da'wah*, preferring to lead by example through their behaviour and conduct. It is not only non-Muslims who are called to Islam. Other Muslims should be reminded of the 'straight path' of Islam if they stray from it.

New Muslims often experience an acute awareness that 'their life is not theirs to be spent in selfish indulgence'; they feel they have gained a purpose in life, whether it is sharing the good news of salvation with others or simply being a loving person who serves others for the sake of God.[86] In Islam, Muslims are expected not only to improve themselves but also to work towards the advancement and betterment of society by contributing productively to their communities. Reverts strive to be active participants in their communities, partly out of a sense of duty and partly from the profound sense of the acceptance, love and joy they experience in becoming Muslim. Many new Muslims understand where they 'fit' in life and the universe, and gain a sense of mission. The love they feel embracing them can be so powerful that they feel empowered to love and serve others more fully.[87] For Indigenous Muslim Justin Agale, Muslims have a role to play in 'mak[ing] humanity a better place, trying to nurture humanity, rather than trying to get what's best for them. One of the things we're taught ... [is] love of service ... I cook for the homeless, which is one of the highlights of my month.'

Conversion is a profound revolution, both in the way individuals view themselves and in the way they view humanity, the world and the universe. The sense of belonging new Muslims experience as part of the local and international community of Muslims builds a new identity as well as creating a network of people to serve. Many new Muslims feel they have become better, more patient, loving and giving people. They also report a new sense of wholeness, claiming that their formerly fragmented self or soul is now united.[88] The questions they had about the meaning and purpose of life have largely been answered, and they often experience a deep sense of inner peace and calm. Although many reverts note that their journey of spiritual enlightenment has not always been easy, they agree it has been worthwhile. The following statement by Alinta Smith is typical of the way many Indigenous Muslim respondents feel: 'At first I thought this religion was requiring so much of me. I thought, I'll be a Muslim [but] I'll still be the same person. And I am the same person, I'm Alinta, but I'm changing inside. And it feels good. It feels like it's the right thing to do. I'm still the same person, but learning about my religion every day has changed me; it's made me a better person.'

SIX

SPEAKING TO THE CONVERTED

In chapter 5 we looked at the personal experience of Indigenous conversion to Islam. However, it is difficult to segregate psychological and spiritual factors from broader biographical circumstances. Although there is a turning about in the heart, the catalyst of it could be external circumstance. Inner and outer worlds constantly flow through each other, and what happens in one environment is easily transformed into an event of immense symbolic significance in the other. This is not surprising because conversion is, as we have seen, above all motivated by a search for meaning, and meaning involves both a reordering of personal priorities and a new understanding of one's milieu. The milieu described in chapter 5 – encounters with texts and the flowering of friendships, often set against a background of disappointment or disillusionment – are circumstantial factors and were presented as secondary to the main theme of conversion. In this chapter the perspective is somewhat reversed, as we pass from the microcontext of conversion to a consideration of the macrocontext in which it occurs.

The macrocontext refers to the larger cultural, political and social environment. In Australia it includes the invasion of Aboriginal and Torres Strait Islander people's lands and waters and the devaluation of their cultural and religious heritage through processes of missionisation and Christianisation. It also incorporates industrialisation, the advent of mass communication, large-scale immigration and the shrinking of Christianity's traditional hegemony. The current portrayal of Islam and Muslims in the mainstream media is another important element of the local and global meta-context. Of course micro- and macrocontexts interact: the influence of media stereotypes on the views some interviewees held about Islam before they examined its claims for themselves is a case in point.

Monika Wohlrab-Sahr argues that any assessment of conversion to Islam must take account of what she terms the 'double frame': 'The religious, cultural and social frame that converts turn away from, but stay related to, on one hand; and on the other, the new religious, cultural and social frame they have chosen, but with which they cannot completely merge.'[1]

This is a useful starting point for our discussion. The microcontext of conversion was often unpropitious: disillusionment with received belief systems, family difficulties and personal disappointments are all factors in triggering a search for meaning. But, as Wohlrab-Sahr suggests, behind this immediate sense of void, there is likely to be a larger context of tradition, belief or self-understanding to which the new faith is seen to relate. Otherwise, it is hard to imagine why Indigenous people, in becoming

Muslim, would fashion themselves into a *double* minority, or what Robert Dannin, writing about experiences of African-American Muslims, has called 'a minority within a minority'.[2] What is it about Islam and the Holy Qur'an that a growing number of Indigenous men and women in Australia find attractive? What does Islam provide that Christianity does not? Is there anything distinct about the phenomenon of Indigenous Muslims?

Reverts and cultural convergence

In fact, it emerges that cultural convergence or compatibility – the degree to which elements of a new religion mesh with and reinforce existing micro- and macrocontextual elements – is an important determinant of whether conversion will occur.[3] The Indigenous Muslims I interviewed perceive a very high degree of convergence between the major tenets of Islam and traditional Indigenous beliefs and practices. We saw in chapter 3 that for Indigenous Australians the issue of reversion has a double significance because a number of those who identify with Islam today have Muslim ancestors. The idea of returning to a former state also has special significance for Indigenous people without Muslim heritage because it is consistent with their interest in reconnecting with their Indigenous ancestry. The Indigenous Muslims I have met perceive such a neat cultural fit between their traditional Indigenous beliefs and the teachings of Islam that many hold that, in 'going back' to Islam, they are simultaneously going back to their Indigenous roots.

Indigenous Muslim respondents discern cultural parallels in the shared practices of male circumcision, promised or arranged marriages, polygyny, and the fact that men are usually older than their wives in both Islamic and traditional Indigenous societies.

Dainggatti woman Alinta Smith believes that 'Islam connects with [her] Aboriginality' because of a shared emphasis on gendered roles and spheres of influence.[4] 'In Islam', she claims, 'men have a clear role and women have a clear role and with Aboriginal people that's how it was, too.' She adds: 'The [Aboriginal] women would prepare food, they would pick fruit and berries and all that type of stuff, but the men would go hunting for the meat. They would kill it, and bring it back, and the women would cook it. And we would have children – their role was clearly defined, and it never changed. It's the same with Islam; they really enforce that, that this is your role. This is what you do, and that's that.'

Several Indigenous Muslims observe a correlation between the Islamic and Indigenous approaches to menstruation. 'Ramiz', for instance, likens the gendered separation practised in some Indigenous communities to the Islamic restrictions applied to women who are menstruating. 'I know', he says, 'that in some traditional clans and tribes there was also the separation of women during menstrual cycles, [and in Islam] women aren't allowed to pray during their menstrual cycle, [so] you can draw all those similarities [too].'[5] Alinta also discussed this apparent convergence in our conversation. It is yet another way in which, she claims, 'being Muslim has encouraged my [Aboriginal] culture'. As she observes:

> When Aboriginal women would get their monthly period they would go away from the tribe and in Islam when it's that time of the month you don't pray, you don't have to do your five daily prayers, you don't go into the mosque … [and] you don't have sexual relations. And it's the same with Aboriginals, the women were secluded, they were kind of kept away. I mean, women have PMS [pre-menstrual stress], they have mood swings and that type of

thing. Islam says that's part of being a woman, and it's the same with Aboriginality; they were kept away from the group so that there was no conflict or anything like that. So I thought, 'Wow, that's quite similar to what we thought.'

Numerous interviewees also commented on the similar attitudes Muslims and Indigenous people have towards the environment. Muslims are obliged to protect and maintain the fragile equilibrium of the earth's many bounties that Allah has bestowed on them. The Prophet Muhammad told his followers that they would be rewarded by God for taking care of the earth. Indigenous Muslim Nazra Wali notes that 'in the Qur'an it tells you very clearly don't waste what is not needed … and the Aboriginal community's the same, you know, water and food, anything which is nature is so precious, you only take what you need'.[6] Anthony Anderson emphasises that 'traditionally we [Indigenous people] worship the earth … we have earth ceremonies just so the earth will be fertile and so forth. [And Islam is] a religion that does exactly the same thing and tells us to treat the land and our people the same way. It's just reiterating [our traditional beliefs].'[7] Eugenia Flynn confirms that 'Aboriginal people, we believe that we're custodians and … we have a very strong connection to land and Islam complements that'.[8] She adds that, in Islam and Indigenous societies, 'There is that same notion that humans are just custodians because Allah is the sovereign over the earth and he lent it to us, and therefore we have to take care of it … and Aboriginal people we take care of the land because we're the custodians looking after it. In that way, it's exactly the same as Islam.'

Another similarity often cited is the high esteem in which elders are held in both Islamic and traditional Indigenous societies. Muslim youth are enjoined to pay due honour and respect to their elders and in a well-known Hadith (prophetic saying) the Prophet Muhammad declared, 'He is not of us who does not have mercy on young children, nor honour the elderly.' According to Nazra Wali, 'In Islam elders are very much respected, and the Aboriginal community is the same.' Alinta Smith elaborates further:

> In the Aboriginal culture your elders are so respected because they're the ones that carry down our traditions, our stories that are passed down through the generations. Anyone that's older than me, I would call them Aunty – it's purely out of respect. They have a lot of wisdom, I mean it's died out quite a bit these days, but as in Islam you're supposed to respect your elders and look after them, and it's the same with the Aboriginal culture. Our elders are everything. The older you get the more respect people have for you.

One interviewee also discerned a degree of cultural convergence in the attitude of Muslims and Aboriginal people towards, respectively, the depiction of divinities and the departed. Muslims refrain from making visual representations of Allah because they would never be able to convey the true meaning, grandeur and wonder of God. To attempt to capture the image of Allah by human hand is seen as an affront to the ineffable majesty of Allah. Muslims also avoid making images that depict Muhammad, any of the other prophets, or any animate beings, human or animal, lest they become objects of veneration or idolatry.[9] Nazra observes a correlation between these beliefs and the Aboriginal prohibition against showing (at least for a prescribed time) images of the deceased. In Aboriginal cultural and religious beliefs, images of an Aboriginal person who has passed away can capture the spirit of the dead and cause trauma to the spirit and Aboriginal people generally. Nazra acknowledges that the Aboriginal and Islamic practices are not identical, but her perception of a correlation reinforces her identity as Indigenous *and* Muslim. In Nazra's words: 'Islam accepts technology, photos and cameras, but Islamically people don't display photos in their houses, of any image, and in Aboriginal culture, once a person dies, the image is hidden away, it's not to be seen, so there's similarities but in a different form. In Aboriginal culture when you are alive, it's still okay, but once you die, you know, whereas in Islam, you have your photos but you keep them away, you don't display them.'

Other Indigenous Muslims believe that Islam and Aboriginality are, as Alinta claims, 'very close together' because of a common sense of community mindedness. Sulaiman Menzies, who was introduced to Islam in the workplace, maintains that, in contrast with the 'Western way [which] is every man for himself, dog eat dog … the Aboriginal native way is we look after each other. And Islam is exactly the same, we look after each other.'[10] This cross-cultural affinity is also evident in what Alinta calls a shared emphasis on 'generosity and hospitality': 'When you visit a Muslim's house they're always trying to feed you. And they want you to enjoy yourself, they want to be hospitable and it's very similar to how it is [being Aboriginal]. In Islam you should want for others what you want for yourself. That is truly generous. It's the same with Aboriginals, you do what you can to help each other out because you're Aboriginal. I am here for you.'

The way cultural similarities or convergences facilitate the conversion of Indigenous Australians to Islam is particularly evident in Justin Agale's case. On Justin's ancestral home of Mer (Murray Island) in Torres Strait, local identity, custom and spirituality come from Malo's law, derived from the culture heroes Malo and Bomai. According to local belief, Malo and his maternal uncle Bomai made a long journey over the seas from western New Guinea across to Mer in the east. Resembling an octopus in form, Malo had eight tentacles that represented the eight clans of Mer. Malo set out the rules for all Meriam people, including gardening practices, property rights, social norms, rules and obligations. At first Justin's belief in Malo's law prevented him from identifying with Islam: 'I felt that I was betraying my past and my ancestors if I became Muslim and that I'd be selling out the things that they fought for and that they stood for.'[11] But when he read about Islam, and engaged in a dialectical process of comparing and contrasting Meriam and Islamic perspectives, the strong parallels he noticed led Justin to conclude: 'I already believe in this. The difference was I didn't know who Muhammad was. But all the other spiritual stuff, I already believed in.'[12] He elaborates: 'I still consider myself a traditionalist, because I use my traditional beliefs as a yardstick and I measure everything else up against them. And nothing measured up against them except Islam ... So I'm actually fulfilling my tradition, my traditional beliefs. I am fulfilling what my ancestors were following by becoming Muslim. It's sort of like the natural step to take.'

Justin distinctly recalls when he decided to become a Muslim. It followed his revelation about the connection between Islam and his traditional Indigenous beliefs: 'I was sitting down one night, and I began praying to Malo, and it dawned on me that Islam is actually an extension of Malo's law, like the final chapter of it. And so I decided to become Muslim that night.' Around six weeks later Justin learned of the Muslim belief that Allah sent 124 000 prophets into the world to preach the Oneness of God (*tawheed* in Arabic). Muslims believe that all races, nations and peoples have had their own prophets, all of whom gave the same basic message to surrender to God in their own languages. This teaching further reinforced Justin's conviction that a cross-cultural convergence existed between Islam and his Meriam beliefs. He now considers this formal similarity as confirmation that 'Malo must have been one of those prophets who received the divine message'. As he says: 'Even though I found out [about the 124 000 prophets] after I became Muslim, it drew me more into it. Every time I met Muslims and I said "I'm Aboriginal–Torres Strait Islander", they'd say, "You know, you must have been sent prophets by God because you have this similar belief, you have that", so, you know, there has to have been a prophet.'

Rocky Davis embraced Islam more than ten years ago after meeting Aboriginal Muslims in prison. For him, too, the story of Allah's sending of prophets to all peoples and races helps explain why 'intrinsically in Aboriginal culture we have Islamic principles'.[13] Wiradjuri descendant Anthony Anderson is also 'certain' that some of Allah's prophets visited Indigenous people. Otherwise, as he claims, 'we wouldn't know how to look after each other, we wouldn't know how to treat each other. We wouldn't know how to interact as tribes unless somebody gave us guidelines.' He elaborates, 'So somewhere along the line we have been given guidelines ... here's the trees, and here's how this works and you catch this and turn it into that. We know all those things from previous knowledge, so somebody gave it to us.'

Others perceive a commonality that goes well beyond parallels between Indigenous culture and Islamic ethics. They identify spiritual as well as cultural parallels. Ramiz, for instance, sees a connection between the Islamic concept of *tawheed* (the belief in a unique, independent and universal God) and the fact that Indigenous people traditionally believed in 'a single Creator'. Different Indigenous communities honoured their own creation figures but, Ramiz maintains, 'because they were dependent for their survival wholly on creation, they would have been thanking the creator for the kangaroos, goannas, trees, the sunrise. They wouldn't have been praying to the sun, or to a sun God.' They believed, he says, 'that there was a Creator, one Creator'. Rocky also emphasised this similarity, citing evidence that reportedly shows that the Aboriginal warrior Pemulwuy believed in 'a transcendental God, one that's not confined by time and space'. Born around 1756, Pemulwuy was a member of the Eora people from the Sydney area who, according to Rocky, believed that their world was brought into being by a transcendental creator, a notion that he finds consistent with Islam's assertion that God is omnipotent, has no beginning and no end, and is outside the limits of time and space.[14] These apparently identical teachings lend support, Rocky states, to his claim that the 'attributes that live in the predisposition of Aboriginal people are Islamic values'.

Anthony Mundine embraced Islam a decade ago after reading the autobiography of Malcolm X – a key text in Indigenous male conversion, and one we discuss in chapter 8. He also firmly believes that 'back at the start Aboriginals were Muslim. They were believers in one Creator.' Shahzad (Shaz) Rind, of Baluchistani and Aboriginal descent, links Islamic theology and the Indigenous concept of the Dreamtime – a notion of eternal, omnipresent creativity:

> A lot of Aboriginal tribes did believe and still do believe in a higher creator, and Muslims believe there were 124 000 prophets that came down to all the peoples, and believe there was a message sent to every people, to believe in a creation. And Aboriginal people have that belief in the creation and we call it Dreamtime in the sense that it happened at a time when it's not in our relevant memory, but dreams are still in your mind and in your body.[15]

Cultural (or theological) reciprocities of the kind detailed above are certainly an important factor in religious conversion, but they are not the only considerations. Besides the before and after systems of belief (in this case, a range of Indigenous beliefs and an Islamic theology), in Australia there was, and is, another factor: Christianity. This tripartite spiritual environment structures the conversion experience almost regardless of the particular choices converts make, and in different macrocontexts the roles played by Christianity and Islam can be reversed. Thus, Charles Kraft's study of the Higi people in Nigeria shows that besides the cultural and theological fit perceived between prior beliefs and a new spiritual orientation, shifts in Higi religious sentiment also reflected their prior relationships with the representatives of the new faith.[16] The Higi are a tribal people living in north-eastern Nigeria. Their positive disposition – towards Christianity in this case – arose partly from the special respect for white people within Higi culture. The traditional Higi world view links whites with God rather than humanity, which is evident in the Higi proverb, 'Fear God, fear the White Man'.[17] Given that the Christian missionaries were white, they were received with great respect by the Higi.[18] Moreover, the Christian God was a figure who closely resembled Hyelatamwe, a god in Higi traditional religion. The Christian message about God and Jesus resonated deeply with the Higi because they believed that Hyelatamwe had a son and that he had departed because his son had been killed.

Other factors further reinforced this perception of cross-cultural homology and its consequence: the prestige accorded to Christianity. In the 1950s leprosy was relatively common among the Higi; sufferers were sent to a leprosarium operated by the Church of the Brethren Mission in Garkida, about 130 kilometres away. Relatives and friends who remained behind at first assumed that their relatives had been taken away to die. Instead, with the help of sulpha drugs, they survived. Further, while at Garkida, they met lepers from neighbouring tribes who were enthusiastic Christians. When the cured relatives returned, friends and family thought they were witnessing a miraculous resurrection. According to Kraft, 'when, therefore, the returnees continually spoke of their new relationship to [the Christian] God, their countrymen were strongly disposed to listen'.[19] In other words, just as Indigenous people in Australia find coincidences in theory and practice between Islamic and Indigenous beliefs so, in this African example, Indigenous peoples rationalised a special relationship between their own and Christian belief.

There is an additional point of particular relevance to the Indigenous Muslim context. The positive disposition of the Higi towards Christianity might not have resulted in conversion were it not for the fact that the 'people were, for historical reasons, negatively disposed toward Christianity's competitor, Islam'.[20] Essentially, it appears, the Higi had three religious options: remain committed to their tribal religious allegiance; convert to Islam; or convert to Christianity. Even though Muslims lived close to the Higi, the Higi generally did not consider conversion to Islam because the Muslims were members of the Fulani tribe, long-term enemies of the Higi. Islam was brought to the Higi area in the nineteenth century by Fulani warriors who captured and enslaved many of the (non-Higi) indigenous people. The association in Higi minds between Islam and enslavement arose from their observation or direct experience of the use of force to bring about either conversion or enslavement. Kraft notes that many Higi to this day still 'believe that even voluntary conversion to Islam is synonymous with detribalisation and/or enslavement to the Fulani'.[21]

In short, then, the decision to adopt Islam, Christianity or any other spiritual belief also depends on the potential converts' historical relationship to the proponents of the insurgent religion. Those invaded by a particular religious group might resist the beliefs of their conquerors; others might identify with them because they confer higher social status, material and educational advantages or political cachet. Indigenous Muslim reverts not only resist Christianity but also embrace an alternative faith that, through its enhancement of their Aboriginal values, confers on them a range of moral, intellectual and social gifts.

Perhaps in understanding the macrocontextual structuration of Indigenous conversion one further overseas instance may be permitted. An even more complex scenario relevant to our discussion is provided by Quentin Gausset's research. In Cameroon in sub-Saharan Africa, two neighbouring communities, the Wawa and the Kwanja, respectively embraced Islam and Christianity.[22] Their choice stemmed from their relationship to the Fulbe people, a pastoral group who brought Islam when they conquered the area in the nineteenth century. In order to secure certain privileges the Wawa collaborated with the Fulbe, but the Kwanja resisted. The Wawa's decision to embrace Islam required their Fulbe-isation, and a rejection of traditional rituals and identity, without full integration into the Fulbe.[23] Becoming a Muslim did, however, confer higher social status, and the process of conversion was relatively straightforward. By contrast, the decision of the Kwanja to respond to another insurgent religion, Christianity, while it facilitated the preservation of traditional rituals and beliefs, had obvious drawbacks: conversion required lengthy Bible studies and, for those living in areas with a high Fulbe population, a capacity to withstand strong social pressure to become Muslim.

In this example it was not a simple convergence of belief

systems that determined conversion: there had to be a convergence of interests as well. Gausset's example highlights the fact that conversion, individually or collectively, is driven by two desires. It involves a desire for reintegration as well as a longing for differentiation. These two impulses meet in a higher search for recognition. With due respect for the obvious differences of time and place, the structural analogy with Indigenous identification with Islam plays out in the willingness of converts to become members of a double minority, for this is desirable if at the same time as it further differentiates, it also enables them to become recognised as part of a larger world community.

Christian missionisation

If many Indigenous Muslims find Islam appealing because of the high degree of cultural overlap they perceive between it and their traditional beliefs and practices, it is partly because, in the Australian context at least, it represents an alternative faith and ideology to the religious beliefs of their subjugators. The majority of Indigenous Muslim converts I spoke to have come from Christian backgrounds of one kind or another. Although they had 'abandoned the cross for the crescent', not all Indigenous Muslims considered Christianity unsympathetic.[24] Some were ambivalent, others indifferent; a few bitterly rejected it. Adelaide-based Eugenia Flynn has fond memories of attending her local Catholic church with her family every Sunday. Her Tiwi grandmother worked as a housekeeper for the Bishop of Darwin after leaving the Catholic mission on Bathurst Island (80 kilometres north of Darwin in the Arafura Sea). The fact that Eugenia does not harbour 'any resentment towards the Catholic Church' has come largely from her father who, she notes, has always said that in his individual experience, the Mission helped his mother and her twin sister and gave him and his sister an education and advantage in life that many other Aboriginal people did not have in those days. Therefore, unlike many other Aboriginal people who, rightly so, lament the interference of the Catholic Church in Aboriginal communities, I do not. My conversion to Islam is not a rejection of Catholicism as the religion of the Oppressors as it may be for some or many.[25]

Certainly, it is difficult to generalise about the history of contact between Christian missionaries and Indigenous people in Australia. Aboriginal and Torres Strait Islander communities came into contact with a range of missionaries from divergent denominations in various regions and at different times during the nineteenth and twentieth centuries.[26] Some of the more enlightened missionaries tentatively tried to incorporate Aboriginal people and ritual into the expression of Christianity.[27] Others condemned Indigenous people's traditional stories and practices, seeking to prohibit ceremonial observances. Even so, many Aboriginal people regarded mission stations as bulwarks against racism, violence, hunger and exploitation. Whatever the missionaries' expectations of conversion, it has been suggested that the interest Aboriginal people took in the mission stations focused on the opportunities they offered to establish trade and exchange relations with the materially endowed newcomers. It was not about 'surrender[ing] their identity and autonomy'.[28] When it became obvious that the missionaries were not going to allow them to continue their traditional lifestyle, many Aboriginal people, including the ancestors of Marjory Hall, 'went walkabout'.[29]

Just as Indigenous Muslims find cultural and theological convergences between Islam and Indigenous spirituality, so the anthropological literature affords many instances of the same associative logic being used to rationalise the insurgence of Christianity into Indigenous lives. Maranguk woman Linda Ford notes that her forebears discerned a high degree of compatibility between introduced Christian concepts and their pre-existing beliefs, in particular finding 'a lot of the ten principles of Christianity similar to indigenous knowledge'.[30] Lyndel Robb, from the Kairi people of Queensland, suggests that traditional Aboriginal beliefs 'probably prepared indigenous people for learning about the virgin birth, life after death and ... other Christian concepts'.[31] In his detailed study of Edward River Aboriginal people (in Queensland's tropical north), anthropologist John Taylor found they identified God with the mythic culture hero Poonchr, who lived in the sky world and occasionally visited earth in human form. He was often referred to as Poonchr-God and, even when the term 'God' was used by itself, his association with Poonchr was understood.[32]

In a further parallel with our findings in an Indigenous–Islamic context, Noel Loos observes that while the first generations of Aboriginal Christians creatively incorporated the new religion into their own world views and cosmologies, in later generations some Aboriginal Christians came to see their old belief system as a forerunner to Christianity. Aboriginal Christians came to regard their former belief system as related to Christianity in the same way as the Old Testament is to the New Testament.[33] Christianity, Loos claims, was seen as augmenting, 'completing or fulfilling their old belief system, not destroying it ... the missionaries had tried to force a complete replacement [but] they had failed and many Aboriginal people retained those aspects of their old religion which they still found relevant and acceptable to their new understanding.'[34] Similarly, in his research into the religious affiliations of Aborigines from Lockhart River (on the east coast of Cape York Peninsula), David Thompson found: 'It is evident that Aborigines of Lockhart River did not see the acceptance of the Christian faith to be in conflict with the continuing performance of traditional ceremonies ... In fact they detected real parallels between their ceremonies and the ceremonies of the Church. This is reflected in some of the English words used to describe the [Lockhart initiation ceremony] to outsiders, e.g. godparents, godchild, baptism and confession.'[35]

Research conducted in Torres Strait suggests a similar capacity among Indigenous communities there to continue their former beliefs and customs in the wake of Christianisation. Nonie Sharp's interviews with Murray Islanders, or Meriam people, indicate that despite 'the destruction of the Malo-Bomai sacred order (or "cult") as an institution, Malo's Law continues to carry the force of a religious commandment'. She adds, 'Meriam people who are especially well versed in matters of law and tradition say that Malo's laws are like those of the Christian religion, so in this respect their conversion to Christianity made no fundamental difference.' The late Sam Passi, former chairman of the Murray Island Council, spoke of his ideas about Malo and Christianity with Sharp between 1982 and '84. In common with his mainland Aboriginal Christian counterparts, he likened his traditional beliefs to the Old Testament and Christianity to the New Testament. In this view, according to Sharp, 'Christianity did not mean an abrupt change, but an extension of the old religious–moral order.'[36] In much the same manner as Indigenous Muslim and Meriam descendant Justin Agale, above, characterised Islam as the 'final chapter' of Malo's law, Sam's younger brother, Anglican priest Reverend Dave Passi, 'came to "see Christianity as the fulfilment, the extension of Malo"'.[37]

This said, other Indigenous communities could not be reconciled with Christianity. Perhaps this is not surprising if, as Robb asserts, Aboriginal people generally had no understanding of hell, no conception of the places in which the events of the Bible took place and 'no comprehension of Christian parables about flocks and shepherds for they had never seen sheep'.[38] The Book of Genesis asserts that man shall 'subdue the earth' and have 'dominion over' every living thing that moves, but traditional Aboriginal mythology teaches Aboriginal people that they are the stewards of the land and environment, which are gifts from their ancestral heroes. Consequently, as Graham Paulson states, what is valued 'is adaptation to the environment rather than change or manipulation of the environment'.[39] Moreover, Aboriginal people believe that all creatures come from human beings, and that people are part of, not above or superior to, the animal kingdom.[40]

There are further points of what would appear to be irreconcilable difference. Aboriginal people's identities are rooted in place. The Indigenous world view insists that one's connection to a particular piece of land gives that person an identity, sense of security, 'a reason for living, a sense of history and an approach to the future'.[41] In the late Kevin Gilbert's words, 'no Aboriginal person is without a place in the Dreaming track'.[42] The notion of being spiritually (if not physically) tied to a particular place contrasts sharply with the Christian concepts of exile, migration and homelessness. In the book of Exodus (the second book of the Old Testament) we are reminded of the flight of the Hebrew slaves from Egypt under the leadership of Moses. For forty years the Israelite refugees wandered in the wilderness, and the motifs of displacement and dislocation remain important in the Christian sensibility.

Despite many years of exposure to missionary pressure, conversion among the Pitjantjatjara, one of the largest Aboriginal language groups in the western desert of Central Australia, has been almost non-existent. According to Aram Yengoyan, the stark differences between the essential tenets of Christian dogma and 'the moral and categorical assumptions that underlie Pitjantjatjara social and collective life' make the Christian conversion of 'individuals or groups a virtual impossibility'. A critical difference is Christianity's emphasis on the individual. Unlike Christianity, which posits a strong sense of the individual and 'the ability to move between group identity and individual identity', in Aboriginal society the individual is *always* embedded in a complex matrix of groups, relationships and structures. Unlike Christianity, which stresses the future and salvation in the hereafter, the Pitjantjatjara are concerned with the here and now, and believe that the eternal is always present. 'For the Pitjantjatjara', as Yengoyan observes, 'salvation, damnation, and the future of each person are non-issues. It is not the future which is important but the message of the ancient past that lives in the present to determine what will happen.'[43]

Still other Aboriginal people, of course, have reason to feel that Christianity is not simply irreconcilable with their values but has also acted to destroy them. Robb maintains that 'Aboriginal communities everywhere across Australia saw the Bible as a weapon', adding, 'the reputation of the Australian churches held in the hearts of Aboriginal people is that damage has been done in the past two centuries of Australian missionisation: the disintegration of our Aboriginal culture'.[44] For Aboriginal Muslim Shaz Rind, 'Christianity was used, and we all know it was used to colonise, it was used to take people away from their traditional lands and values and cultures.'

Countering 'the hurt of colonisation'

One reason Indigenous Australians are attracted to Islam is that, at least in the subaltern role it occupies in contemporary Australia, it does not insist on the kind of spiritual subjugation and cultural assimilation preached by Christian missionaries. The Qur'an states that Allah made human beings into different nations and tribes and that these differences, far from being wrong, are a sign from God: 'And among His Signs is the creation of the heavens and the earth, and the difference of your languages and colours. Verily, in that are indeed signs for those who know' (30:22).

In embracing Islam Indigenous Muslims have found a religious identity that does not entail renouncing their Aboriginality. According to Shaz:

> Islam recognises tribes and nations. It gives you identity, a purpose. It doesn't just say, 'You're Muslim, that's it.' It says yes, all Muslims are the same, but it does recognise we belong to different tribes and nations, so it doesn't do what Christianity did to a lot of Aboriginal people [which] was try and make them like white people. So it allowed you that identity and it still does today. Islam allows you your identity, your tribe and nation, and that is quoted in the Qur'an.[45]

On this argument, by identifying with Islam Indigenous Muslims attach themselves symbolically and philosophically to an alternative world view that closely mirrors their own. Robb notes that missionaries sought to enforce Christian marriages and to prevent Aboriginal people from engaging in polygyny.[46] The missionaries withheld food and other rations from Aboriginal people to prevent their engagement in these activities. They rather arbitrarily chose whom they deemed appropriate Christian marriage partners for young Aboriginal men and women but, as we have seen, in Aboriginal communities, as in many Muslim societies, it was customary for the parents or other elders to arrange promised marriages. As noted, it was also acceptable in both Aboriginal and Muslim traditions for a man to have more than one wife. Through frequent lecturing and daily Christian routine the missionaries reminded their charges that monogamous marriage had been decreed by God, thus instilling a sense of guilt and shame in their Aboriginal charges.[47]

Aboriginal people were made to feel inferior for engaging in practices that, in their culture, were acceptable. They were also made to feel inferior on account of the colour of their skin. Shown biblical pictures, Aboriginal people 'saw only a white God, a white Jesus, white angels and a black devil, and they were naturally alienated by the symbolism of white as good and black as evil'.[48] Forty-year-old Aboriginal Muslim Rocky Davis recalls how his mother and her generation were taught to believe that:

> Black was equal to dirty and heathen and devil and white was pure and heaven and snow and God … That's why there's so many light-skinned Aboriginals, not just from rape and assimilation, but from the Christian doctrine they taught us, because we are ashamed of who we are and if you tell someone for so long that they're negative, they're going to believe it. I know guys [who] have tried to scratch their skin with a stick to get the colour off.

The long-term impact of these experiences is an important factor in Islamic conversion. Present-day family breakdown, sexual and domestic violence, substance abuse, criminality and material, cultural and spiritual impoverishment are widely understood to be the legacy of what Shaz calls 'a lot of the hurt of colonisation'. Indigenous people want to see change: there is no going back, but the prospects for going forward are limited. The models of community offered up by 'whitefella' society – Christianisation, assimilationism, integrationism and multiculturalism – have largely failed to 'uplift' Aboriginal people. How can people who have been separated from culture, ceremony and country engage in a spiritual life? And how do they do it in a way that does not mean they have to choose between their Indigenous and their religious identities?

The Aboriginal Muslims I have met firmly believe that Islam is, as Anthony Mundine says, 'not an answer, it's *the* answer'. In Alinta Smith's opinion, 'If a lot more Indigenous Australians turned to Islam they would solve a lot of their problems, [including] the anger they have towards the white community' (we return to this theme in chapter 8).

Islam helps Indigenous people cope with the ongoing pain of colonisation through its emphasis on forgiveness. Forgiving other people, even one's enemies, is one of the most important teachings of Islam. In the Qur'an Allah describes the believers as those who 'avoid major sins and acts of indecency and when they are angry they forgive' (42:37). This teaching has helped to dissolve the anger Alinta formerly felt. As she explains:

> [In Islam] we're encouraged to forgive, because how can God forgive you for your sins if you can't forgive another person for theirs? So you've just got to accept what happened [i.e. colonisation] … I am becoming more conscious of my actions, and more conscious of God, and more kind when people look at me or say things to me or whatever. I don't retaliate like I used to. Now I just smile because I know that God will reward me for my patience and for controlling

myself, controlling my actions. Islam is all about perfecting yourself – becoming more of a giving person, more of a charitable person and bettering yourself. And I know that God's watching me and guiding me and I feel safe with him – I feel very content. I was always very strong in my Aboriginality. I belong to a community of very special people. We are Indigenous Australians and our culture is very unique, but now I belong to a religion that is very fulfilling and it has made me very happy.

The inner contentment numerous interviewees described reflects the *integration* of their Indigenous and Muslim identities. Many also feel that their faith gives them a clearer sense of responsibility for their decisions and actions. 'It's up to me, and there's not one person in this world around here that can do anything to change that. It's all up to me in my world and whatever I do,' says Ramiz. Christian missionaries often viewed Indigenous people as child-like and incapable of taking agency. They were further infantilised when forced to rely on 'the system' for such basic necessities as food and clothing. One legacy of this is the dependence of many Indigenous people on unemployment benefits, or 'sit down money'. Islam, however, emphasises that individuals are accountable for their attitudes and actions. This is not the same as promoting individualism; on the contrary, it is an injunction to serve and reconnect. Teaching that each person has been given freedom of choice and is responsible for (changing) their own life, Islam has helped Indigenous Muslims to rediscover a sense of self-worth. In particular, the Qur'anic injunction (13:11), 'Verily never will Allah change the condition of a people until they change what is within themselves' empowers Indigenous Muslims to see that the future is in their hands, and not in the form of a hand-out.

The adoption of a recognisably Islamic name is another way in which Indigenous Muslims symbolically cast off the shackles of colonisation and Christianisation. Muslim reverts often take on a Muslim name in order to be recognised as such by other Muslims, and to renounce their former identities. For Indigenous Muslims, changing their name is also a symbol of their desire to break with a history of racism and colonial conquest. Generations of intermarriage have meant that Aboriginal and Torres Strait Islander Australians have surnames common in non-Indigenous society. But it is also the case that Indigenous people's original names were disregarded by missionaries, bureaucrats and others who rather arbitrarily christened them with new names. In adopting an Islamic name, then, Indigenous Muslims are simultaneously aligned with an international community of believers while reclaiming their subjectivity.

A name change may also address another hurt. Many Aboriginal and Torres Strait Islander people are in the position of Malcolm X: adopting an Indigenous name is impossible because their original languages are no longer known or spoken. In this circumstance, many feel that Arabic offers an alternative language in which they can rewrite their identities. In chapter 5 we noted how Muslim reverts often learn classical Arabic so they can read the Qur'an in its original form. But learning Arabic can have a special appeal for Indigenous Muslims who have 'lost' their traditional languages, and who want to speak a language other than the coloniser's tongue. As Sulaiman Menzies expresses it:

> Well, actually one of my reasons for travelling overseas [to the Sudan] was that I was craving a language. I wanted a language to speak, but I didn't feel I belonged to the English language and I couldn't find [an Indigenous] language here to learn. There are many

languages, many different dialects, but not enough people who know them [well enough] to be able to document them and teach them. I'm a member of the Dainggatti tribe. There are people who still have elements of the language, but it's not a documented language that I can study ... [There's only] little scraps of language.[49]

'Dog-eat-dog' values

Although the long intertwined history of colonisation and Christianisation provides a macrocontext for Islamic conversion, one that casts its shadows across generations and continues to seep into every aspect of Indigenous life, it is by no means the only context in which conversion should be understood. There is also the secular context, the decline of official religion, the continuing upward spiral of mainstream Australia's commitment to consumption and the associated environmental and social fallout of neoliberalist individualism. In recent years the regularity and fervour of Aboriginal participation in Christian activities has decreased as the socio-political context has shifted.[50] With the provision of alternative avenues of employment, social security payments and 'work for the dole' schemes, dependence on the goods and services traditionally supplied by missionaries has diminished. Christian conversion, often although certainly not entirely borne of necessity, has also lessened (as a percentage).[51] This new sense of socio-political identity means, however, that Indigenous people now find themselves living in an increasingly capitalistic and individualistic society in which stable values are hard to find. According to Patrick Dodson, the younger generation of Indigenous people less frequently attend church or worship on a regular basis. He says Indigenous youths are not only 'finding it difficult to reconcile their own experience of being

Aboriginal with Christian church belief, preaching and practice', they are also seeking 'to re-claim and strengthen their own Aboriginal cultural and religious beliefs and values'.[52]

However, this is difficult in the contemporary climate where what Charles Harris refers to as 'so-called "Western civilization"' amounts to 'a dog-eat-dog value system'.[53] Indigenous people today, whether or not they have come from a mission or non-mission, Christian or non-Christian background, confront the further challenge of sustaining their faith 'in a world forged by secular materialism and based on increasing individuation'.[54] Like their non-Indigenous counterparts, Indigenous Muslim Rocky Davis believes Aboriginal people have succumbed to this materialist, consumerist culture. As he says: 'The thing is, [in] Aboriginal culture now, we're basically capitalist and we believe in greed and lust and violence. And it's everywhere, you can't deny it.' Sulaiman concurs, claiming that 'in modern culture, the Aboriginals of today are in the Nike culture'. He adds, 'These days [Indigenous] kids are just consumers and that's it. They're a whole part of this big consuming capitalistic society and they're comfortable in it. They're not worried about the state of Aboriginal people.'

It appears that a number of Indigenous people who identify with Islam today are doing so out of a sense of disillusionment, both with Christian missionisation *and* contemporary materialism. Many Aboriginal people feel that both of these forces have and continue to rob them of their Aboriginal culture and identity. Islam is increasingly being seen as an antidote embodying a range of cultural, ethical and spiritual values that ameliorate this sense of loss and disorientation. Indigenous Muslim Alinta Smith observes that a widespread stereotype of Aboriginal people is that 'we drink and we don't work'. She acknowledges that many Indigenous people have 'fallen into that gap' but stresses 'how Aboriginals live today is not the true identity of Aboriginal people'. She insists that 'instead of living like a white man and falling into these gaps', Aboriginal people need to reclaim their *true* selves. They have to remind themselves 'where they're from, and the beauty of our culture and how special it is; about this land that we were blessed with and the morals of being an Aboriginal person'. Indigenous Muslims firmly believe that because it closely mirrors 'traditional' Aboriginal cultures, Islam provides a symbolic route back to their Indigenous roots and an alternative path to the future.

On a practical level Islam helps Indigenous people from falling into 'gaps'. The adoption of a faith that demands the strict observance of religious *and* social practices, including the avoidance of alcohol, drugs and gambling, has played a positive role in many lives. The clear prescriptions or codes of behaviour are welcomed as a stabilising influence in lives that had often been devoid of a sense of order and focus.[55] Islam is sometimes characterised as disempowering because it circumscribes choice, but followers of Islam disagree, claiming that its clear rules of ethical action empower them to act responsibly. Disciplining their desires does not equal disempowerment: 'it is the desire for discipline that is empowering'.[56] Indigenous Muslim 'Jamila' notes that she has 'been saved' from a number of the social ills that plague some of her fellow Torres Strait Islanders. Not drinking she knows she will not become an alcoholic; not gambling, she can never become a problem gambler.[57] As Aboriginal Muslim 'John' suggests, 'The whole idea of being the slave of God, and I mean slave in a real sense, is that you're not enslaved by other people or other things.'[58]

Islam not only helps Indigenous Muslims to develop an

alternative sense of personal responsibility. It also provides a new and radical vision of social justice.[59] One of the Five Pillars of Islam is the redistribution of wealth to the needy. Muslims do not consider zakat – the obligation to donate to charity each year – to be a burden but a contribution to making a more just community and society. In his last sermon the Prophet Muhammad is reported to have said, 'Allah has forbidden you to take usury [i.e. interest], therefore all interest obligation shall henceforth be waived. Your capital, however, is yours to keep. You will neither inflict nor suffer inequality.' To paraphrase Carolyn Moxley Rouse, for many Muslims conversion to Islam is as much a protest against the socio-economic and socio-political structures of mainstream Western society as it is an embrace of the tenets of Islam. As she says, Islam is often interpreted by converts as a 'counter-hegemonic faith' that provides them with a blueprint for 'a redistributive capitalist system'.[60] Indigenous Muslim 'John' maintains that an important aspect of being a Muslim is 'a political awareness of where you live'. This includes an obligation to try to further the socio-economic principles at the heart of Islam:

> The critical thing in Islam is not how you cut your beard or the clothes you wear; it's not even that we should be respected because we don't drink and smoke. Who cares? But the Qur'an makes it really clear that the great crime is actually for people to amass wealth and then to believe they got it solely through their own agency and to then declare themselves independent of God and their fellow man. Things that are condemned are those that create social disunity. [For instance] Islam forbids usury. Usury is when you loan money and you demand exorbitant interest. These crimes are major social crimes, but they're also crimes against God.

Some Indigenous Muslims even feel that through embracing Islam their status as the rightful custodians of this land is symbolically restored. Several interviewees observed a similarity between their desire to have their connection to land recognised and the Islamic ruling, affirmed by a majority of jurists, that prayers conducted on or in stolen property are devoid of reward or *barakah*, an Arabic term meaning 'blessing'. According to Abu Ameenah Bilal Philips, whenever one of the obligatory five prayers is performed, it generally produces two results: it removes the individual's obligation to perform that prayer, and it earns him or her reward. A general principle of *fiqh*, or Islamic jurisprudence, however, is that prayer 'performed on or in stolen property ... is devoid of reward'.[61] Some Indigenous Muslims interpret this ruling to mean that believers do not derive divine blessing from praying in Australia because they are conducting their prayers on stolen land.

In this context Justin Agale has proposed that Indigenous visas be granted to immigrant Muslims. This, he believes, would serve two purposes. It would mean that the immigrants' presence is acknowledged by the traditional and rightful owners (with the hope that prayers conducted in Australia would then receive *barakah*), and it would act as a potent reminder of Indigenous people's status as the custodians of this land. As Justin explains:

> In Islamic law, it's forbidden to pray on stolen land, it's said that your sharia or law is legally valid but there's no blessing in it, there's no special spiritual benefit to it, so what [some Muslims] have asked me to do is to basically see if they can get visas from Aboriginal people and get their passports stamped, sort of giving them permission to be here, because they feel that they're not gaining anything spiritually by being in this country ... So when they come to Australia they

can go to a Land Council and say, 'I've just come to Australia, I want your permission to be here', and get their Aboriginal visa. And also with citizenship, 'I've accepted citizenship here, but I want your permission to be here.' It's also recognition of our traditional ownership. I don't like that word 'traditional' ownership, but rather rightful ownership.

Here, then, we return to what Wohlrab-Sahr labels the 'double frame' of religious conversion; that is, the religious and cultural frame from which converts turn away, and the new religious and cultural frame with which they choose to align themselves. We have seen that Aboriginal and Torres Strait Islander Australians who embrace Islam perceive that their chosen faith complements their traditional Indigenous identity. But so, it appears, do many Indigenous Christians. They, in common with their Muslim counterparts, perceive strong cultural and theological convergences between their new religious frame and their prior-held convictions. It is not, of course, a question of who is correct. It is first and foremost a matter of perception. At the subjective level Indigenous Christians are just as sure as Indigenous Muslims that their religion of choice matches their traditional beliefs. In this sense we might consider religious conversion, not in terms of a double frame but a *doubled* one. Believers feel that in embracing Islam (or Christianity) one's Indigenous identity is simultaneously consolidated. The difference for Indigenous Muslims, though, is that Islam provides an alternative to the macrocontexts that come 'in between' these two frames: colonisation, Christian missionisation and contemporary capitalism.

In local and international studies of conversion to Islam the act of embracing a minority religion is often perceived as an indication of converts' discontent with the beliefs, attitudes and values they imbibed as they grew up.[62] This is certainly true for Indigenous Australians. Their conversion to Islam can be read as a sign of their disillusionment with Australian society, past and present. But, significantly, Islam also offers Indigenous reverts, in particular, 'the "ultimate protest" – the shedding of the Christianity that had been forced on them but never helped them'.[63] Beyond the spiritual enrichment it offers, Islam helps Indigenous Muslims counter the accumulated psychological scars of colonisation, missionisation and racism. Many Aboriginal people in Australia today are seeking to reaffirm their Indigenous identity by recovering ties to country, culture and community. The retrieval of Indigenous heritage is often narrowly interpreted – and judged – in terms of a capacity to conjure up some ideal of pre-colonial purity. The way some Indigenous people reaffirm their Aboriginality through an identification with Islam offers instead a practical and dynamic way of renegotiating Indigenous subjectivity in a world from which many feel disenfranchised. As a vehicle for the reconstruction of an Indigenous identity, Islam produces not only new connections to the past but also new and creative strategies for connecting with the non-Indigenous world in the present and future.

SEVEN

SISTERS ARE DOING IT FOR THEMSELVES

Most Australians perceive Islam to be anything but liberating – socially, politically or spiritually. Despite possessing little knowledge about the faith, media and political commentators in Australia (and other Western countries) condemn Islam publicly as a theology that promotes violence and fanaticism, rejects modernity and democracy, and oppresses women. The perceived backwardness of Islam contrasts sharply with the apparently modern, democratic and liberal West. In view of the negative stereotypes circulating in the mainstream media, it is perhaps surprising that conversion to Islam is growing in Australia and elsewhere in the West. It is even more ironic that most Western converts should be women. Those subscribing to the stereotype of the oppressed Muslim woman would be surprised to learn that female converts far outnumber men. Recent studies in the United

Kingdom suggest that the female:male ratio could be as high as 2:1.[1] In the United States an estimated 20 000 people convert to Islam each year; almost four times as many being women as men.[2]

In Australia the number of Indigenous Muslim men exceeds the number of women. In the five years between the 2001 and 2006 national censuses the percentage of Aboriginal and/or Torres Strait Islander women who nominated Islam as their religion increased by 55 per cent (from 277 to 432), just below the 60 per cent increase in the number of Indigenous men (from 364 to 582).[3] Why would a growing number of Indigenous Australians, and women in particular, actively choose to embrace a faith that ostensibly oppresses women? How are we to make sense of the fact that, contrary to the stereotypes, all of the Indigenous Muslim women I have met firmly believe that Islam has been an overwhelmingly positive force in their lives? The intelligent and confident women I interviewed were a far cry from the stereotype of Muslim women as oppressed and disempowered. In fact, it is difficult to sustain this view when, as Kate Zebiri (quoting Margo Badran) points out: 'In converting, women exercise agency, bravely and decisively, in going against the grain of their background, family, and culture and in opting for something strange and new.'[4]

The purpose of this chapter, then, is to examine the experiences of Indigenous Muslim women. Given that most non-Muslims in Australia and the West perceive the Islamic headscarf or hijab as a potent symbol of Muslim women's oppression, our discussion begins with it. Of course by focusing on the hijab I run the risk of re-exoticising Muslim women's dress. But its treatment is important because it is the most obvious and accessible (and perhaps misunderstood) symbol of religious faith for those unfamiliar with Islam.[5]

The dialectic of veiling

Commonly understood in English-speaking countries to refer to a head covering traditionally worn by Muslim women, in actuality the Arabic word *hijab* (meaning curtain or cover) refers both to dress *and* demeanour, attire *and* attitude. In the Qur'an *hijab* is used not to denote an article of clothing but a spatial curtain that divides and protects privacy. In 'the verse of the hijab', the Qur'an instructs male believers to talk to the wives of Muhammad from behind a curtain:

> O ye who believe! Enter not the Prophet's houses, until leave is given you, for a meal [and then] not [so early as] to wait for its preparation: but when ye are invited, enter; And when ye have taken your meal, disperse, without seeking familiar talk. Such [behaviour] annoys the Prophet: he is ashamed to dismiss you, but God is not ashamed [to tell you] the truth. And when ye ask [his wives] for anything ye want, ask them from before a curtain: that makes for greater purity for your hearts and for theirs. (33:53)

This verse was revealed to the Prophet following his wedding to Zaynab Bint Jahsh. According to al-Tabari, a companion of the Prophet, some impolite guests remained in the Prophet's house lingering outside his marriage chamber after all the other guests had departed. The Prophet, being too polite to ask them to leave, waited until the remaining guests finally left of their own accord. While drawing a curtain between himself and another companion, Anas ibn Malik, the Prophet recited 'the verse of the hijab'. This curtain or hijab was not a means of putting a barrier between a man and a woman but of separating two men and demarcating the public and private spheres of life. However, in later Muslim societies this instruction, specific to the wives of Muhammad, was generalised, leading to the segregation of the sexes.[6]

The meaning of *hijab*, and the status of requirements to wear it in public, are widely debated within the Muslim community, and the diversity of views is considerable. Some, like Fatima Mernissi, interpret 'the verse of the hijab' to be about politeness and order. She insists that it is used in the Qur'an to 'express a spatial dimension, marking a threshold between two distinct areas'.[7] Through an historical and etymological re-reading of the requirements of hijab, Mernissi ultimately concludes that wearing the veil is *not* a religious requirement. Others use the following passage from the Qur'an to argue that the headscarf is a religious obligation for all Muslim women:

> Say to the believing men that they should lower their gaze and guard their modesty; that will make for greater purity for them; And Allah is well acquainted with all that they do. And say to the believing women that they should lower their gaze and guard their modesty; that they should not display their beauty and ornaments except what [ordinarily] appear thereof; that they should draw their veils over their bosoms and not display their beauty except to their husbands, their fathers, their husbands' fathers, their sons, their husbands' sons, their brothers or their brothers' sons, or their sisters' sons, or their women, or their slaves whom their right hands possess, or male attendants free of sexual desires. Or small children who have no carnal knowledge of women. And that they should not strike their feet in order to draw attention to their hidden ornaments. And O ye Believers! Turn ye all together towards Allah in repentance that ye may be successful. (24:30–31)

All the Indigenous female converts I interviewed wore the hijab. Various personal, religious, social and political factors contributed to their decision to veil. For most it was not something they arrived at immediately. It sometimes took years before these women felt ready to 'take the step'. As discussed in chapter 5, the conversion or *converting* process involves the gradual adoption of the practices of Islam. In common with Zebiri's study of British convert women, there existed among my interviewees 'a reciprocal or dialectical relationship between wearing hijab and progressing in one's faith'.[8] Eugenia Flynn (see figure 15) postponed wearing the headscarf for a number of reasons:

> For me, I know as Muslim women it's something that we have to do [wear the headscarf]. But it wasn't something that I felt strong enough to do – I guess because my family had such strong objections. So at the beginning of last year [2006] I decided that I was finally going to do it. I felt that I was in a place where I'd been a Muslim for long enough, and it was something that I had intended to do, something that I wanted to do; I knew that it was obligatory and I felt strong enough in my faith, and strong enough as a person to be able to do that. And therefore to be able to deal with anything negative that might come as a result of that. So I felt strong enough to be able to deal with my family's reaction and with people in general. So that was the point that I had to reach. It's one thing to say that on the inside you're strong enough, but it's such an outward expression of your faith, you need to be really strong on the outside to be able to deal with that.

Deciding to wear the hijab is obviously both a private and a public matter. Whether they veil in the company of friends, fellow Muslims, family or strangers, women who wear the hijab are, observes Margot Badran, 'assertively putting religion back into public space'.[9] 'Jamila' voiced the opinion of several interviewees when she spoke about feeling comfortable wearing the hijab in some public spaces but uncomfortable in others. Like Eugenia, she felt anxious about wearing the veil in front of her family, opting to remove it when in the company of her grandmother, in particular. Born in the early 1970s on Badu Island in Torres Strait, Jamila was raised largely by her grandmother. At the time of our interview in 2005 she had been a practising Muslim for many years and lived in Sydney's Muslim heartland of Lakemba. She felt very much at ease wearing the hijab there, but it was a different story when she visited Badu. As she recounts:

> When I go up to visit [my grandmother] I still don't wear the scarf in front of her. Down here is when I wear the scarf, but when I go to visit my grandmother, because I'm not used to wearing the scarf in front of her, I feel uncomfortable. And every time I go up there for holidays she says to my cousin, 'Oh, I hope she doesn't come here and wear those clothes.' So I feel a bit uncomfortable when I go there.

Even if their families interpret it differently, Muslim women who wear the veil certainly do not intend it as a rejection of 'home and hearth or kinship relations with their non-Muslim families and parents'.[10] Wearing the hijab is, rather, a matter of faith. Donning the headscarf is among the most visible ways a woman can express and affirm her religious identity and spirituality.[11] Indigenous convert Alinta Smith articulated the attitude of many interviewees when she commented that she wears the hijab primarily as 'a form of worship to God'.[12]

The hijab is not only worn as a form of worship, it also symbolises and communicates modesty. In covering, Muslim women are freed from having to portray themselves as sexually desirable and/or available. The veil might symbolise sexual and social oppression in Western societies, but Muslim women argue that, far from being oppressed, they are liberated from both unwanted sexual attention and the dictates of fashion. Taking on the hijab becomes a way for Indigenous Muslim women to reject the West's increasingly superficial and subjective standards of (white) female beauty and desirability. Rather than trying to win in the contemporary beauty stakes, they opt out of the competition altogether.[13] In an environment of negative representations of black female beauty this is particularly salient for Aboriginal and Torres Strait Islander women. Like their African-American Muslim sisters, in wearing the hijab they simultaneously resist the projections of 'Eurocentrism, Western patriarchy, and capitalist market-values onto the organization and understanding of women's bodies'.[14]

Female allure is certainly not undervalued in Islam, but it is reserved for one's husband.[15] In the words of Katherine Bullock, hijab 'does not smother femininity or sexuality'. Rather, it 'regulates where and for whom one's femininity and sexuality will be displayed and deployed'.[16] Zebiri suggests that Western and Islamic norms are 'inverse mirror images of each other' in terms of both religion and sexuality. In Western society, she notes, religion is largely considered a private matter whereas sexuality, on the other hand, has entered the public sphere, becoming an integral part of identity politics. For the majority of Muslims, though, 'religion is not just a personal and spiritual affair' but a social – and to some extent political – phenomenon whereas 'sexuality is a very private matter'.[17] Alinta Smith, who embraced Islam in 2005, publicly demonstrates her religiosity while trying simultaneously to privatise her sexuality:

> [In wearing the hijab] not only am I identifying myself as a Muslim, I'm fulfilling a command from God. But it has other benefits as

well. You know in today's society, or in the Western world, women get all dressed up to go outside and then when they get home they take off their make up and their nice shoes and clothes – they're not dressing up to look beautiful for their husbands, but for other people. Maybe because of my mind-set growing up in this world, I thought that's how it was, [but when I found Islam] I thought, 'Wow, that does make sense' [i.e. looking beautiful only for one's husband]. In the Qur'an it says that the hijab protects women from men being attracted to you, and wearing the scarf, people will look at me, but no men have tried to talk to me, and it is like a barrier. When you have it on, it's like you're saying I'm not open to being spoken to, or to have a general conversation, or for you to try and pick me up, as you would do. I'm Muslim, and this is my belief, and I believe in it so strongly that I dress like this, to show the rest of the world as well.

All Muslim women who veil appreciate not being seen as sexualised objects who are subject to the male gaze, but this is perhaps especially pertinent for Indigenous women who have long been labelled wanton and sexually available. Eugenia emphasises the veil's special significance for Indigenous women: 'As an Aboriginal woman, one of the things I found incredibly liberating about Islam is that you are modest and that it's about treating yourself with respect, and having other people, and men in particular, treating you with respect.'[18] While the stereotype of the sexually available black woman largely emerged to excuse their widespread rape and sexual abuse by white settler men, Eugenia's veil communicates her unavailability to Aboriginal and non-Aboriginal men alike: 'I want to be a modest person, and I don't want men, particularly Aboriginal men, to view me in that way, and this is the line that I'm drawing.'

Indigenous Muslim women who veil also free themselves from

the negative labels applied to Indigenous people because the headscarf functions to conceal their Indigeneity. African-American Muslim Amina Wadud notes that wearing the hijab increases her 'ethnic anonymity'. As she says, 'It has hidden my African origins, allowing others to identify me with several Muslim ethnicities.'[19] While, like Wadud, the Indigenous Muslim women I met are certainly not trying to conceal their racial and cultural identity, they find that the hijab operates similarly in Australia. Jamila mentioned that in her encounters with shopkeepers and others in the public realm she is often praised for how well she speaks English. Her headscarf acts as a visual cue of her assumed outsider status, and most take for granted that she comes from the Sudan or elsewhere in Africa. It is ironic that it is often Anglo-Celtic Australians, immigrants themselves (even if generations ago), who assume Jamila's immigrant status.

Halima Binti Hassan Awal has had comparable experiences. As she recounts, 'Non-Muslims, they always seem to have this idea that I am from overseas [because of] how I'm dressed – not knowing that I'm actually an *Indigenous* Australian from the Torres Strait.'[20] When Halima's late Lebanese–Australian Muslim husband was ill and paramedics came to their house, Halima recalls, 'They didn't know how to approach me because I was covered ... "Should I speak English? How do I approach this woman?"'[21] In, as she says, 'breaking the ice' by speaking English, Halima was promptly asked where she came from! Her inquirer was probably surprised at her answer: 'Well, I was born north-west of Brisbane, at a place called Cherbourg ...' (Halima was born at Cherbourg's Aboriginal Mission following her family's evacuation from Thursday Island during World War II.)

It is not only non-Indigenous Australians who assume the immigrant or outsider status of veiled women. Aboriginal Muslim

Nazra Wali regularly engages with Indigenous people as part of her community-based work. Over the years she has encountered their sometimes inflexible attitudes towards Aboriginality and authenticity. In her experience some Indigenous people 'can't see beyond' the veil.[22] When Nazra is wearing it they automatically assume she is non-Indigenous, and at times some have resented what they perceive to be the intrusion of an outsider into their affairs. Discussing with me the assumptions that (particularly younger) Indigenous people sometimes make about her on the basis of her veil, Nazra also alluded to the differences between converts and kinverts:

> The [Indigenous people I engage with] sort of welcome you and thank you for coming to support them and support their cause, and I find that, especially the women, they'll come out of their way and say, 'Thank you for coming to help and for being here with us' and 'Thank you for being part of this', and sometimes you want to say to them, 'It's also my path as well', but because you're wearing a scarf, they've already sort of identified you as somebody from outside; they don't include you as an Aboriginal person. So a lot of times you just say, 'Yes, I'm happy to be here' rather than trying to explain, you know, why you are there, because a lot of times people are not ready to accept that there can be a person who wears a hijab and is Aboriginal. Though a lot of older people know, because they've grown up with people who were married to Muslims and have kids and, especially when you go and look at some of the names, you know, they reflect Afghani names or Indonesian names, but people have lost where it came from.

While veiling conceals, it also exposes. One positive manifestation of this dialectic is that the hijab helps Muslim women recognise one another. As Jamila says, 'It's good when you see a Muslim lady in the street, you say salaam.'[23] Alinta Smith, as observed, stresses that she wears the scarf primarily to fulfil a religious requirement, but she also appreciates the sense of connectedness she feels when acknowledged in the street by other Muslims. In her experience, 'You feel that you're one of them.' Halima notes that when she wears the hijab she is 'recognised. People know straight off I'm a Muslim.'[24] In Eugenia's words: 'A guy walked past [today] and said *salaam 'Alaikum*. You know, it's nice when people do that. I guess for me [wearing the hijab is] also about other Muslims recognising that I am a Muslim as well.'

Of course non-Muslims also identify scarf-wearing women as followers of Islam. Wearing the hijab places Muslim women in the full light of the public gaze.[25] Paradoxically, while they hope that wearing the headscarf will put an end to the objectification of their bodies, they often find, instead, that they become more frequent 'objects' of the Western gaze.[26] Halima, like Jamila above, notes that when she is in public, people do not know whether she speaks English. Either way, non-Muslims have often made disparaging comments within earshot. Recalling an incident at the local supermarket, Halima states: 'I heard a remark, "Oh, that's disgusting how they dress." But you just let it in one ear and out the other. They don't know. They don't know me as a person. They only see how I'm dressed.'

Jamila found negative comments directed at her 'especially around the time when there was the bombing in America'. The high incidence of verbal and physical abuse Muslim women suffered post-9/11, which almost invariably manifested itself in the tearing off of the hijab, serves as a potent reminder of the way self-concealment also exposes. Most of the Indigenous Muslim women I interviewed reported cases of having been verbally abused when wearing the veil. Ironically, more than one has been exhorted to go back to where she came from. In short, although Indigenous Muslim women who choose to veil are, on the one hand, freed from some of the stereotypes applied to Indigenous women, they can simultaneously be victimised by the application of the negative associations of Islam that circulate in the broader community. The dialectic of veiling means that the hijab both isolates and secures, both curtails access to the broader community and enlarges agency in claiming allegiance to another community.

Negotiating identity

The only act entirely forbidden in Islam is the association of Allah with other gods, beings or things. The Arabic word for this, *shirk*, refers specifically to the sin of polytheism (believing in more than one god), but *shirk* can also encompass the practice of associating partners with Allah, or assigning Allah's characteristics to those other than Allah. Excepting one's engagement in *shirk*, there is a great deal of forgiveness in Islam, even for those who neglect obligatory acts of worship. Given this openness, (Indigenous) Muslims have to decide for themselves which acts of worship are important and 'how to perform those acts without compromising other values'.[27] A woman's individual interpretation of the Qur'an and the Sunna (ways and manners of the Prophet) will inform how she practices her faith. To make sense of Islamic theology and practice, Indigenous women engage in an active process of religious exegesis or interpretation, known in Arabic as *ijtihad*.

Nazra's decision to forgo wearing the hijab in the presence of the Indigenous community is an example of one woman's *ijtihad*. After embracing Islam in the 1980s Nazra initially fulfilled the stereotype of the religious convert who is stricter in religious practice than those born into a faith. For years she was extremely devout in her practice; she always wore a scarf or hijab (for more than two years she wore a full-face veil or *niqab*); she refused to frequent places that served alcohol; and was always careful only to eat halal food. After performing the pilgrimage or *haj* in Makkah, she recalls: 'I put the religion and my life together and [they] couldn't be separated and I sometimes made it miserable for everybody else around me, because I wouldn't take it any other way, you know, the two had to come together and if whatever else I was doing in my life didn't fit in the religion, I wouldn't do it.'

As mentioned Nazra felt she was not accepted as an Aboriginal woman by other Indigenous people when she wore the headscarf. After reading, contemplating and critically engaging with the sacred text and the traditions she concluded that she could best serve the interests of the Indigenous community (and, she hoped, please Allah) by fitting in with them – even if this meant forgoing her headscarf in their company and agreeing to cook (but not consume) bacon. As she says:

> When I started looking more in the Aboriginal community and when I started going and feeling that I'm not being accepted with the hijab, I thought, 'Well, I'm not going to cause anybody harm but myself if I take the hijab off, that way I can get their trust, and be part of the community.' I've even cooked bacon and eggs at the Aboriginal Advancement Week events. People know that I don't eat it, but they don't know why I don't eat it. Most Muslims will frown at me for doing that, but when you talk to the people of knowledge, the Muslim teachers, they say if you're doing that [cooking bacon], and that's the least thing you are doing, the rest of the community work you are doing outweighs it.

Like Nazra, all of the Indigenous Muslim women I spoke to exhibited a degree of flexibility towards their implementation of Islamic norms, particularly when interacting with non-Muslims. They demonstrated, in the words of Zebiri, 'a willingness to adapt to different situations and contexts and to apply the spirit and not just the letter of the law'.[28] Several interviewees described how, in their daily encounters with unrelated men, they tried at all times to avoid touching them or shaking their hands, to lower their gaze in their presence and, if possible, not to be alone with them in a non-public place. But they also recognised that it was difficult, if not impossible, to practise gender segregation in a modern Western society. 'I try to avoid shaking hands [with men] as much as possible,' Halima says, 'but sometimes you can't avoid it. But I try the best I can to do everything that is halal [permissible].'[29] According to Alinta, 'I don't shake guys' hands. Before [I converted] I used to, but Muhammad (peace be upon him) he never touched a woman unless he was married to her … I try and follow the Sunna as much as I can, but living in a Western society it's a bit harder.'

Trying to engage scrupulously only in religiously sanctioned behaviour, the women are also aware that Islamic norms can be 'misunderstood or construed as hostile' by non-Muslims.[30] In declining to shake a man's extended hand Alinta, for instance, explains that she is not 'want[ing] to be rude', she is trying to live by her religious beliefs. She is keen not to alienate people or add to Islam's 'bad name' and hopes that in taking the time to explain her position she 'creates awareness, so maybe if they meet another Muslim woman, they won't try to shake their hand'. Beyond engaging in *da'wah* (inviting people to understand the worship of Allah), Alinta emphasises her desire to be part of the larger Australian community. 'I also want to integrate to a certain extent', she says, even if this occasionally means compromising a specific teaching. Invoking the Islamic principle of *maslaha* (public interest) provides the basis for Alinta's desire to act according to the laws of the country she lives in – even if they are social customs, not legal precepts.[31]

Depending on how it is construed, the Qur'an can be interpreted as a liberating or oppressive moral code. It all depends, as Mernissi maintains, 'on the person who invokes it'.[32] Every exegetical and critical engagement with the Qur'an and the Sunna reflects the intentions of the text as well as the 'prior text' of the one who makes the 'reading'.[33] To paraphrase Zebiri, a convert's original socialisation will influence their interpretation of Islamic teachings.[34] The colonial and social history of Indigenous people in Australia contributes substantially to the view of Indigenous Muslim women that Islam is a faith with the potential to liberate them from sexism, racism and classism.[35]

As observed, veiling has a special significance for Indigenous women who continue to confront the image of the sexually promiscuous black woman, a stereotype that has had currency since the earliest days of colonisation. The widespread practice of the forcible removal of Aboriginal and Torres Strait Islander children from their families also contributes to the appeal of Islam for Indigenous women. Islam's emphasis on the sanctity of marriage and family is especially attractive to Indigenous women who want to provide their children with a sense of security and stability. They firmly reject the claims of Western feminists who view the nuclear family as a major source of women's oppression. Instead, they argue that freedom, for them, entails the ability to form families, given that the long history of racism and colonisation in Australia has resulted in the break-up of their families, communities and social networks.

Jamila is one Indigenous revert who values highly Islam's emphasis on morality and family values. Coming from Torres Strait where, she notes, there is a high incidence of family breakdown and single motherhood, Jamila feels that a Muslim marriage is a viable way of countering the increasingly precarious structures of Indigenous family life. The special emphasis in Islam on the importance of a happy and peaceful marriage is especially significant for Indigenous Australian women, given the reality of the high number of broken and fatherless homes in their communities. According to Jamila:

> I think [my life's] changed for the better because … in the [Torres Strait] Islands a lot of girls grow up, they take drugs, they take alcohol and they become pregnant and things like that. And for me … I've been saved. Like, I came here [to the mainland], I got married and I've got proper children from my husband, you know, not from this man and this man and that man. So, I think in a way I've found that it's better for me [being a Muslim].

The goal of a secure and stable Muslim family is not something Indigenous revert women desire for their personal satisfaction alone. They also hope it will have a positive effect on their children and, in time, the wider Indigenous community. Aboriginal and Torres Strait Islander Australians are painfully aware that racism and colonisation have left deep-seated, cross-generational psychological scars in their communities. They also believe that these scars have had an adverse effect on their ability to prosper. The vast majority of Indigenous Australians suffer extreme economic hardship, and most have little hope or expectation of improving their lot in life. They are also well aware that living without the means 'to exercise meaningful agency over one's material life is a situation that invites addiction'.[36]

Islam can help circumvent this familiar trajectory because it endows believers with a sense of purpose and, through the recreation of self, a means of combating self-hatred. Islam's emphasis on personal responsibility has helped many Indigenous Muslim reverts improve their psychological well-being and, as a result, their material status. Eugenia stresses that it is incorrect to 'assume that [simply believing in] Islam is going to save you'. But it can, she says, equip one with 'the tools to be able to save yourself ... [Islam teaches that] you're only as good as what you can make yourself.' Islam has also helped Indigenous Muslims like Eugenia 'in decolonising the mind, where your mind is free enough to be able to reject those things that are bringing down our people and to take on other values that are good'. Islam provides Indigenous people with a much-needed framework of positive symbols and rituals within which they can reorient their personal and group identification. The pride and confidence they feel in their new identity act as an antidote against the destructive stereotypes of Indigenous people that circulate in Australian society.

Western forms of feminism 'tend to view the assertion of difference between the sexes as implying male superiority'.[37] By contrast, the Indigenous Muslim women I met were attracted to Islam's emphasis on male/female differentiation. Far from perceiving men as superior, they adopted a 'different but equal' understanding of gender roles, stressing complementarity and equity, rather than strict equality. In Halima's words, 'The man is the head of the family and he's there to protect me and my children, but women do have equal rights.'[38] Similarly, Alinta insists that while 'men and women are created differently, just because I'm a woman doesn't mean I'm any less than a man':

> I embrace the fact that I am a woman. I don't have to do a man's job, or live up to the expectations of what a guy does ... to prove that I'm equal. And I don't want my husband to stay home and look after the kids; I'm the one who's more nurturing. God has made us certain ways with our certain roles and we fit perfectly into [them] ... I don't have to have a job and then look after my kids, plus clean my house and cook for my family, and do all the washing and all that stuff. I find a lot of women in today's society, that's what they have to do. But in Islam, my right is that I don't have to work, that's the man's role. So I have rights that a lot of Western women don't.

In her study of African-American Muslim women's understanding of Islam, and how it relates to their personal and social history, Carolyn Moxley Rouse suggests that African-American Muslims, although not engaged in a revolutionary movement calling for sweeping reform, are active participants in articulating an empowering social narrative that is poised to change the way 'African-Americans look at themselves, their race, their gender, economics and politics'.[39] Indigenous Muslim reverts in Australia are similarly engaged. They are part of a small but growing movement that, through religious praxis, is strategically repositioning the meaning of race, class and gender in (Indigenous) Australia. In their individual efforts to liberate themselves from the negative characterisations of Indigeneity, Indigenous reverts simultaneously protest against the treatment of their community as a whole. Their sense of self is deeply entrenched in the collective experiences of their people. Although, as Magnus Bassey argues, the white concept of self can exist independently of the larger community, for the oppressed, who have a different perception of history, 'individual consciousness is inextricably linked to the collective'.[40]

Engaged surrender

According to Rouse, African-American Muslims manipulate cultural symbols in the interest of challenging the legitimacy of secular, hegemonic notions of race, class and gender. But women, in particular, are simultaneously engaged in a process of critiquing the sexism they sometimes encounter within the Muslim community itself. Using the same tools of religious interpretation and Qur'anic exegesis, African-American women use Islam to negate sexist attitudes within their families and the wider Muslim community.[41] The women have surrendered to Allah, but they continue to engage with the non-Muslim and Muslim communities for their rights. Indigenous Muslim women in Australia are also taking part in what Rouse calls a process of 'engaged surrender'. Qur'anic exegesis provides them, like their African-American counterparts, with a means of critiquing both Western normative views of gender and femininity *and* patriarchal readings of and practices in Islam.[42]

In Islam, unlike Christianity, Adam and Eve are equals in order of creation and degree of sin. In the Islamic creation story the first man and woman (unnamed in the Qur'an) were produced out of one living entity (*nafs*) and the mate (*zawj*) was created from the first. Since, as Rouse explains, the terms *nafs* and *zawj* are gender neutral, one gender cannot claim superiority over the other on the basis of the order of creation.[43] If, as Riffat Hassan proposes, woman was not created *from* man, then nor was she created *for* man; her existence is significant in itself.[44] Scholars such as Hassan and Wadud also maintain that the first man and woman were equally responsible for the fall from the Garden of Eden. According to Hassan, only oral tradition, and not the Qur'an, nominates Eve as responsible for expulsion from the

Garden.⁴⁵ Wadud's Qur'anic exegesis shows that with the noteworthy exception of two verses in *sura* (chapter) 20, the Qur'an always uses the Arabic dual form to describe Satan's tempting of both Adam and Eve, their mutual disobedience to God and their joint ejection from the Garden. Notably, she says, the 'exception to the Qur'anic use of the dual form to refer to the temptation and disobedience of Adam and Eve in the Garden singles out Adam'.⁴⁶

The Qur'an also provides clear-cut evidence that woman is equal with man in the sight of God in terms of her rights and responsibilities. It is not gender that determines who earns Allah's grace; 'it is faith and the desire to serve and obey him'.⁴⁷ The sacred text grants women the right to be educated, to conduct business, to maintain property and to keep their maiden names upon marriage.⁴⁸ Muslim women can work outside the family home if they choose to, but their money is their own. Unlike their husbands, Muslim women are not obliged to contribute their earnings to the running of the household. In addition, women cannot be forced into marriage; husbands do not acquire the property of their wives upon marriage; women can initiate divorce, and they have the right to set the dowry or *mahr*. In Islam women also have the right to vote and can hold positions of authority over men.⁴⁹ Of course in practice the roles and rights of Muslim women and men vary from one country, culture, community and family to the next. For a great many Muslim women, in Muslim majority and minority countries, their lives do not remotely resemble the ideal perceived to be their right or due in Islam.⁵⁰ Muslim women recognise the disjuncture between Islamic ideals and cultural realities, believing that while the religion is perfect,⁵¹ those who practice it are not. For them, 'the roadblocks to liberation are seen not as Islam, but poor readings of Islam'.⁵²

The majority of the Indigenous revert women I interviewed were married to Muslim men who had migrated to Australia in the last twenty to thirty years. Interestingly, at the time of writing, none was married to an Aboriginal and/or Torres Strait Islander Muslim man. Given the relatively small number of Indigenous Muslims in Australia, and the fact that they reside in different areas of the country (the majority in Sydney), Indigenous Muslim women have perhaps had greater contact with members of the Muslim diaspora.

The most recent census figures give some idea of the relative sizes of the Indigenous and non-Indigenous Muslim communities in Australia. In 2006 there were a recorded 582 Indigenous Muslim men in Australia (out of a total 1014), whereas non-Indigenous Muslim men comprised around half of the 340 000 Muslims in this country. On the basis of these figures, an Indigenous Muslim woman is more likely to meet and marry a Muslim man who migrated to Australia (or who is the Australian-born child of Muslim immigrant parents) than an Indigenous Muslim man. The married women I met had married Muslim men who were born and raised in various countries, including Pakistan, Lebanon and Somalia; another was married to an Australian-raised convert of Indian descent. As such, the Islam the men practised emerged from cultural milieus that were distinct not only from each other but also from 'mainstream' cultural values in Australia.

At the time of her marriage to her Pakistani-born Muslim husband in 1989, Torres Strait Islander revert Jamila knew nothing about Islam, but she gradually became more interested in the faith. In Islam a Muslim man is permitted to marry a Muslim, Christian or Jewish woman (Muslim women, on the other hand, can only marry Muslim men), so Jamila's Christian upbringing did not prevent their marriage. But, according to Jamila, nor was there any 'pressure on his side whatsoever' for her to embrace Islam. Jamila reached this decision after independent study, attending classes and comparing and contrasting Christianity and Islam. Although she never felt comfortable with Christianity's Trinitarian theology, Islam 'made a lot of sense' to Jamila and, in becoming Muslim, she decided, as she says, 'to follow my heart'. We saw earlier that through a Muslim marriage Jamila feels she has 'been saved' from many of the social and marital problems that afflict her fellow Torres Strait Islanders. But this, of course, does not mean she always sees eye to eye with her husband. Their difficulties stem, in part, from what Jamila perceives as her husband's culturally derived assumptions about women. As she states: 'It's difficult for me to adjust because my husband expects me to be more like a Pakistani woman [laughter]. Sometimes I tell him I'm not a Pakistani woman, so he can't expect too much. I think in his sense, women in Pakistan have to listen to their husbands, no matter what he says, right or wrong. But I tell him, "You can't make me like a Pakistani woman!"'

Jamila's husband's resistance to the notion of female self-determination is perhaps not only culturally determined. It might also be attributable to his particular interpretation of the sacred text. Of all the Qur'anic passages about men and women, perhaps the most vulnerable to different readings (by Muslims and non-Muslims alike) is the following in which Allah states, in part: 'Men are the protectors and maintainers of women because Allah has given the one more preference than the other, and because they support them from their means. Therefore the righteous women are devoutly obedient, and guard in the husband's absence what Allah would have them guard' (4:34).[53]

Men in this verse are *preferred*. Elsewhere in the Qur'an they are described as having 'a degree above' women (2:228). Those I interviewed interpreted the special treatment given men not in terms of male privilege or superiority but of added responsibility and a duty to protect and support one's wife and children.[54] According to Islamic doctrine, as the head of the family, Muslim men are not only the caretakers of the family's well-being and safety, they are also responsible for supporting them financially.[55] As Jamila states, 'In Islam, a husband has to support the wife.' According to Alinta: 'I mean, there are certain rights that a husband has over a wife … I shouldn't hang around people that he doesn't approve of, or go to places that he doesn't approve of, that type of stuff.' The man 'also has more control over the money'. But not, she insists, 'my money – if I work my money is solely spent on me. I don't have to pay for any bills, that's his responsibility.' So, she adds, 'there are some rights that he has [but] more than anything men are [obliged] to look after us and protect us'.

This same Qur'anic verse describes righteous women as devoutly obedient. The Arabic word *qanitat* (the feminine plural of *qanit*), meaning submissive or obedient, is often interpreted (by men, in particular) to mean that women must obey their husbands. But *qanit* is a word used in many other verses in the Qur'an, and in each case it refers to one's obedience and subservience to Allah. Many Muslim women argue that there is no reason that verse 4:34, alone, should depart from this convention and decree that women should be devoutly obedient to their husbands. They interpret this verse to mean that women (just like men) must remain obedient to Allah. As Alinta adroitly points out, being obedient to your 'husband, and not God, where's the reward in that?'

Most of the women I spoke to upheld the general principle of wifely obedience to their husbands, but they tended to see it in rather qualified terms.[56] Jamila, for example, refused her husband's request that she seek paid employment on the basis that he was asserting his (assumed) right of obedience, without fulfilling his obligation of providing for her and their children. As she says: 'Recently we had another argument and he mentioned to me that he wants me to get a job, but I've learned that in Islam a husband has to support his wife, you know.' She continues, 'So sometimes it's difficult now because we have arguments. We go back to the money issue and he tells me to get jobs and all that, and I find it very hard now.' In Islam a woman's marital responsibilities are understood to lie with the maintaining of the house and the raising of the children. But the underemployment of those from non-English-speaking-backgrounds in Australia is a material reality that can cause Muslim men to be poor financial providers. As Rouse suggests, 'The dissonance between the ideal and the practical can cause tension.'[57]

Jamila's unwillingness to accede to her husband's entreaties is perhaps also attributable to what she interpreted as his lack of respect for her role as a mother. In Islam mothers are held in high regard. The Prophet Muhammad reportedly said that paradise lies at the feet of mothers. According to another Hadith or tradition, it is related that a man asked the Prophet Muhammad to whom he should render kindness. The Prophet instructed him to be kind to his mother. He asked, 'Who is next?' Again the Prophet replied, 'Your mother.' He put the question to the Prophet a third time and was again given the same answer. When he asked the question the fourth time he was told to be kind to his father, indicating that mothers are to be given three times the honour and respect shown fathers. According to Alinta, 'If anything, the role of a mother is one of the most important jobs in Islam.'

Her husband's decision to take another wife has also been a

cause of tension in Jamila's marriage. Jamila understands that Islam permits Muslim men to marry up to four women (on the proviso that they can provide for each of them equally). However, according to Jamila, her husband's decision to marry a second wife during a return trip to Pakistan was due to cultural pressures as well: 'It's not because my husband wanted to marry overseas, but he had to marry there because, I don't know, like in their culture, our children were born here, and they will grow up here and they will stay here. He will have nobody back there if he goes overseas. He has no children there. It especially has to do with land and things like that so that's the main reason why he had to get married.'

Either way, Jamila struggles with the thought of sharing her husband with another woman. She notes that in 'Pakistan when women grow up, they expect these things, it's in their culture, but for us, like here in a Western society, we marry a Muslim man and like, you have to get used to it'. She adds, 'Some women, they find it easy, but I don't. I find it difficult.' The thought of living together with her husband and his new wife in a single dwelling is not one Jamila relishes. When she and her husband discuss the prospect of her accompanying him on his trips back to Pakistan, 'He says to me, "I'm sure if you go over there, we can't all stay together."' According to Jamila, this is because, as her husband says, 'she [his second wife] can hack it, but I can't. And it's true. I don't think I can [laughter].'

Jamila was raised in a family environment that would not have countenanced polygyny. Although she has chosen to embrace a religion that sanctions it (if particular conditions are met), she was, at the time of our conversation, 'finding it very difficult'. Like other revert women I met, Jamila combined her Islamic faith with many of the values found in Western society. One consequence of the conflict she now perceives between the conventions of her adopted faith and her own cultural values has been a tendency to withdraw from Islam. As she says, 'Now, I've gradually slowed down. I don't pray as much as I used to, and I find it difficult now, so I have a lot of arguments with my husband and things like that.' In fact, she elaborates, 'I've lost interest in praying right now. I felt like God was not helping me, but [recently] I have started praying again and I want to go back to feeling like God was very close to me, I was very close to Him, you know, before.' Unfortunately I have since lost contact with Jamila. The last I heard she was still committed to Islam but was no longer living with her husband.

Indigenous revert Nazra Wali also found that her Muslim husband made demands she could not meet. Nazra was born in Townsville in 1963. Her Aboriginal mother, originally from the Tiwi Islands, met her Fijian–Indian father during one of his many trips to north Queensland. At that time he regularly travelled between Fiji and Australia on business, bringing in kava and copra (coconut meat), and taking other goods back to Fiji on his return journeys. Not long after Nazra's birth, her young unmarried mother was approached by child welfare officers. According to Nazra they notified her mother that unless she could prove she was married, 'she was not entitled to have the child in her care'. Nazra's mother asked her father to take the baby back to Fiji with him. Nazra spent her childhood and adolescence in Fiji, living with her paternal grandmother, and at other times with her father, stepmother and half-siblings. Her father, who had married in Fiji just before meeting Nazra's mother, was ashamed of his duplicity and forwent telling Nazra about her Aboriginal mother until she was much older.

In 1982, still unaware of her Aboriginal heritage, Nazra

returned to Australia to attend university. She shared a house with some fellow Indonesian students who were Muslim. It was then, according to Nazra, that 'Islam sort of became interesting to me'. Living and interacting with her Muslim housemates, observing them at prayer and appreciating 'their inner peace', Nazra 'slowly, slowly' began to consider Islam as an option. With her housemates and some other Indonesian people in what she called 'a little gathering one night', Nazra took the *shahada* in 1984. That same year she met her future husband when he came to Australia as a refugee of the Ethiopian famine. He self-identified as a Muslim but, according to Nazra, 'he wasn't really practising, but he grew up in the religion. He knew the religion, but I can't say that he was praying five times a day.' As a new Muslim revert, Nazra was puzzled by the differences she perceived between the way her former Indonesian housemates practised Islam and the behaviour of her future husband and his Muslim friends. For Nazra it was through trying to understand these differences that 'Islam became more a part of [her] life'. As she says: 'I started comparing the two groups. I started to read more and research more and tried to see which one of them was right ... Until then I sort of read very little and observed more, but from then on I started to find out more about the Qur'an and the Hadith.'

In time Nazra's father told her about her Aboriginal heritage. Ashamed of an extra-marital sexual relationship, he had also wanted to protect Nazra and her Aboriginal mother from any further intervention from child welfare officers. In any case, having been told the truth, Nazra wanted to know more. As she recalls: 'If you know that you are Fijian, you accept it. But when somebody comes and tells you, yes, that's who you are, but you have this other [heritage] in you, and there are reasons why you were not told about this, you know, and it was to protect everybody around you, and yourself in some ways ... then I started to want to know more, and to identify my kids and myself [as Aboriginal].'

While Nazra's husband initially supported her interest in her newfound heritage, he soon resisted her growing identification with her Aboriginality. After the birth of the couple's second child Nazra's husband strongly opposed her wish to identify herself and their children as Indigenous. Nazra recalls this difficult period in her life:

> [My husband] discouraged me from knowing anything about it. That only became very clear when I had my kids, and when I wanted to identify [as Indigenous] ... When I was first told he did, you know, support me in some ways, but then when I started to want to know more, and identify my kids and myself, he sort of said, no, you just have to leave that there because that's another past [sic] of your life, so, I didn't do a lot for a long time. When I did start researching and finding out more, our relationship really broke down. So in some ways I had to lose one to get the other.

Her husband's attitude is, Nazra notes, particularly perplexing in 'somebody who's from a mixed marriage and mixed background'. Whatever the cause, this painful experience has in one sense been instructive. It has shown Nazra the folly of trying to 'be so controlling'. She has since adopted a more flexible and lenient attitude towards life, faith and identity. Her more relaxed interpretation of Islamic norms is a far cry from the days, discussed earlier, when she refused to participate in any activity that she felt even remotely compromised her religious beliefs or practices. Nazra now picks and chooses when she wears the hijab. Her more open and compromising attitude is also evident in the way she engages with her children:

At the moment I've let them choose what they want to do. They're not the best examples of Muslim kids, but it's something I want them to say, you know, and choose if they want that. A lot of Muslims will frown at me for saying that, because it's not acceptable in a lot of Muslims' minds that you let the child choose, but I am in this situation where I don't want to use force. They have been taught the religion, they know the basics, they know what's right and what's wrong ... My middle child at the moment is asking if going to the mosque is the most important thing, or whether there are other things in his life which he needs to correct or do, which are more important. And I try to rationalise with him, and say, you know, 'You can work both together and they both will help [on the Day of Judgement]', but at the end of the day it's his decision. And that's where their father and I differ a lot. Because when they're with him he wants to enforce things, and I've become the way I have become with the religion because [of] my ex-husband. He doesn't practice what he preaches, he just preaches, and I've become very tired of that way of living. I'd rather see it practised and for the kids to follow the example, rather than saying, 'This is what you have to do', and then, I do whatever I want.

In our interview Nazra spoke passionately of her desire to meet her Tiwi Islander mother, but was very mindful of the impact any meeting might have on her: 'My biggest issue, which I always say, is that I don't want to upset her in any way or form, or disturb her life', adding, 'even if she doesn't want to tell everybody who I am, as long as we can have some time together'. Nazra's Indigenous identity has been hard won. She has had to overcome child welfare intervention, the strenuous resistance of her ex-husband and people's assumptions that a scarf-wearing woman could not possibly be Aboriginal. Her understanding of her religious identity has also been achieved after much introspection.

For Nazra, and all of the women discussed in this chapter, living and self-identifying as an Indigenous Muslim woman is a work in progress. They are each engaged in an active, syncretic and open-ended process of identity formation in which being a woman is inextricably linked to renegotiating differing and sometimes irreconcilable religious and cultural affiliations. Through their creative fusion of Islamic and Western values these women contribute in various ways to both an *Indigenous* and a local, home-grown or *indigenous* Australian Islam.

EIGHT

MALCOLM X DOWN UNDER

Indigenous Muslims experience Islam as a living force. They relate it, and relate to it, in a host of different ways. I have constantly been impressed by the diversity of the testimonies generated by my seemingly generic questions. Some have focused on remote ancestries, others on intimate matters of personal faith, and yet others have shared with me difficult ethical and doctrinal dilemmas. This diversity of experience is not only reflected in the content and style of the stories told – it also extends to the definition of community. If there is an overarching theme, an idea that runs through most if not all the accounts I recorded, it is the journey from a sense of aloneness to a sense of belonging. And, just as ways of relating or storytelling vary from person to person, so does the conception of community. It is clear in chapter 7, for example, that veiling simultaneously closes out one kind of community and embraces another. Yet this is not a simple choice between two opposed but actual societies: women who embrace Islam also embrace an *ideal* of community (one notably resistant to patriarchal pressure).

The meanings that can be attached to the term *community* multiply when, as in this chapter, we factor in the experiences of Indigenous male converts to Islam. Perhaps one can venture the generalisation that both men and women identify community, and their role within it, with nurturing: women emphasise their role as care-givers whereas men, as we shall see, speak more often as providers of protection. But beyond this broad commonality of the social goal Islam mediates in their lives, a considerable diversity of interpretations exists, reflecting the gendering of roles and, exceptionally in the case of my male interviewees, the prominence of a single recent historical role model – Malcolm X – in their decision to convert. And perhaps the powerful influence of the life of Malcolm X on the lives of Indigenous men drawn to Islam is also a clue to the diverse understandings of community that they relate, and relate to. For it appears that one of the attractions of Malcolm X, as his autobiography is communicated to us through the literary skills of Alex Haley, is his inconsistency or, rather, his consistently restless self-reinvention. For him Islam was not a static authority but a living force with which to wrestle; and in the course of his turbulent pilgrimage, Malcolm X also traversed most, if not all, the archetypal stages in a man's growth from aloneness and abjection to the achievement of a oneness both with oneself and with the world.

In 1965 Malcolm X was assassinated in front of his wife, young daughters and a hall full of supporters while giving a speech in a Harlem theatre in New York. At the time of his shooting he was addressing members of his newly founded Organization of

Afro-American Unity, established as a political vehicle to internationalise the plight of black Americans and to move from civil rights to human rights.[1] Before his untimely death Malcolm worked tirelessly in support of restoring black Americans' sense of pride and self-worth by reconnecting them to their African heritage. A skilled public speaker and debater with a sharp wit and charismatic personality, Malcolm argued passionately for the rights of African-Americans to freedom, justice and equality. He articulated the anger and frustration of many black Americans during the major phase of the civil rights movement (from 1956 to 1965) and has been described as one of the most influential African-Americans of all time.[2]

In my conversations with Aboriginal and Torres Strait Islander Muslim men, a high proportion described the inspiration they drew from Malcolm X's life story and the significant role it played in their decision to embrace Islam. In the words of Sulaiman Menzies, Malcolm X's autobiography 'changed many lives out here and in jail as well'.[3] He elaborates, 'A lot of us became Muslim through the autobiography of Malcolm X; he's the one that first encouraged us. If you ask a lot of Aboriginal Muslims and blacks all over the world really, in Western countries, a lot of us start off like that because we can relate to his whole story.' In an interview with Dilara Reznikas, Indigenous Muslim Justin Agale said he had 'only met one Aboriginal who became Muslim whose conversion wasn't connected with Malcolm X'.[4] But, although many Indigenous Muslims, men in particular, credit Malcolm X's autobiography with their identification with Islam, a number were unaware that Malcolm was a Muslim before they read his life story. Chapter 5 showed that Justin was initially attracted to Malcolm X in his capacity as a 'black nationalist'. It was only *after* reading his autobiography that he understood Malcolm's struggle for African-American liberation to be inextricably linked with his identity as a Muslim. It was then that Justin began reading about (and eventually embracing) Islam. Another interviewee, 'Abdul', who is of Torres Strait Islander descent but grew up in north Queensland, was also initially drawn to the speeches and published works of Malcolm X because of his interest in racial politics. As he says: 'I found the works of Malcolm X quite appealing because I think even though the African-American experience is quite different to the Aboriginal or the Indigenous experience, there are quite a few parallels with the dispossession, the loss of the original culture, the original languages and the almost total assimilation into a largely English Anglican cultural norm.'[5]

Through his reading Abdul not only discovered that the experiences of Indigenous Australians recapitulated many of the themes of *The Autobiography of Malcolm X*; he was also introduced to Islam, coming to understand 'why [Malcolm] had chosen to follow what seemed to be a very alien faith'. As Abdul puts it, Malcolm X's autobiography and other published works 'basically opened up a new door and I just went and read whatever I could'. Regardless of their initial motivation in reading about Malcolm X, his life story has undoubtedly inspired many Indigenous men to consider Islam as a viable religious option. But if Malcolm X's autobiography is the initial catalyst, what is it about Islam that finally persuades these men to revert? Is reversion ever finished – or, like community, is it an idea or goal that constantly evolves?

Rainbow coalition

In common with Indigenous women, Aboriginal and Torres Strait Islander men who are engaged by the teachings of Islam find the importance they give to community to be one of their most attractive elements. Islam, they are taught, always situates the individual firmly within the context of a larger social unit, 'providing protection, communal identification and support'.[6] In the words of Aboriginal Muslim 'John', 'I think a lot of [Indigenous] converts – if they haven't been too successful as non-Muslims – they probably find they're affirmed in ways that didn't happen before.'[7] They discover, he says, that 'there's a community, they're welcomed, people want to teach them things. Muslims are very generous and hospitable people.' The fact that fellow Muslims are greeted as 'brother' and 'sister' further reinforces the communal and familial image of Islam.[8] And, of course, their use resonates in Indigenous communities, where 'brother' and 'sister' and such terms of respect as 'Auntie' and 'Uncle', used in reference to elders, are commonplace.

In another manifestation of cross-cultural convergence, Indigenous reverts to Islam are likely to recognise the companionship and solidarity they experience as embodiments of the ideals of community and camaraderie their Indigenous brothers and sisters espouse. Sulaiman is a descendant of the Dainggatti people of northern New South Wales. In our conversation he stressed that Indigenous people in general are highly community and family oriented: 'Every Aboriginal person who meets another Aboriginal for the first time, we start our conversation off with, "Where are you from?" to see if we can find any connection somewhere. Always you'll find that they know someone who you know, who knows someone that they know and they're related somehow. And that's it: you're accepted straight away into their family.' This Indigenous familial orientation, he says, makes 'it easy for us to accept Islam ... because naturally we believe that ... As a people we believe that family and community are everything'. Such companionship and solidarity is also seen to contrast sharply with the individualism of Australian society, often experienced by Indigenous reverts as cold and impersonal.⁹ Sulaiman, for instance, claims that the sense of community-mindedness he perceives among Aborigines and Muslims is something 'we don't see in white culture'. Although 'you will find it', he says, 'it's not prevalent. It's definitely not prevalent in white culture.'

Identifying with Islam, Aboriginal and Torres Strait Islander men, like their female counterparts, become members of more than the *umma*, or international family of believers. They also feel part of the wider human family. A number of the Indigenous Muslim men I interviewed commented that through Islam they have finally learned to consider themselves equal to all other human beings. Individuals may attribute more or less value to one another on the basis of race, ethnicity, nationality, gender and material status, but Allah does not 'and [for Muslims] His is the true perspective'.¹⁰ According to the Qur'an (49:13), Allah made people into 'nations and tribes that you may know one another'. Allah created different races for the purposes of identification, not oppression.¹¹ As Amina Wadud points out, 'If we were all alike, with nothing to distinguish us, we would have no way of knowing each other or being known.'¹² In this case, being Indigenous becomes not a sign of inferiority but of God's will.

Significantly, black skin, which for apologists for racism is proof of inferiority through the biblical myth of Ham, becomes for Muslims of Indigenous descent a sign of divine creation. In *Genesis* one of Noah's three sons, Ham, was supposedly condemned to slavery for witnessing the nakedness of his father. Christian apologists for the slave trade claimed that Ham was specifically black – and that black people therefore were predestined to serve whites. According to Colin Kidd, the curse of Ham was used increasingly throughout the nineteenth century 'as an intellectually serious justification for racial subordination'.[13] The myth of the curse of Ham was so powerful that it was invoked by segregationists in the United States in the 1960s and by South Africa's apartheid government in the 1970s.[14] Indigenous Muslim Khalid Bin Walid recalls that it was also invoked by one of his white foster mothers. In a 2003 letter sent from prison to the Australian Federation of Islamic Councils, Khalid described being 'stolen from [his] tribal family and relations' at the age of six.[15] He spent the rest of his childhood living with different white foster families, where he was 'forced into Christianity'. In the early 1980s, when thirteen years old, one of his foster mothers informed Khalid that because he 'was a descendant of Ham ... [he] and other blacks were cursed to be servants to the white race'. Even as a child Khalid knew 'deep down inside [his] spirit' that he was not doomed to serve 'the white race'. Following his conversion to Islam in adulthood, the Qur'an gave him the words and permission to believe 'what [he] already knew'.

Writing about the experiences of African-American reverts, Robert Dannin argues that the *umma* 'erases the color line by retracing a circle of inclusion around all humanity'. Despite 'complexities of cultural diversity and socio-economic status', what he calls Islam's 'rainbow coalition' helps redeem 'the enforced creolization of slavery'. This is because 'miscegenation is ... an empty term within the *umma*, which disavows racial distinctions'.[16] In the Australian context it appears that Islam's rainbow coalition also helps Indigenous Australians overcome feelings of inferiority arising from the supposed stain of mixed heritage. When I asked Muslim revert Adbul what he found most attractive about Islam, he replied: 'I think the thing about Islam as I understand it ... is that we are, in a sense, one people. We are the descendants of Adam and Eve ... a black person can have a child with a white person [but Islam] acknowledges their common humanity as children of Adam and Eve. So I found that reassuring.'

Abdul's and other Indigenous reverts' sense of a common humanity in Islam is further strengthened by the knowledge that Allah sent prophets and messengers to *all* people. Abdul first encountered Islam through reading about Malcolm X but, as he states:

> If Malcolm X's works opened to me, I guess, a different window, what clinched it for me was that there was this tradition that was willing to accept a few hundred blacks on a tiny island that's going to disappear under the waters in the Torres Straits, as it would accept Han Chinese, as it would accept the Bantus or you know, whatever else people, and accept them all as human, and treat them as human and in sending down a covenant that [was] equally applicable to every one of these nations, if they wanted to accept it.

Before he embraced Islam, Indigenous Muslim Justin Agale did not 'feel that in Australia' he was recognised 'as a human being'. He believed that his identity as an Aboriginal–Torres Strait Islander man symbolised his inferior status to others and himself: 'Whenever I walk[ed] around, I [was] thinking, "I'm an Aboriginal, I'm an Aboriginal", [rather than] thinking to myself, "I'm a human being, I'm a man."'[17] In embracing Islam Indigenous Muslims like Justin feel a sense of freedom from the burden of race. It helps them reorder their identity: they are human first and foremost, and racial distinctions become secondary or incidental. Faith in Allah helped Justin 'realise my own humanity, and that I wasn't Aboriginal, I wasn't black. I'm a human being.' 'Now', he says, I understand 'my Aboriginality and my blackness as things that are in my hands, rather than in my heart. They don't control me, I control them. I'm a human being, and these just happen to be the circumstances that I'm in, rather than being my identity.'

Anthony Mundine also emphasises the universality of Islam 'as opposed to nationalist or racialist doctrines'.[18] He sees his acceptance of Islam as a transition from specific to universal identity, in which his Aboriginality is subordinated to his identity as a Muslim. These days he sometimes feels exasperated by 'people [who] are so caught up in their culture that they don't recognise the greater picture. I mean, we wouldn't be here if it wasn't for God, that's first of all.' Elaborating further, Anthony argues: 'Well, first I'm created from God. So it doesn't matter where you come from, what nationality you are, you're God's son. So he's the most important, first and foremost, and he made me [an Aboriginal man], that's his choice, that's his decision. But I've got to acknowledge him first because without him I wouldn't be here.'

The only distinction Islam makes between people relates to their consciousness of and obedience to God, their piety or *taqwa*. This is clear in the Prophet Muhammad's last sermon in which he states, 'All Mankind is from Adam and Eve, an Arab has no superiority over a non-Arab nor does a non-Arab have any superiority over an Arab; also a white has no superiority over black nor a black has any superiority over white except by piety and good action.' Embracing Islam, situating their Indigenous identity within a larger global spirituality, Indigenous Muslims no longer measure themselves against white Australia's standards, and their sense of self-worth has been restored as a result. As Justin claims, 'This is one of the [places] where the … Islamic faith comes into it, is that it gives me the strength to think, "Yes, I am a man. I am a human being, you're no better than what I am, and there's nothing you can do to me."'[19]

A family affair

Indigenous men find reversion builds self-confidence and esteem. This changes the way they think about their roles as husbands and fathers. Sole parent families are very common in Indigenous communities, and they are predominantly headed by women.[20] External forces acting on the Indigenous community often contribute to this. These include the fact that one in four Indigenous men will die by the age of thirty, and that two of the remaining three will be incarcerated at one time or another or otherwise caught up in the justice or mental health systems.[21] The low self-esteem many Indigenous men suffer impairs their ability to sustain intimate relationships. In this context, the beauty of Islam, many reverts claim, is to recognise the importance of defined leadership roles for men in their families and communities – roles largely lost through a combination of past and present practices that serve to institutionalise racial discrimination and loss of opportunity. According to Sulaiman Menzies, Islam taught him 'how to cry. It taught me how to love, taught me how to forgive, taught me how to care, taught me responsibility, taught me how to be a good father; because I'm a son of a deadbeat [Sudanese-born] Dad who I met for the first time when I was twenty-six years of age. So Islam taught me all these beautiful things and if anyone's got anything good to say about me, credit it all back to Islam.'

Islam helps Indigenous Muslim men deal with what Shahzad (Shaz) Rind calls 'the [psychological] burden' of living in white Australia as a black man.[22] Every day, in subtle and overt ways, Indigenous people are reminded that they have few rights in (white) Australian society. Not only are they a small percentage of the overall Australian population (around 2.5 per cent) but also the 'difficult thing', as Sulaiman stresses, 'is that [the descendants of the British colonists] are still occupying our country'. The rights bestowed on men in Islam to some extent counteract this sense of powerlessness. As the head of the family, Muslim men protect and maintain their wives and families. As Shaz says:

> Islam allows me to lift a lot of that burden off my shoulders. It connects me to my community, it connects me to my tribe and my nation, it gives me strength as a man. It says as a human being, as a man you have all these duties and rights, and those duties and rights extend to your family, to your women, to your children, to your grandparents, to your mother and father. And that helps me. It gives me guidelines; it gives me structures; it gives me a solid foundation to be a man.

As observed in the previous chapter, the Qur'an (4:34) not only describes men as the protectors and maintainers of women; it also says they are *preferred*. Elsewhere, as noted, the Qur'an states that 'men have a degree above' (women) (2:228). Some Muslims take these passages to mean that men have an everlasting superiority over women. In research on black Muslim converts in Britain, though, Richard Reddie found that his male interviewees did not appear to entertain any notions of the deferential wife or assert a 'hyper masculinity' over their wives and families.[23] This tallies with the way the Indigenous Muslim men I spoke to characterised gender relations in Islam. Anthony Anderson, a descendant of the Wiradjuri people, says he is confounded by the widespread belief that 'the Muslim man is the boss of all things'. He acknowledges that men tend to take responsibility for issues and events that occur outside the home, but once a man walks 'across that threshold in the front door, there's no boss in that guy at all. He does what he's told', Anthony declares.

The Indigenous Muslim men I met stressed that being the

head of the family brought with it responsibilities. Speaking of his children, Anthony Anderson says 'my job as their father is to make their life as good as possible'. He believes that on Judgement Day, when an individual's book of deeds is used to determine whether they are sent to paradise (*jannah*) or hell (*jahannam*), the father alone will bear the blame for any failure to protect his family.[24] Exhorting men to look after and provide financially for their families, Islam, reverts say, combats any tendency to adopt the position of victim – and this, according to Shaz, is a message many Indigenous men need to hear. As he says, 'I think a lot of brothers out there have to be men, realistically. Get off your arses, don't play the victim. Be a man; take control of your life.'

In the latter part of verse 4:34 of the Qur'an, Allah says, 'And as for those [women] from whom you fear disloyalty and rebellion, admonish them [first], [next] refuse to share the same bed, [and last] beat them. Then if they obey you, take no further action against them.' Does this mean that a husband has a God-given right to chastise a recalcitrant wife physically? According to Indigenous Muslim Anthony Anderson, 'The Qur'an says you can admonish your wife [only if you can do so] without marking her. But you can't even touch anybody with the lightest touch without changing the colour of [leaving an imprint on] their skin, therefore, you can't do anything physical to her at all.' While acknowledging that this verse is interpreted in different ways, Justin maintains that one only has to look at the everyday practices and sayings of the final Prophet to see why men should be 'very protective of the sisters'. He continues:

> In *Wretched of the Earth* Franz Fanon talks about when a people are colonised the ones who usually cop the brunt of it are the women because the men feel that they can't rise up against their coloniser,

so they lash out against the women. It's really sad that that's the case because in Islam we're taught that the Prophet said paradise lies at the feet of your mother,[25] and that the mother is to be honoured. Like you have God, and then the Prophet, and then your mother, and [according to the Prophet Muhammad] she's to be honoured three times more than your father.

The Qur'an also directs people to 'cherish the wombs that bore you' (4:1). Accordingly, many Muslims emphasise the power that Allah gave women to teach and nurture the next generation. Significantly, there is no equivalent assertion in the Qur'an that men are due the same reverence. As Justin points out:

> And when you really look at it, the man, the father – all I would be doing is just putting the food on the table, or providing the house, which really isn't a big deal. Those things aren't really that important at the end of the day, whereas [the mother], she's nurturing the children and, as Malcolm X put it, the woman is the first teacher of the child, so if you have strong women, then you end up with a strong society. But when you oppress the women, that's where a lot of the problems in society stem from because the women are not given the opportunity to be able to nurture children, to teach them right from wrong and to make them good human beings.

The Indigenous Muslim men (and women) I interviewed also attribute considerable significance to the Qur'anic verse in which Allah permits men to marry more than one wife. Such permission is, as noted, conditional on the provisos that men marry no more than four women and that they treat each of their wives equally. In verse 3 of chapter 4 Allah says, 'Marry women of your choice, two, three, or four; but if ye fear that ye shall not be able to deal justly [with them], then only one.' Given the impossibility of treating different women in exactly the same manner, Indigenous Muslims including Anthony Anderson understand this verse to mean that Muslim men should only marry once. As he says, 'The Qur'an says you can have multiple marriages, but you have to have the ability to treat both women the same as you can treat one. [But it's] impossible. You can't even keep [one] wife happy all the time [laughter].' His interpretation is backed up by a verse that appears later in the same chapter or *sura*, which says: 'You are never able to be fair and just between women, even if it is your ardent desire.'

Angry Black Men

In numerous interviews Malcolm X described himself as 'the angriest black man in America'.[26] Highlighting the subhuman treatment of African-Americans, he attacked the racist attitudes and policies of white Americans that perpetuated the oppression of his people. Against a background of four hundred years of enslavement, humiliation and continuing prejudice Malcolm struggled to restore a humanity that had been distorted and brutalised. Although he criticised the social and economic exploitation suffered by African-Americans, his main focus was on the liberation of consciousness.[27] To restore the self-esteem and human dignity of his fellow African-Americans, Malcolm repeatedly argued against externally imposed definitions of African-American identity, wanting black Americans themselves to define their humanity and take responsibility for changing their own conditions.[28]

Long before encountering the anti-white teachings of Elijah Muhammad's 'Nation of Islam' (NOI) while imprisoned for burglary (from 1946 to 1952), Malcolm Little, as he was then known, suffered humiliation and privation.[29] Born in Nebraska in 1925, he moved with his family to Wisconsin and, following death threats from Ku Klux Klansmen, to East Lansing, Michigan, where so-called Negroes were not allowed on the streets after dark. Malcolm's Baptist minister father was brutally murdered by white supremacists after the family's third relocation. With no husband, provider or protector to take care of her or their nine children, Malcolm's mother relied on welfare. State welfare workers intervened in the family's affairs, visiting regularly and 'asking a thousand questions'. Malcolm's mother suffered a mental breakdown and was institutionalised for twenty-six years.[30] Malcolm and his siblings were made wards of the state and sent to different white foster homes, a process akin, as he states, to 'legal, modern slavery – however kindly intentioned': 'I truly believe that if ever a state social agency destroyed a family, it destroyed ours. We wanted and tried to stay together ... But the Welfare, the courts and their doctors, gave us the one-two-three punch. And ours was not the only case of this kind.'[31]

Indigenous Muslim Sulaiman Menzies' experiences mirror those of Malcolm X. Among daily humiliations he has suffered, Sulaiman recalls, 'the police bashings and the woman who you walk past in the street at twelve years of age and holds her bag as if you're going to grab it when you're only walking to school'. Justin Agale mentions 'getting harassed by the police all the time', and the sense of unease he feels when going 'to places where they're just all [white] Aussies in that area'. Rocky Davis, also known as Shaheed Malik, rues the fact that 'as an Aboriginal person you have to be twice as good as ... a white person to get a job'.[32] These men not only identify with the ideological and institutional racism that Malcolm X endured; they also empathise with his response of having 'no mercy or compassion ... for a society that will crush people, and then penalize them for not being able to stand up under the weight'.[33]

A high proportion of the Indigenous Muslim men I spoke to identified themselves as former Angry Black Men. Incensed by a continuing history of oppression, they adopted an oppositional stance, regarding Anglo-Australian people and society with contempt. Troy Meston noted that he initially constructed an identity that was the product of anger and hatred: 'I guess for a lot of years I was mad. I thought, "Stuff them [white Australians]."'[34] According to Justin, 'Well, before I was the typical black angry man. I was just consumed by anger, everything was fuelled by anger.' Rocky claims that he 'used to be an angry violent person' who 'couldn't care if [he] lived or died'. After a life of put-downs Sulaiman also succumbed to these feelings of hatred and anger:

> You're called an animal, you're a coon, you're a monkey, you're a dog. You hear these things time and time and time again and you love to hate people after that, you enjoy it, you enjoy hating because you think, "Fuck them. I can give back as much as they give me"
> ... So there's a plague, an epidemic that goes on, a sick cycle ...
> You're established with the mentality that this is not your country, established with it your whole life. And if I was to dwell on this ... it could turn me to react, which I did for many years. I rebelled against society, rebelled against the government, rebelled against many things for years and years and years just because of the way they treated me.

Malcolm X left the NOI in 1964 and that year undertook his haj (pilgrimage) to Makkah, where he experienced a second conversion, to what he called 'the true religion of Islam'. During his pilgrimage Malcolm encountered Islam's 'rainbow coalition'. He met Muslims from all nations and walks of life, witnessing true brotherhood between black and white: 'There were tens of thousands of pilgrims, from all over the world. They were of all colors, from blue-eyed blonds to black-skinned Africans. But we were all participating in the same ritual, displaying a spirit of unity and brotherhood that my experiences in America had led me to believe never could exist between the white and the non-white.'[35]

This experience of universal brotherhood caused Malcolm to renounce the separatist beliefs of the Nation of Islam and to embrace the *umma* or community of orthodox (Sunni) Islam, adopting the name El-Hajj Malik El-Shabazz. His 'thinking had been opened up wide in Mecca' and although, as he states, 'I was no less angry than I had been', the true white and black brotherhood 'I had seen in the Holy World had influenced me to recognize that anger can blind human vision'.[36] Malcolm's new vision of racial equality, in particular his insistence that there are good white people, has influenced Indigenous Muslims in Australia. Sulaiman notes that he and some of his fellow Aboriginal Muslims 'were fired up people until we read that Malcolm went to haj. And his time there made us sort of think, "Hold on a minute, I know what he's saying is right. There are white guys out there that are good."' He continues:

> Malcolm helped us see there are white people that are good to us, they don't all hate us and they're not all against us. And so by him mentioning that in his book, it made us really realise, yes, it's true. We could point a finger at a million people who are hating us, but there are still a lot that are not hating us, and it's too easy to focus on the ones that are hating you. When you're influenced so much by somebody and he goes, 'Hey, wait a minute [some whites are good]', it really made us feel the same way, so thanks to Malcolm for that.

Many of the men I spoke to found that identifying with Malcolm's post-haj views on race and equality helped them manage the anger they felt. Embracing Islam's vision of universal equality has brought about a process of spiritual healing. Rocky Davis likens it to a panacea for the ills that continue to afflict his people, claiming, 'Allah is the supreme doctor and the script is the Qur'an and the medicine is Islam.' In a newspaper article he further emphasised the need for this self-prescribed 'medicine': 'If you're an alcoholic, you go to AA. If you're a drug addict, you go to rehab. But if you're colonised where do you go? Aboriginal men are becoming Muslim because ... we need a new ideology if we're going to be free.'[37]

In the post-9/11 era Islam has been increasingly conflated with terrorism and violence. The circulation of media-inspired terms like 'Islamic terrorist' and 'violent jihad' has prompted many non-Muslims to suppose that Islam supports terrorism. As a result, the conversion of Indigenous Australians to Islam has been viewed as a serious threat to national security. These fears are, if nothing else, extremely ironic given that many Indigenous Muslim men attribute their *renunciation* of violence to Islam. In fact, as a result of conversion, men formerly on the margins of society and at risk have 'become "model citizens" whose discipline, focus and integrity make them ideal role models' for today's Indigenous youth.[38] While Troy defined himself as 'mad' before finding Islam, he stresses that 'everything's different for me now. I'm much calmer. I see the world through different eyes.' Justin similarly emphasises that Islam gives him the 'strength to endure it [Australia's colonial legacy] and not to get angry and to just lash out at all the things we've been through',[39] while Sulaiman Menzies stresses that he considered terrorism *before*, not *after* becoming a Muslim:

I could very well have become a terrorist, without Islam, through the way I've been treated ... Now if people are going to blame Islam, Islam actually stopped me from reacting against society. [Before becoming a Muslim] I was very much at a stage where I was ready to give up my life and I was going to go down with many people, just from the pain of growing up. This is just as an Aboriginal man without Islam. Islam came into my life and actually said, 'Hey, hey, cool down a little bit. It's all right. Justice will be served eventually.'

Sulaiman also perceived the folly of judging *all* white people by the deeds of a few. He recognised that Allah alone has the right to judge:

Before [embracing Islam] I wanted to hurt people, I wanted to hate you. Islam gave me the reason to see good and say, 'Hey, what about the good in that person? Why are you focusing on the negative? Why are you judging the whole white race for Captain Cook's crimes?' Islam taught me not to judge the whole nation because of the crimes of one ... Islam says [that] everyone's accountable for their own sins. You can't judge everybody. So it really started making me think, 'Stop being a reactionary person. Focus on what I'm doing, how I'm affecting people's lives, stop worrying about how [other] people are.' A special saying in Islam is that when you point one finger there's three pointing back at you. Even though there might be someone doing bad things, just look at all the things you're doing first, so it really takes the attention off those people who are oppressing me and makes me focus on me more and my actions and how I'm treating people. So if anything, Islam should be praised.

Prison Islam

It is difficult to obtain an accurate estimate of the number of Indigenous Muslim prisoners in Australia. Part of the problem is that the religious beliefs of prisoners are not always recorded when the inmate is first admitted to jail. Even if they are, the prisoners' religious affiliation can change during their period of incarceration, and these details are generally not updated. More than a third of the reported 1014 Indigenous Muslims in Australia reside in New South Wales.[40] According to the NSW Department of Corrective Services, while the only data available at present is based on the inmates' nominated religion (if provided), even these rather limited statistics indicate that the number of Indigenous Muslim prisoners is growing. Recent figures show that nearly fifty of the roughly 700 Muslim inmates in New South Wales prisons are of Indigenous descent; this number has almost doubled since 2005.[41]

At the age of fourteen Rocky Davis was sent to a juvenile detention centre for shooting at the police (see figure 17). Four years later he received a minimum eight-year prison sentence for armed robbery. He was sent to Grafton prison but, following his participation in a prison riot, was removed to the High Risk Management Unit, or 'Super Max' facility, within Goulburn jail.[42] Here Rocky encountered Aboriginal Muslim prisoners who introduced him to Islam, an event that 'turned [his] life around'.[43] In common with many Indigenous Muslim prisoners, Rocky's first introduction to Islam came through reading *The Autobiography of Malcolm X*. As he recalls:

> I ended up in Goulburn and I was yelling out to these guys through the peep holes in the big steel doors, and I yelled out, 'Can you get me some books?' I went out to the yard and done some exercise and come back in and there was Malcolm X's autobiography, which I was pretty happy about.[44] I knew who Malcolm X was as a teenager from watching movies and I watched *The Black Panthers* and [my Aboriginal friends

and I] all liked it, we all thought we were militants and shit like that and after reading Malcolm X the [Aboriginal Muslim prisoners] started telling me about Islam.⁴⁵

Malcolm X's experiences resonated with Rocky. Growing up in what, in an interview with Dilara Reznikas, he described as 'a racist period in Australia, where just before I was born [late 1960s] Aboriginal people weren't allowed in towns', he 'really resented that we weren't allowed to be on our land because someone used force to take it off us and I was angry, really angry, like so many other [Aboriginal] kids'.⁴⁶ Like Malcolm X in his pre-haj incarnation, Rocky initially defended his criminal behaviour by blaming it on white racist ideologies and policies. However, again in line with the evolution in Malcolm's self-narrative, his rhetoric later changed. In fact, embracing Islam brought about a dramatic shift in his self-perception, his view of the prison administration and white society more generally. Rocky underwent what Tony Barringer, in his thesis on black-American Muslim prison converts, labels 'a perspective transformation'.⁴⁷

This transformation is also clearly evident in the changed outlook of current Indigenous Muslim prisoner Terry Sampson. Terry (who is twenty-five) has served more than six years of a twelve-year prison sentence (with a non-parole period of eight years) handed down for discharging a firearm with intent to inflict grievous bodily harm. In a recent letter I received from him, he described himself as an 'Indigenous revert' who embraced Islam more than five years ago.⁴⁸ He spent a year reading about and contemplating Islam before making the *shahada* (declaration of faith) in 2004, reporting that 'ever since that day my life started to change for the better'. His correspondence continues: 'I was once a brutal man, in part I still am. I have hurt a lot of people, and those acts of anger and aggression, I am deeply ashamed of. But by the guidance of Allah, I have learned to control my anger and aggression, and I have gained discipline, obedience, tolerance, most of all compassion towards my family and fellow man.'

In a 2003 letter called 'I don't hate white people' sent from Broken Hill prison to Bilal Cleland at the Australian Federation of Islamic Councils, Khalid Bin Walid (whose foster mother informed him that he was destined to serve the white race) also emphasises the sobering effect of conversion. When he wrote his letter Khalid had served ten years of a fourteen-year prison sentence. The 'crimes [he had] committed', he wrote, 'were done through hate and disrespect for white people and their government'. He expanded, 'If someone from Africa or Arabia said to me back then to come and join them to fight against the capitalist white man, I would have gladly [gone].'

Then, in 1995 while in Goulburn prison, Khalid met some Lebanese–Australian Muslim inmates, one of whom gave him an English translation of the Qu'ran. Khalid 'read it constantly for a period of twelve months. I read late into the night alone in my cell.' He, like others, was drawn to Islam because of the cultural convergence he perceived between it and his Aboriginal spiritual beliefs. As he says, the 'Holy Qur'an ... was speaking to me in a spiritual way and it was like I was relearning what I already knew'. Describing the positive perspective transformation evident among many Aboriginal prison converts, Khalid reflected: 'Through Islam I have increased in knowledge and my eyes and heart have become softer. Now I do not hate. I reason and try to understand people, including the white race ... I hope that if there is another black brother or sister out there confused, angry and hurting because of the constant racial abuse and discrimination they are put through, I say to you people – let it go – find your love, peace and strength in Islam and Allah.'

Dr Soliman Gilany, a Sydney-based Muslim prison chaplain, recalls what one Aboriginal prisoner said about his cousin and fellow inmate's change of heart upon conversion:

> He said I see my cousin after he become Muslim, I saw changes in him, in his manners and his qualities. He doesn't get angry, he doesn't swear anymore, he gave up smoking, he's not doing drugs. And so when I saw changes in my cousin I say, 'OK, cousin, what happened?' And he say, 'Well, don't you know I'm a Muslim and Islam doesn't accept those wrong things?' He said I saw my cousin he used to think the white man is his enemy but I find my cousin a different man. He eats with the white man and drinks, he sits with them and they have conversations, then I ask him, 'Cousin what's going on?' He say, 'Well, I'm a Muslim, and Islam doesn't accept discrimination so I cannot be a Muslim and hate anyone.' So he said that was enough for him to think about [embracing] Islam.

Khalid's experience, described above, is not unique. A former (non-Indigenous) Goulburn jail inmate observes that Lebanese–Australian and Aboriginal prisoners share a particularly close bond. Interviewed on the ABC's *Four Corners* program (aired in 2005), Christopher Binse stated that friendships and alliances form between certain groups within the prison system. According to him, 'the Lebanese and the Aboriginals, they hang out together',[49] and he suggested, plausibly enough, that one reason a growing number of the Koori inmates were embracing Islam was because of the connection they shared with Muslim Lebanese prisoners: 'I know a lot of people, a lot of Kooris in particular, have [identified with] Allah ... They've been hanging out with the Lebanese and maybe their faith's touched them.'

Wider social interaction is not only a reflection of Aboriginal converts' sense of inclusion in Islam's rainbow coalition; it also indicates a higher degree of emotional integration. Islam, as observed in chapter 6, encourages people to take responsibility for their actions through the Qur'anic verse 'Verily never will Allah change the condition of a people until they change what is within themselves' (13:11). It instructs people to look to Allah for guidance, and gives believers hope that they might gain entrance to paradise. Speaking of another Aboriginal Muslim inmate, Gilany recalls:

> I met a man, he say look, I had no life in the jail, or out of jail. A lot of time I do crime because I want to come back to jail. So I say, 'Well [what do you think] now you are a Muslim?' He say after I become Muslim, I put all that aside, I have a hope and if I get enough chance to go out and do the right thing, I have a hope of going to paradise, to *jannah*. He says so I do not live in the past any more because … after I join Islam I left my past, but before I was always angry, at night time I don't sleep, many time I tried to kill myself, but now because I join Islam I put all that behind, I'm a different person and … my aim when I finish my time is to go outside to continue in this.

Many are attracted to Islam because, they say, it is a pure, logical, rational and easily understood faith. Prison converts understand this practically. Answers to their philosophical questions go hand-in-hand with many helpful pieces of advice. The commandments and prohibitions are clear, simple and adaptable to modern life. The Islamic religion recognises One Creator, and believers have a direct relationship with the Almighty not mediated by any other individual or dependent on church hierarchies. All these conditions converge on another that appeals to institutionalised Indigenous men: believers do not have to attend a particular place to worship but may perform the acts of daily prayer in their cells. In this sense, Islam may help reverse a double dislocation, cultural as well as physical. Many Indigenous Muslims, as we have seen, stress that a further virtue of the Islamic faith is the convergence they perceive between it and their 'traditional' Indigenous beliefs and practices. Melbourne-based Muslim prison chaplain Aziz Cooper hears from 'many of the Muslim Koori prisoners ... that Islam makes sense [because] a lot of the Islamic spirituality is in alignment with Koori spirituality, especially in the area of traditional law'.[50] He elaborates: 'Islam teaches that *nabis* or prophets of God were sent to all tribes and nations before the Prophet Muhammad (peace be upon him), and some Muslim Koori prisoners have said to me that there were prophets visiting our people thousands of years ago and teaching monotheism, [belief in] one God.'

However, in many cases, cultural knowledge is tenuous, and access to it is rendered even more difficult inside prison. Thus, some, particularly younger, Indigenous men find that Islam fills the void left by their ignorance of their Indigenous heritage and culture. Soliman Gilany remarks that in his experience 'the majority of Aboriginals who are becoming Muslim are all young men. And you ask them about Aboriginality, they don't know much ... so they don't come to Islam because Islam is close to [their] traditions.' Some Indigenous Muslims outside the criminal justice system make similar comments. Sulaiman Menzies emphasises that Islam helps compensate for 'the lost knowledge' of his ancestral customs:

> For me my Aboriginality was a mixture of culture that I was brought up in [and] that culture itself was deprived of Indigenous culture. We only had crumbs of Indigenous culture to sift through and try

to make up who we were, establish who we were from this little bit of knowledge that we had, so my Aboriginality was not established anyway, being an Aboriginal. I was just holding on to little bits of culture that we had left, trying to establish the culture in my life, but Islam came along and … once I became a Muslim I became this now full entity … I'm not saying I'm not Aboriginal any more but … there's many questions that my Aboriginality couldn't answer for me, that were answered through Islam.

Islam helps repair psychic fragmentation. It addresses ills of the soul by reconnecting these converts to the spirit of the past. It does not replace what has been taken away but places the experience of colonisation and ongoing systemic disadvantage within a larger, cosmic framework. But the efficacy of this spiritual uplift is measured in the here-and-now. It is the clarity of Islam's moral injunctions and the simplicity of its codes of behaviour that make it so attractive, especially to a group of people susceptible to destructiveness. Islam pronounces an unequivocal program for bodily purification: drugs and alcohol are forbidden. Given that these are a major factor in violent behaviour, and that their use leads inexorably to criminal sentencing, the stark command to avoid them is a kind of wish-fulfilment. Coming from on high, these prohibitions give converts the strength to take responsibility for themselves and others. As Justin Agale explains:

> One of the things that comes with a lot of Indigenous men is the sort of depression that you can't do anything about [your situation], and you're feeling sorry for yourself, so you turn to drink or drugs to try and take the edge off that pain. And I think one of the good things about Islam for Indigenous people, especially for the men, is that because you can't drink or do drugs, they're taken out of the picture,

so then you're forced to look at yourself and to deal with [your life] ... It's no good just sort of sitting around talking about problems, it's about going out, finding solutions and implementing them.

Soliman Gilany similarly observes that Islam inspires the Indigenous Muslim prisoners he meets to make amends for past misdeeds, and many are motivated on release to contribute to the well-being of their communities. Recalling the words of one Muslim revert in particular, he says: 'He told me, "My people need what I learn about Islam. My people need to give up alcohol, my people need to give up abusing or disrespecting, my people need a lot of help and I'm very excited to go out there" ... So a lot of [Indigenous Muslim converts] not only aim to help themselves but they say, "Well I'll go there, I'll try help my community." So yes, this is a big thing for them.'

This is not to deny that some Indigenous prisoners may be drawn, initially at least, to Islam for other, less salutary reasons. In a 2006 article in the *Australian*, 'Radicals brainwashing Aboriginals in prison', Indigenous Muslim inmates are described as a 'serious national security time bomb'.[51] Despite the fact, reported in the article, that Sydney-based Muslim cleric Khalil Shami, who is authorised by NSW Corrective Services to visit prisons, claims he is not aware of any radical Muslim clerics converting Indigenous inmates, Rocky Davis raises concerns that some Indigenous prisoners are finding so-called Wahhabism attractive. Wahhabism or, more correctly, Salafism is dominant in Saudi Arabia, Kuwait and the United Arab Emirates.[52] It is a conservative form of Sunni Islam that advocates a return to the Islamic practices of the first three generations of Muslims. According to Indigenous convert Rocky: 'If you're disenfranchised and you're oppressed and you've got no economy and you've always been discriminated against, you're the most likely to become a terrorist, you're the most likely to become a fanatic – and that's the thing that I have to worry about because my people are disenfranchised, they're oppressed.'[53]

'Khalid' was one of five men featured in a report on Indigenous Muslims aired on the SBS program *Insight* in 2003. When discussing the world's most infamous terrorist leader, he had this to say: 'Wherever you are, Osama Bin Laden, I love you brother, and I do it for you and I pray for you, because you're just a spiritual warrior standing up for Islam and propagating freedom around the world.' This would appear to be legitimate cause for concern. But when asked whether he would seriously consider using terrorism to fight for Aboriginal people's rights Khalid responded: 'It's not really relevant to our situation, where we are geographically, politically and population-wise, no. But yes, I'd fight them [the Australian government] back in a political way now.'[54]

Speaking with Sulaiman Menzies, it was apparent that he is also concerned about Indigenous Muslims being drawn to terrorist activities. Like Rocky, Sulaiman is highly aware that 'there's a lot of hatred, there is a lot of pain' in Indigenous communities. These feelings of desperation and despair might well lead to one's engagement in acts of violence. As he says, 'If you ask me, the Palestinian suicide bomber who jumped on a bus in Israel, he's feeling the same pain [as Aboriginal people].' But he is equally adamant that politically inspired acts of terrorism have nothing to do with Islam, even when they are committed in its name. Some people, he argues, 'are using the religion as their political agenda but if someone is sincere [in their Islamic beliefs] they will never do that'.

In the United States the term 'Prislam' is used to denote the 'convergence of criminal activity with a distorted version of the

Koran and of [the Islamic] faith ... where charismatic criminal leaders' use 'the Koran as [a] cover to perpetuate ... goals that they may have or that their group may have'.⁵⁵ Soliman Gilany has had some experience with Prislam or so-called Jailhouse Islam in the Australian context. Whether they have been influenced by media reports that conflate the anti-American and anti-Western views of some Muslims with Islam as a whole, the pre-haj vitriol of Malcolm X, or the misguided 'religious' views of other Muslim prisoners, Gilany has encountered some Indigenous men who believe that 'I could gain power through Islam and get my country back ... They say I could become a Muslim and Islam is going to help me to get more rights for my people.' In his role as a provider of pastoral care Gilany takes very seriously his obligation to help prisoners understand 'the true Islam'. He is aware that Indigenous Muslims are sometimes influenced by other prisoners, 'jihad and all these things', but, he says, 'when they come to me [they realise] this guy is totally the opposite to what I have learnt'.

Gilany instructs his charges that in Islam, Allah honours *all* of 'the children of Adam'.⁵⁶ So, he says, 'Muslim or non-Muslim, they all have a right to live in justice and in peace and in love together.' Here he recalls an Indigenous Muslim inmate's response to his teachings:

> So they take a step back and say, 'But imam, I didn't hear that.' And I say, 'Well, this is a verse of the Qur'an.' So a lot of time they really have a debate with me, then I come back some time after ... a few weeks later, and he says, 'Imam, do you know you were right? About living with others together? Because I read about Malcolm X, that's the reason he gave up the Nation of Islam, so you are right. Now I shake hands with the non-Muslims, now I think we're all Australian. It doesn't make a difference what is your colour.'

In another case Gilany met an Aboriginal Muslim prisoner still angry that 'they [white Australians] took my grandma away, they took this away, they took that away', to which he responded, 'Look, brother, the true Islam hasn't reached your heart.' Despite his protestations that he had asked Allah for forgiveness for his sins and prayed five times a day, Gilany told him, 'It's not enough.' He elaborates:

> So I tell these Aboriginals that, I say look this is how it is. You cannot be a Muslim and have hate in your heart. And when I went back a couple of weeks later, he said, 'Imam, all night long I couldn't sleep, I was thinking about what you said, yes I got rid of the hate. Before I was not talking to white men much, now you can see me, I will go and have a good chat with everybody.'

In the 2005 *Sydney Morning Herald* article, 'Hard men turn to Islam to cope with jail', journalist Stephen Gibbs lists in graphic detail the various violent crimes committed by a number of Indigenous men imprisoned in Goulburn jail. Noting that these men (whom he calls 'monsters') who converted to Islam in prison, 'are all jailed under A1 security classifications – one below the AA rung reserved for terrorists', Indigenous identification with Islam is represented as an apprenticeship in terrorism.[57] This inference is made despite the admission of the Commander of Security Services in NSW jails, Brian Kelly, reported on *Four Corners* (and in the *SMH* article) that while 'we see some efforts to convert inmates to Islam for probably the wrong reasons, we haven't really had evidence for terrorist purposes in itself' [*sic*].[58] According to the article Ron Woodham, Commissioner of NSW Corrective Services, told *Four Corners*, 'We're worried where certain prisoners ... denounce their Aboriginality for Islam ... We monitor them very closely. To us they're not terrorists in the real sense but they talk the talk.'[59] Of course Indigenous converts neither denounce or renounce their Aboriginality; nor is it clear what non-real terrorists could be.

The Indigenous Muslim 'monsters' described in the article include one Peter Buchanan, blamed, the journalist reports, 'for attacking a prison officer at Lithgow [prison] ... and accused (then acquitted) of stabbing and bashing another prisoner to death at Long Bay'.[60] Can this be the same Peter Buchanan whom Indigenous Muslim Sulaiman Menzies recently described as 'a lovely, humble guy ... who has really taken on Islam properly. He properly understands Islam and its purpose?' Is it the same individual who, years after his release from prison, is lauded by incarcerated Indigenous Muslim men as a role model? Muslim prison chaplain Soliman Gilany recalls hearing about Buchanan, who is now married with children and living 'a very humble life', for the first time:

> He was wild and uncontrollable. He was a man well known in the prison system. I never met him, but the first time I heard his name an Aboriginal man was arguing with an officer ... he told them, 'What's wrong with me being a Muslim because you see how I am changed, I was always segregated, I was always in trouble. As soon as I took Islam on have I ever said anything wrong? What about Peter Buchanan? He was uncontrollable in the jail but when he became Muslim his life changed.'

Nor is Peter Buchanan's reformation unique. In an interview with Dilara Reznikas, a former Muslim prison chaplain (who wishes to remain anonymous) recalled complaining to an Indigenous Muslim inmate about what he perceived as the insincerity of many Indigenous Muslims. The chaplain's confidant acknowledged the truth of what he said, but counselled him to be patient. According to the former prison chaplain:

> I said [to an Indigenous Muslim inmate] 'Look, a lot of these [Indigenous Muslims] are not genuine', and he agreed with me, but he said something I'll never forget, he said, 'Yeah, imam, some of these guys turn to Islam [and] in the early days it's quite disappointing, but then give them two or three years and they grow in Islam, and become very good, such as so and so.' And he was right. When [so and so] first became a Muslim, he was no different than current Aboriginal converts, but then over the years, he was excellent, and he was heart-warming, and today he's released, he's married to a girl, and he's working full time, and he's doing extremely well for himself.[61]

The jihad in which these Indigenous Muslim men are engaged is not the kind the mainstream media seeks to popularise. The Arabic word *jihad* means struggle. Jihad requires Muslims to struggle or strive in the way of Allah, and to struggle to improve themselves as individuals. Gilany teaches inmates that, according to the Prophet Muhammad, 'the greatest jihad is the jihad of *nafs* [self, psyche], to fight your own desires, your own soul, struggle not to do wrong things. If you want to steal something, try not to, that's jihad. If someone harms you, try to forgive them, that's jihad.'

Islam provides Indigenous Muslim men not with bombs but an arsenal of ideological weaponry that, in restoring their sense of self-worth, teaches them to value all others. Reversion to Islam brings these men a sense of self-worth and belonging that radiates outwards. From being nobody nowhere, they become people with roots and proud origins as well as the protectors of others. By way of brothers and sisters, they extend care to a cosmopolitan community. In the Australian context the redemptive power of this is movingly recognised by the immigrant imam Soliman Gilany:

> [One Indigenous Muslim prisoner] he say, 'Imam, it was my aim, that I have to gain my country back.' He say, 'But after I join Islam I thought no, we are all human beings, it's a big country, there's room for everybody here. Now I think it's our country.' And my tears start coming down. He says, 'Why are you crying?' I say, 'Well, I'm thinking of my own kids and my grandchildren. Probably this is their country. So it's good that people like you who thought of my children as invaders, now you think not. [Now you think] it's a big country, we all live together as one family. I'm glad that Islam has changed something in your heart.' And I grabbed him and hugged him. It was good to meet [him].

CONCLUSION

Attractive as it might be to focus on – and celebrate – the extraordinary evidence of social resilience and spiritual survival the stories of my interviewees represent, it would be naive and irresponsible not to acknowledge one macrocontext that hitherto we have largely downplayed: the worsening environment of reception for both Islamic and Indigenous claims to inclusion in what is defined as Australia's national identity. As a brief review of the first decade of the twenty-first century quickly reveals, balanced discussion of Islam's place in Australian life has become almost impossible. Politicians have shamelessly exploited the collective trauma that 9/11 induced and, in what is possibly a unique Australian twist, the prospect of attacks on our territorial integrity from outside have regularly been twinned with increasingly acerbic attacks on Indigenous cultures. Evidently, in this unpropitious context, voluntary identification with a double minority is an act of some temerity. The point, of course, is that Indigenous converts do not see it in this way; unfortunately, though, they cannot entirely insulate themselves. In the light of the impoverishment of cross-cultural dialogue evident in what follows, their commitment to a process that, as we have seen, is never ended, and always susceptible to change, renewal and renegotiation, is all the more remarkable.

Muslims come from an extremely diverse range of social, political, economic, racial and ethnic backgrounds. They constitute around a fifth of the world's population (approximately 1.3 billion people), hail from dozens of countries and societies, speak a myriad of languages and have had an infinite number of different experiences. Diversity in terms of religious practice also needs to be considered. Not everyone in the 'Muslim world' is religious. 'Islamic countries and communities of origin, like other communities, comprise practising individuals and non-practising skeptics, along with secular, laic and even atheist members.'[1] It is a mistake to assume that Islam is a monolithic religion.[2] Saeed Rahnema notes that beyond the major division between the majority Sunnis and minority Shi'as there are significant sub-sects and divisions within each. Moreover each of the many sects and schools among both Sunnis and Shi'as has developed their own versions of sharia or Islamic law and expanded upon these to produce their own specific Islamic jurisprudence or *fiqh*.[3] Notwithstanding this variation, Islam and Muslims are often represented in the media as 'one-dimensional political fictions'.[4] And in the wake of the terrorist attacks in New York and Washington in 2001, Islam and Muslims have increasingly been coupled with violence in the Western collective imagination. Widespread usage of the media-inspired terms 'violent jihad' and 'Islamic terrorist' means that many non-Muslims now take for granted that Islam promotes terrorism and suicide-bombing. Needless to say, acts of terrorism have nothing to do with Islam, even when they are committed in its name and the vast majority of the world's Muslims are horrified by them.

In Australia two events in 2001 added fuel to the Islamophobic fire that blazed after the Twin Tower bombings that year. The first involved the castigation of those held to be 'of Middle Eastern Appearance'. The gang rapes of two white Australian women by some Lebanese–Australian Muslim youths (who were widely accused of preying on white women in a symbolic attack on all white Australians) resulted in the pinning of the 'sexual crimes of a group of men on to an entire racial minority'. The violent attacks provided further proof, if the Australian public needed it, of the violence and depravity of Muslims the world over. Suddenly the entire Muslim community in Australia was held accountable for the heinous crimes of a few young men who, incidentally, did not identify with Islam or their Lebanese culture.[5]

The second event that saw Muslims characterised as Australia's public enemy number 1 was the so-called 'children overboard' affair, which 'presented Islam as an alien culture in which parents were so barbaric [read un-Australian], so subhuman that they would endanger their children by throwing them into the sea'.[6] This claim was 'used by the [Howard] government to demonstrate that "they" did not love their children and respect family values as "we" Australians do'.[7] A Senate inquiry found that the Howard Government's claims were completely unsubstantiated and that no such event took place. But by then the damage had been done and many Australians believed that Middle Eastern asylum seekers, the majority of whom were Muslim, were hostile to Australian values.

In late 2001, and largely in response to the so-called *Tampa* 'crisis', the Howard Government introduced its 'Pacific Solution' (operative until the election of the Rudd Labor government in 2007). It sought to negate the threat that asylum seekers allegedly posed to white Australian territorial sovereignty through a remapping of the Australian nation-state. National borders were simultaneously expanded and contracted through, respectively, the placing outside the nation of detention camps and the excision of Australia's outer islands from the migration zone.[8] The Pacific Solution saw an expansion in what Suvendrini Perera (quoting Bernard Cohen) has labelled 'not-Australia'.[9] Not-Australia extended beyond national borders with the establishment of detention centres on distant shores, including the tiny island nation of Nauru and Manus Island in northern Papua New Guinea, to which asylum seekers were to be removed while their claims for refugee status were processed. Through the Howard Government's excision of Ashmore Reef, the Cocos (Keeling) Islands, and Cartier and Christmas Islands from Australia's migration zone not-Australia expanded further, swallowing Australia's outer islands so that, as Perera contends, 'asylum seekers who arrive here will be deemed not to have arrived'.[10] The willingness to cut out parts of Australian territory from the national body not only represented a rather remarkable commitment to shoring up Australia's borders but also exposed an acute border disorder, a national mind that was, according to Graeme Turner, 'riddled with fear and paranoia'.[11]

In recent media and government reports Indigenous people have also been charged with aberrant, anti-social behaviour that is hostile to Australian standards of decency. Aboriginal people's apparent failure to live up to 'Australian values' also stems from their lack of regard for their children's welfare or safety. Media reports on the high incidence of child sexual abuse in some remote Northern Territory Aboriginal communities have seen

Indigenous people as a whole held responsible. Aboriginal people are blamed for these attacks and are accused of not keeping their men in check – something we also witnessed with the Muslim community's apparent failure to control the supposedly voracious sexual appetite of Lebanese–Australian youths. Indigenous communities, like their Muslim counterparts, have also been accused of threatening Australia's territorial integrity. Recent land rights claims have been seen by some as the forerunner of an invasion from within. Native title was back in the headlines as recently as 2006 following a successful claim made by Western Australia's Nyoongar community over metropolitan Perth. Headlines like the *Australian*'s 'Perth hit by native title claim' were evocative of the mood that prevailed in the 1990s when a highly emotive and fear-filled debate raised the spectre of native title claims being made on people's suburban backyards.

Once people believe that our national security and our 'uniquely' Australian values are under threat, they are less likely to oppose the 'harsh and hubristic forms of instrumental action' taken by the government to safeguard them.[12] The demonisation of asylum seekers played a critical role in the previous government's ability to persuade the Australian public of the need to take tough action to keep them at bay. Similarly, the reinforcement of negative stereotypes of Indigenous people as inherently pathological was an important ingredient in the Howard Government's ability to garner public support for its militaristic humanitarianism. Describing the militarised intervention in Northern Territory Aboriginal communities as 'black children overboard', an (unnamed) Indigenous commentator made a direct link between the negative portrayal and treatment of Aborigines and that of (Muslim) asylum seekers.[13] Australia's first Indigenous female Cabinet minister, Northern Territory Community

Services Minister Marion Scrymgour, also made this connection. She labelled the Howard Government's measures to stop Indigenous child abuse the 'black kids' *Tampa*.[14] In his assertion that Aboriginal mission camps are the predecessors of contemporary detention centres, Dinesh Wadiwel also insists on the structural similarities in the ways in which Indigenous communities and Muslim asylum seekers experience Australian sovereign violence.[15]

The election of the Rudd Labor government in 2007 seemed to mark a significant symbolic (if not actual) shift away from lumping Muslim and Indigenous Australians together with border security policy. The Rudd Government got rid of Temporary Protection Visas, dismantled the Howard Government's Pacific Solution and closed the Nauru processing centre. Rudd further differentiated his approach from that of former Prime Minister Howard by offering a formal apology to the Stolen Generations. Despite these apparent shifts, though, it is not clear that public opinion has similarly shifted and, in my experience, sections of the press remain remarkably attached to the stereotypes of their own fantasy.

In 2001 in a front-page article, under the headline 'PM sends in the troops', the *Australian* printed a large colour photograph of one of the Indigenous Muslim women I interviewed. Nazra Wali was depicted, in full cover, with Janette Howard, wife of former PM John Howard, at a 'meet and greet' event at a Melbourne mosque as part of the federal election campaign (see figure 18). The caption read: 'Standing quietly to one side of the pack gathered around the Prime Minister and the imam, covered from the world in all but her eyes, Nazra Ibrahim ['Ibrahim' is Nazra's ex-husband's surname] whispers to Janette Howard about family and children. It is four hours since John Howard has committed

Australian troops to the war against terrorism.'[16] According to Alia Imtoual, the image and caption were designed to represent Muslim women as cloistered in black, concerned solely with family and domestic affairs, as too oppressed to speak above a whisper and 'as inferior to Janette Howard who was presented as the embodiment of "liberal", tolerant, sophisticated and liberated "western" women'.[17]

During our conversation Nazra told me that a number of journalists subsequently contacted her to do a follow-up story. One flew from Sydney to Melbourne to interview her, but when Nazra, who was asked to speak further about her life, identified herself as an *Aboriginal* woman, the journalist refused to go ahead with the story. In Nazra's words: 'She said, "Please don't open that chapter." I said, "Why?" She said, "Well, I can't do a story if you want to insist on [identifying] yourself as an Aboriginal, fully covered and with Janette Howard, you know, just in the middle of the campaign ... No, I can't do that, it's not going to sit well with my editor."'[18] In short, the journalist was only interested in portraying Nazra as a victimised (immigrant?) Muslim woman, not as a local (and an *Indigenous* woman at that) who had actively chosen to convert to Islam, and who opted to wear the *niqab* (face veil). For Nazra the journalist's intention was completely transparent. As she claims: 'John Howard was sending troops to Iraq and if I was identified as a Muslim woman, fully covered, you know, John Howard is sending the troops to protect Muslim women like myself.' Somehow it does not have the same ring to it if Howard is sending Aussie troops to the 'war on terror' to protect *Indigenous* Muslims.

Much media commentary on Indigenous Muslims characterises them as fanatical extremists intent on destroying the fabric of 'our' society. It appears that Indigenous people who identify with

Islam symbolise the 'joining of forces', as it were, of Australia's enemies within and without. Imtoual suggests that Indigenous people who also identify as Muslim 'are viewed with confusion, suspicion and bewilderment by white Christian Australia'. They are, she says, 'double-troubling the dominant view of the nation which sees two binaries with regard to identity: Australian (white) vs Indigenous and Australian (Christian) vs Muslim'.[19] In the words of Anthony Mundine, Australia's best known Indigenous Muslim, 'being Indigenous and being Muslim, you know, not really [a] good combination, in this society'.[20] According to 'Khalid', an Indigenous man who was introduced to Islam in prison, there is nothing the Australian Government fears more than for Indigenous people to convert to Islam and create a Muslim state 'because they know we've got the land to do it'.[21] It is telling that Khalid should associate the white Australian fear of Indigenous Muslims with land rights. The apparent shift from *terra Australis* to *terror Australis* is a point we return to below.

A sign of a more mature media representation of Islam, and Indigenous Muslims, occurred in May 2007 when the *Sydney Morning Herald* ran a seven-day series called 'The Face of Islam'. Each day different articles explored the diversity of Muslim life and opinion in Australia. The newspaper won a Media Peace Award for its promotion of multicultural issues. One article in particular, 'A new faith for Kooris', went some way towards redressing the one-sided media representations of Indigenous Muslims.[22] For a start, it included an interview with a woman, Eugenia Flynn. Australian Bureau of Statistics figures from the 2006 census reveal that Indigenous Muslim women account for 42 per cent of the total number of Aboriginal and/or Torres Strait Islander Muslims in Australia.[23] Given this, it is disappointing that their voices are rarely heard. Among other things Eugenia provides a pointed rejoinder to the reportage discussed in the previous chapter: 'My issue is that people like to stereotype black Muslims as angry militants who did jail time and left behind a life of crime and violence. The more typical story is an Indigenous person was searching for a spiritual way and found Islam to be incredibly liberating.'[24] The other (male) interviewees also described how they came to Islam, with Anthony Mundine, like Eugenia, stressing that his motives were spiritual, not political. Initially introduced to the faith by his Muslim manager (who gave him a book on Malcolm X), Mundine discussed the positive effect it has had on him, claiming, 'Islam is my life, it's helped every aspect of it' (see figure 19).[25] Rocky Davis, who was also inspired by the story of Malcolm X, predicted that conversions would continue to rise in the Indigenous community and emphasised the significant role Islam could play as a cure for economic and social disadvantage.

Nuts and bolts

Still, it would be naive to suppose that the media macrocontext has undergone wholesale conversion. Commenting on the above article in his *Herald Sun* blog, conservative journalist Andrew Bolt opined that, far from providing Indigenous people with a way out of unemployment and drug addiction, 'Islam offers an underclass something more primitive and dangerous – a revelling in an us-against-the-world victimology, and a legitimising of anger and force. No wonder that so many Aboriginal converts are convicted criminals and boxers.'[26] Ninety readers posted comments on Bolt's blog. One warned that it is only 'a matter of time before we have a terrorist attack in Australia perpetrated by an Aboriginal Muslim'. Another reader claimed that 'Australia is under attack from Islamists and ... the land belonging to Aboriginals (that most white Australians never see and are not permitted to enter without a permit) eventually will be under Muslim control'. Yet another questioned whether or not it was a coincidence that 'Muslims who wish to see the flag of Islam flying over Australia have joined up with the very group whose members own large parts of the country'. In these paranoid projections Indigenous Muslims are imagined as the embodiment of the 'double jeopardy' of the threat of Indigenous land rights coupled with the danger of terrorism. Paranoiac fantasies of a Muslim land grab are also clearly evident in the postings offered up on anti-Islamic website *Australian Islamist Monitor*. The first in their three-part series 'Islam destroys Aboriginality' is called 'Destructive Muslim fishermen' and looks at the pre-colonial connections between northern coastal Aboriginal communities and Muslim Makassans from Sulawesi in Indonesia.[27] One reader expressed concern that Muslims might use their pre-colonial encounters with Aborigines to challenge 'Mabo for THEIR land rights to Australia'. Another commentator agreed, noting, 'I guess that's the game plan. There is an aggressive programme to convert Aborigines, and then of course, as the original owners of the land, they can claim Australia on behalf of Islam. You have to hand it to Islam – it's fiendishly, devilishly cunning.'

In the words of Michael Humphrey, 'national security [is] an issue that now reaches into the everyday life of all citizens'.[28] Nowhere does the truth of this observation impinge more viscerally on personal safety than in the group this book describes. Many interviewees have felt, at one time or another, terrorised by the so-called war on terror. Johari Bin Demin notes that his Malaysian father, who has lived in Australia for more than fifty years, was too frightened after the 2005 Cronulla riots 'to go out on his own' for fear of reprisals.[29] On a recent trip to Malaysia to visit relatives Johari, perhaps because of his Muslim surname and what he terms 'Arab' appearance, was continually singled out for explosives testing. As he says, 'I flew out from Broome and got tested for explosives in Broome, flew out to Perth and I got tested for explosives in Perth and I got tested again in Singapore on the way back.' He adds wistfully, 'Yeah, well, it was ironic because I got picked every plane I caught that trip and the only one I didn't get picked out of was in Malaysia because [there] I look like everyone else.'

Muhammad Hassan Mokak is the brother of Aboriginal–Malay sisters Semah and Halimah. Known by his family and friends as Hassan, he decided after a family trip to Malaysia to start using the name Muhammad instead. He and his siblings travelled to Malaysia to take part in a feast held in honour of their late father. Semah recalls that the trip had a significant influence on Hassan, who began to take great pride in his Malaysian ancestry. His decision 'to start calling himself Muhammad after being in Malaysia' was a symbol of his effort to try 'to find out who he is'.[30] In normal circumstances this highly personal decision would not have been a cause for concern, but Semah and her sister were well aware that it could be construed differently by those with suspicious minds. Recalling a conversation with her sister Halimah, Semah said:

> I'm really concerned about Hassan using Muhammad because – but then I thought about it and I thought that *is* his name. He's just made the links; he's proud and now I'm fearful that someone's going to grab my brother, drag him off and think he's connected to some terrorist cell … It scared the living daylights out of me. And I just thought that was really unfortunate that here he was really embracing

[his identity] and we're, as his older sisters, saying, 'Hey, can you tone down on this stuff?'

Whether intentionally or not, in the current Islamophobic climate, conversion to Islam assumes a political meaning. In one of our many telephone conversations Aboriginal Muslim Rocky Davis recalled being stopped and searched by police one day on his way back from the local library, from which he had borrowed a number of books about Islam. When the police found them in his bag they automatically assumed Rocky was a terrorist and proceeded to interrogate him about his beliefs and associates. During the course of researching and writing *Islam Dreaming* I was frequently in possession of books about Islam, but somehow I don't think their presence in my bag would arouse the same suspicion (if I were stopped and searched in the first place). Another interviewee, Sulaiman Menzies, was prevented by the Australian Security Intelligence Organisation (ASIO) from undertaking a study trip to Africa (where he hoped to learn Arabic in order to read the Qur'an in its original form) because of alleged involvement in terrorist activities. Sydney-based Sulaiman planned to travel to the Sudan in 2002 but was arrested at the Perth airport, the first stop on his journey. As he says, ASIO officials 'put a bag over my head and duck taped me and drove me [around] for hours and questioned me. They were some of the most stupid questions you've ever heard in your life: "Do you know Saddam Hussein? Do you know Osama Bin Laden?"'[31]

Before his detainment Sulaiman had been under surveillance following an anonymous tip-off claiming that he was intending to travel to Africa to attend a terrorist training camp, and that on his return he planned to blow up Sydney's MLC building. When asked by reporter Julie Nimmo on the SBS *Insight* program whether there was any truth to these allegations, he replied: 'No, not at all – this is my country.'[32] Despite the absence of evidence of involvement in a terrorist plot, and despite the fact that Sulaiman's father lives in the Sudan, ASIO was not persuaded of his innocence, and for two years he was barred from overseas travel. After the ban was lifted, he resumed his travel plans. In our interview I couldn't help asking whether, if he *had* been a terrorist, wouldn't he still be one two years later?

Just rewards

In embracing Islam, Indigenous Muslims adopt a cosmopolitan identity simultaneously at home in Australia and part of a larger international spiritual community. Their sense of identity and being is not threatened but, rather, strengthened through their membership of more than one community. In being citizens, concurrently, of Australia and the world, Indigenous Muslims' sense of belonging is effectively multiplied. Of course elements of the Australian Government and public remain highly fearful and deeply suspicious 'of any Australian with multiple cultural and national allegiances'.[33] In the eyes of some commentators Indigenous Muslims' doubled identity doubles the security threat they purportedly pose to national security. In arithmetic terms, from the paranoid position, Indigenous Muslims have multiplied their insecurity potential by being Indigenous *and* Muslim. However, from Indigenous Muslims' point of view, in doubling their identity they have halved their own sense of insecurity and isolation. Through the discovery of what they perceive to be a high degree of cultural convergence between 'traditional' Indigenous society and the major tenets of Islam, Indigenous Muslims have achieved a stronger sense of identity and, thereby, security. Their doubled identity, the very thing that makes them suspicious to the Andrew Bolts of this world, is a strategy of self-securing that Indigenous Muslims have employed to achieve a new sense of belonging.

Indigenous Muslims construct their hybrid identities self-consciously and dialectically. They constantly compare and contrast Indigenous and Islamic perspectives to understand their lives and subjectivities. Through the process of religious reversion Indigenous Muslims exploit points of resemblance between Aboriginal and Islamic spirituality that justify a radical simplification of faith. Tending to invoke a romanticised and decontextualised Indigenous spirituality, they also often call upon a rather essentialised and dehistoricised notion of Islam. Some respondents identified themselves as Sunni Muslims. A couple said they were attracted to Sufism, but the following comments of Anthony Mundine are typical of the vast majority of interviewees. When asked whether he subscribed to a particular school of Islamic thought he responded, 'No, not really, I just follow the Qur'an, that's it. Nothing else, [or] any other sects. I follow God's law, God's word.'[34] Alinta Smith said that whenever she is asked, '"Are you Shi'ite or Sunni?" I say, "No, I'm Muslim, I'm Muslim, that's it."'[35] It is this 'pure' and unmediated Islam that helps interviewees reclaim what Alinta calls 'the true history behind being Aboriginal'. The points of resemblance between Indigenous and Islamic spiritual beliefs make it possible to ignore or jettison the cultural differences between the two traditions. Significantly, Indigenous Muslims see their traditional belief systems validated and mirrored in Islam and in forms that give them a place in the contemporary world.

The Indigenous men and women featured in this book have come to Islam via different paths. Some found faith while in prison, others were introduced to Islam by friends or co-workers, several engaged with Islam textually; still others reaffirmed spiritual beliefs practised in their families generations ago. Whatever the route, whether as kinverts or converts, Islam has a profound influence on them as individuals and on their families and friends. Any religious conversion typically results in a shift in attitudes, beliefs and behaviour. Within Islam this generally manifests itself in a change in name, attire and abstinence from certain practices.[36] These changes, while strengthening a Muslim's local and global ties to fellow believers, can be seen to diminish one's connection with other groups or communities. Elements of the wider Anglo-Australian community perceive Indigenous people's identification with Islam as un-Australian, at best. Some Aboriginal people assume that it is incongruous for Indigenous people to become Muslims, and that those who do so forgo their Aboriginality. As Justin Agale says, 'I know of Aboriginal brothers who have converted who have been told by Aboriginal leaders that they're sell-outs, that they have no right being Muslim.'[37] A number of Aboriginal people hold very negative views about Islam, particularly if, like the majority of Australians, they get their information from the mainstream media. People are willing to accept one's being Aboriginal and Christian at the same time but not, it seems, Indigenous and *Muslim*.

While Indigenous converts might be attracted by the *idea* of the multicultural and multiracial nature of Islam, they often find, in practice, that the Muslim community is far from non-racist. Kuranda Seyit, a Turkish-born Muslim community journalist and advocate, says it is 'really sad' that 'a few Aboriginal Muslims have experienced' rejection by other Muslims, being asked at mosques: 'Who are you? We don't want you here.'[38] Several Indigenous Muslims, disheartened by the factious nature of the broader Muslim community, have withdrawn, opting to practise their faith in private. Eugenia Flynn is dismayed by what she labels 'the lack of understanding and solidarity between the Indigenous peoples of Australia and the largely immigrant-based Muslim community in Australia'.[39] She cites a recent Gaza rally where a speaker made a connection between the plight of Palestinians and the situation of 'Indigenous Australians [who] know all too well what invasion, occupation and dispossession mean'. It drew a confused and muted response from 'the majority of Muslims and Arabs in the crowd'. Why, they wondered, was a politician 'speaking about Aboriginal Land Rights issues' at a *Muslim* event? For Eugenia the incident dramatised the 'ignorance and covert racism' that she believes 'exists within the Muslim community towards Indigenous Australians'. The fact, she says, that most Muslim Australians either do not know about or rally against the 'disadvantage experienced by Indigenous Australians in this country' renders them 'complicit in the continued injustices carried out against Indigenous Australians'.

This research might be best understood as a 'snapshot' in time of the various ways in which Indigenous Muslims characterise their connection to Islam. This has been true in a number of ways. It is partly a reflection of the relationship the researcher has to her materials and her human informants. Where I have been privileged to conduct two or more interviews with the same person, it has been impressed upon me that their Islamic faith is a dynamic, evolving and mutating body of belief. It is a sounding-board for the vicissitudes of life, and grows with them. What I have written here has already been superseded in the lives of the people I spoke to by new experiences, reflections and understandings. In a small way *Islam Dreaming* itself has changed the landscape, as I was able on occasion to introduce Indigenous Muslims who had not formerly been aware of one another's existence. Islam in Indigenous

Australia is an unfolding conversation: as it reaches further back into the past, so it weaves a web of stories, commitments and mutual recognition that create a pattern of future identity formation, one in which history, biography and the life of the spirit are integrated and find new meaning.

What of the future? Unlike their kinvert counterparts, most convert Indigenous Muslims had little contact with Islam or Muslims in their youth. The vast majority have embraced Islam in the last ten to fifteen years.[40] How will their children self-identify? Will they take on their parents' spiritual beliefs and become practising Muslims or will they, like those before them, treat Islam as one among many strands in their cultural heritage? The prospect of Indigenous Muslim men and women marrying and carrying forward a new understanding of postcolonial Indigeneity is intriguing. The potential of Islam to act as a catalyst of new conversations between Australia's oldest cultures and the most recent arrivals to these shores should not be neglected. Nor should the capacity of Indigenous Muslims to act on the world stage be overlooked. It is clear that new ways to engage the Muslim world are needed: Indigenous Muslims are in a position to address global issues of intercultural cooperation from a unique point of view. As Indigenous–Islamic connections engage the broader community, greater social cohesion and renewed multicultural self-confidence may be hoped for – and even perhaps a culture where security is based on mutual trust rather than fear.

Beliefs evolve, mature and deepen. In chapter 6 we quoted Justin Agale's views on the meaning of prayers performed on stolen land. While his 'general view has not changed', he writes that 'the depth of my understanding has developed substantially'. He now sees that connection to country – necessary if those who pray are to 'receive *barakah* [blessing] in their prayer and action' –

is not simply a question of formally acknowledging Indigenous land rights. It involves an active 'striving for the betterment of this country and nation in areas such as social justice'. He also acknowledges now that the 'legal position' is not for him to decide, 'it's Allah's (swt) business not mine'. These remarks (in an email sent to me in April 2010, six years after our first interview) show '*alhumdulillah* [all praise is due to Allah] that I have not become stagnant, for that would mean the death of my path'. It is fitting to close this book with the wise words of one who was among the first to befriend me and put me on the path of Islam in Indigenous Australia. The result has been, as I say, a snapshot, but I hope it participates in a process of changing perceptions and growing understanding.

Interviews

'Abdul', 22 July 2009, location unspecified.
Agale, Justin, 27 November 2004, Sydney, NSW.
Ahmady, Rasoul, 27 April 2007, Adelaide, SA.
Ahmat, George Abdul, 28 January 2007, Thursday Island, Qld.
Ahwang, Ronny, 31 March 2005, Brisbane, Qld.
Akbar, Johnny, 20 April 2007, Quorn, SA.
'Ali', 15 July 2005, Broome, WA.
Anderson, Anthony, 19 August 2009, Ipswich, Qld.
Binawel, Abdul (Karim) 26 January 2007, Thursday Island, Qld.
Bin Bakar, Mark, 14 July 2005, Broome, WA.
Bin Demin, Johari, 4 September 2006, Broome, WA.
Bin Demin, Sally, 5 September 2006, Broome, WA.
Bin Juda, Ambrose (Binjie), 30 January 2007, Hammond Island, Qld
Bin Juda, Rosemary (Mary), 29 January 2007, Thursday Island, Qld.
Bin Swani, Majunia, 3 September 2007, Broome, WA.
Bin Swani, Rose, 3 September 2007, Broome, WA.
Binti Hassan Awal, Halima, 30 March 2005, Brisbane, Qld; 26 January 2007, Thursday Island, Qld; 14 December 2009, Sydney, NSW.
Boerkamp, Beatrice, 9 June 2007, Adelaide, SA.
Cooper, Aziz, 11 March 2009, Melbourne, Vic.
Davis, Rocky (Shaheed Malik), 17 August 2006, Sydney, NSW.
Demin, Anthea, 5 September 2006, Broome, WA.
Dowling, Julie, 11 April 2006, Perth, WA.
Esgin, Tuguy, 11 November 2009, Adelaide, SA.
Flynn, Eugenia, 6 December 2005; 10 June 2007, Adelaide, SA.
Gilany, Soliman, 21 July 2009, Sydney, NSW.
Hamidani, Kamal, 20 July 2009, Sydney, NSW.
Hathaway, Daphne, 19 April 2007, Whyalla, SA.
'Jamila', 25 April 2005, location unspecified.
'John', 11 August 2005, Melbourne, Vic.
Jones, Philip, 4 December 2007, Adelaide, SA.

Kenny, Anna, 10 December, 2007, Alice Springs, NT.
Khadem, Mojgan, 8 December 2005, Adelaide, SA.
Khan, Azeem (Johnny), 13 December 2007, Alice Springs, NT.
Kite, Esther, 12 December 2007, Alice Springs, NT.
Mahomed, Dean Gool, 23 April 2007, Port Augusta, SA.
Menzies, Sulaiman, 19 July 2009, Sydney, NSW.
Meston, Troy, 31 March 2005, Brisbane, Qld.
Mokak, Halimah, 14 August 2008, Melbourne, Vic.
Mokak-Wischki, Semah, 15 August 2006, Brisbane, Qld.
Mundine, Anthony, 4 December 2006, Sydney, NSW.
Nasir, Joanne, 17 December 2007, Darwin, NT.
O'Shea, Assan (Ken), 16 March 2008, Caboolture, Qld.
'Patricia', 15 July 2005, Broome, WA.
Rajkowski, Pamela, 6 December 2005, Adelaide, SA.
'Ramiz', 15 December 2009, Sydney, NSW.
Rind, Shahzad (Shaz), 27 November 2004, Sydney, NSW.
Robertson, Marilyn, 9 June 2007, Adelaide, SA.
Rogers, Des, 12 December 2007, Alice Springs, NT.
Ross, Balfour, 26 December 2005, by telephone.
Sahanna, Rosie, 2 September 2006, Broome, WA.
'Sarah', 17 December 2007, location unspecified.
Shibasaki, Hismile, 6 February 2007, by telephone.
Sultan, Eric, 21 September 2005, Alice Springs, NT.
Smith, Alinta, 18 December 2005; 15 December 2009, Sydney NSW.
Stevens, Christine, 14 February 2006, Sydney, NSW.
Wali, Nazra, 9 July 2008, Melbourne, Vic.
Wilson, Mona, 21 November 2005, Kyneton, Vic.
Wilson, Shirley, 8 April 2006, Perth, WA.

Notes

Introduction

1. Mona Wilson quoted by Pamela Rajkowski in a letter to the author, 10 April 2010.
2. Peshawar is located on the edge of the Khyber Pass, near the border of Afghanistan. It is now a regional city in Pakistan but before Pakistan's creation in 1947, Peshawar was part of the North-West Frontier Province of British India.
3. Rajkowski, *Linden Girl*, p. 226.
4. Marilyn Robertson (née Khan) in interview with the author, 9 June 2007, Adelaide. Unless otherwise indicated, all quotations from Marilyn come from this interview.
5. Originally established in 1826 by the British East India Company, the Straits Settlements came under British rule from 1867. The Settlements (dissolved following the end of World War II) included Malacca, Penang (or Prince of Wales Island), Singapore and, from 1907, Labuan, off the coast of Borneo. With the exception of Singapore these territories now form part of Malaysia.
6. 'Koori' is a regional term used to refer to Indigenous people from southern New South Wales and Victoria. The current status of the Koori Muslim Association is unclear.
7. Tsiolkas, *The Slap*, p. 19.
8. Stephenson, *The Outsiders Within*.
9. See Macknight, *The Voyage to Marege*, and McIntosh, 'Allah and the spirit of the dead'.
10. See Shnukal, '"They don't know what went on underneath"'.
11. See Rajkowski, *Linden Girl*; Rajkowski, *In the Tracks of the Camelmen*; and Stevens, *Tin Mosques*.
12. Reddie, *Black Muslims in Britain*, p. 10.
13. Gallagher, *Expectation and Experience*, p. 28.
14. Reddie, *Black Muslims in Britain*, p. 164.
15. Zebiri, *British Muslim Converts*, p. 197.

ONE The beginnings

1. Sutton & Vertigans, *Resurgent Islam*, p. 131.
2. Clarke, 'The "Moormans Trowsers"', p. 317.
3. Ganter, 'Muslim Australians'.
4. Mulvaney & Kamminga, *Prehistory of Australia*, p. 411.
5. Morwood & Hobbs, 'The Asian connection', p. 197.
6. Macknight, *The Voyage to Marege*, p. 29.
7. Mulvaney, *Encounters in Place*, p. 24.
8. Russell, 'Aboriginal–Makassan interactions', p. 8.
9. McIntosh, 'The Birrinydji legacy', p. 76.
10. Russell, 'Aboriginal–Makassan interactions', p. 9.
11. Gerrit Knaap and Heather Sutherland quoted in Macknight, 'Harvesting the Memory' in Veth, Sutton & Neale (eds), *Strangers on the Shore*, p. 136.
12. Reynolds, *North of Capricorn*, p. 14.
13. Stephenson, *The Outsiders Within*, p. 164.
14. Searcy, *In Australian Tropics*, p. 46. See also Mulvaney, *Encounters in Place*, p. 182, and Macknight (ed.), *The Farthest Coast*, p. 182. However, linguistic studies reveal that Melville Island languages contain a considerable number of Makassan loanwords (see Russell, 'Aboriginal–Makassan interactions', p. 4, and Evans, 'Macassan loanwords in Top End languages', pp. 51–2).
15. Lamilami, *Lamilami Speaks*, p. 26.
16. Russell, 'Islam', pp. 89–95.
17. See Gervaise in Swain, *A Place for Strangers*, pp. 102, 182.
18. Russell, 'Islam'; Milner, *The Malays*, p. 43.
19. Berndt & Berndt, *Arnhem Land*, p. 45.
20. Ibid., pp. 45–6.
21. Walker, 'Macassan influences on the Aboriginal language and culture of Northern Australia', p. 33.
22. Christina Mayer, email to author, 27 January 2010.
23. McIntosh, 'The Birrinydji Legacy', p. 71.
24. Burrumarra quoted in McIntosh, *The Whale and the Cross*, p. 18.
25. McIntosh, 'Pre-Macassans at Dholtji?' in Veth, Sutton & Veale (eds), *Strangers on the Shore*, p. 171.
26. McIntosh, 'Allah and the spirit of the dead', p. 133; McIntosh, 'Islam and Australia's Aborigines?', p. 55.
27. Ganter, 'Muslim Australians'.
28. McIntosh, 'Islam and Australia's Aborigines?', p. 55; Palmer, 'Negotiating the ritual and social order through spectacle', p. 2.

295

29 Palmer, 'Negotiating the ritual', p. 3.
30 McIntosh, 'Allah', p. 133.
31 McIntosh, 'Islam and Australia's Aborigines?', p. 55.
32 McIntosh, 'Allah', pp. 134–5. *Wurramu* also refers to Aboriginal people's salvation in Allah.
33 Burrumarra quoted in McIntosh, 'Islam and Australia's Aborigines?', p. 63.
34 McIntosh, 'Islam and Australia's Aborigines?', p. 56.
35 Warner, 'Malay influence', p. 492.
36 Warner, *A Black Civilization*, p. 420.
37 Warner, 'Malay influence', p. 492.
38 Warner, *A Black Civilization*, p. 421.
39 There are many differing views on how this phrase should be transliterated into English, but it also appears as *Bismi Allah ir-Rahman ir-Rahim*. Muslims often say this phrase when embarking on any significant endeavour, and all but one of the *sura* or chapters in the Qur'an begin with it.
40 Warner, *A Black Civilization*, p. 423.
41 Isaacs, *Australian Dreaming*, p. 275.
42 McIntosh, 'Allah', p. 134.
43 Isaacs, *Australian Dreaming*, p. 275.
44 McIntosh, 'Islam and Australia's Aborigines?', p. 68.
45 Ibid., p. 74.
46 McIntosh, 'Allah', p. 137.
47 Ibid., p. 137.
48 McIntosh, 'Islam and Australia's Aborigines?', p. 76.
49 Macknight, *The Voyage to Marege*, p. 293.
50 In 1838 the British established a settlement (called Victoria) at Port Essington on the Coburg Peninsula (see Ganter, *Mixed Relations*, pp. 19–20, and Macknight (ed.), *The Farthest Coast*, p. 13). In 1849, after eleven years, it was abandoned (like Forts Dundas and Wellington before it).
51 Earl, 'An account of a visit to Kisser', p. 116.
52 McIntosh, 'Islam and Australia's Aborigines?', p. 67.
53 McIntosh, 'Allah', p. 137.
54 McIntosh, 'Pre-Macassans at Dholtji?', p.174.
55 John Algar, email to author, 28 January 2009.
56 Stevens, 'Afghan camel drivers', p. 49; Jones & Kenny, *Australia's Muslim Cameleers*, p. 9; Loois, 'Afghans and Indians in Western Australia', p. 398.
57 Willis, 'From indispensability to redundancy', p. 40; Scriver, 'Mosques, ghantowns and cameleers', p. 24.
58 Cigler, *The Afghans in Australia*, p. 11.
59 Stevens, 'Afghan camel drivers', p. 49.
60 Rajkowski, *In the Tracks of the Camelmen*, p. 29.
61 Cigler, *The Afghans in Australia*, p. 98.
62 Jones & Kenny, *Australia's Muslim Cameleers*, p. 9.
63 Scriver, 'Mosques, ghantowns and cameleers', p. 25.
64 Quoted in Koch & Koch, *Kaytetye Country*, pp. 22–3.
65 Hercus, 'Afghan stories', p. 39.
66 Quoted in Richards, Hudson & Lowe (eds), *Out of the Desert*, pp. 73, 75.
67 Hercus, 'Afghan stories', pp. 40, 47.
68 Quoted in ibid., p. 47.
69 Hercus, 'Afghan stories', p. 40.
70 Ibid., p. 39.
71 Jones & Kenny, *Australia's Muslim Cameleers*, p. 19.
72 Ibid., p. 23.
73 Scriver, 'Mosques, ghantowns and cameleers', pp. 25–6.
74 Rajkowski, *Linden Girl*, pp. 50, 64.
75 Rahman, 'Islam', p. 303.
76 Ibid., p. 303.
77 Jones & Kenny, *Australia's Muslim Cameleers*, p. 111.
78 Stevens, *Tin Mosques and Ghantowns*, p. 213.
79 Ibid., p. 152; Mulvaney, *Encounters in Place*, p. 177.
80 Jones & Kenny, *Australia's Muslim Cameleers*, p. 111.
81 Malyapuka cited in Richards, Hudson & Lower (eds), *Out of the Desert*, pp. 63–9. See also Dadleh, 'Fair devil sticky beak', pp. 101–2.
82 Rajkowski, *In the Tracks of the Camelmen*, p. 167.
83 Jones & Kenny, *Australia's Muslim Cameleers*, p. 111.
84 Stevens, *Tin Mosques and Ghantowns*, p. 152.
85 Dadleh, 'Fair devil sticky beak', p. 110.
86 Julie Dowling in interview with the author, 11 April 2006, Perth, WA.
87 Rajkowski, *In the Tracks of the Camelmen*, p. 169.
88 Quoted in Rajkowski, *In the Tracks of the Camelmen*, p. 169.
89 Hercus, 'Afghan stories', p. 40.
90 Rajkowski, *In the Tracks of the Camelmen*, p. 169.
91 Ibid., p. 169.
92 Quoted in Shaw (ed.), *Our Heart is the Land*, pp. 68–9.
93 Jones & Kenny, *Australia's Muslim Cameleers*, p. 121.
94 Mulvaney, *Encounters in Place*, pp. 176–7.
95 Cigler, *The Afghans in Australia*, p. 41.

96 Rajkowski, *In the Tracks of the Camelmen*, p. 168.
97 Ibid., pp. 50–1.
98 Stevens, *Tin Mosques and Ghantowns*, p. 232.
99 Rajkowski, *In the Tracks of the Camelmen*, pp. 54–5.
100 Stevens, 'Afghan camel drivers', pp. 53–4.
101 Stevens, *Tin Mosques and Ghantowns*, p. 167.
102 See Dadleh, 'Fair devil sticky beak', p. 111.
103 Ibid., p. 111.
104 Jones, 'Muslim impact on early Australian life', p. 40; Manderson, 'Malay', p. 579.
105 Milner, *The Malays*, p. 201.
106 Manderson, 'Malay', p. 579.
107 Choo, 'Asian men on the West Kimberley coast', p. 96.
108 Sickert, *Beyond the Lattice*, p. 60; Burton, *General History of Broome*, p. 2.
109 Reynolds, *North of Capricorn*, p. 132; Balint, *Troubled Waters*, p. 23.
110 Manderson, 'Malay', p. 579.
111 Sickert, *Beyond the Lattice*, p. 39.
112 When Europeans in Western Australia's Pilbara region observed Aboriginal people's use of pearl-shell they concluded it must be locally available. Aborigines were initially willing to collect shell in shallow tidal reaches for white people in exchange for food and clothing. But as the demand for pearl-shell grew, unscrupulous whites engaged in a practice known as 'blackbirding': forcing Aboriginal men and women to 'skin' dive for shell, and keeping them in captivity on the pearling boats or on offshore islands. See Sickert, *Beyond the Lattice*, p. 25, and Reynolds, *North of Capricorn*, p. 131.
113 Shnukal & Ramsay, 'Tidal flows', p. 39.
114 Choo, 'Asian men on the West Kimberley coast', p. 97; Choo, 'The impact of Asian–Aboriginal Australian contacts', pp. 303–4.
115 Shnukal, '"They don't know what went on underneath"', p. 88.
116 Choo, 'The impact of Asian–Aboriginal Australian contacts', p. 304.
117 Quoted in Balint, 'The pearling families of Broome'.
118 Choo, 'Asian men on the West Kimberley coast', p. 96.
119 Chase, '"All kind of nation"', pp. 8, 12.
120 McGann, '"Malays"', p. 46.
121 'Patricia' in interview with the author, 15 July 2005, Broome.
122 Shnukal & Ramsay, 'Tidal flows', p. 45.
123 Halima Binti Hassan Awal in interview with the author, 30 March 2005, Brisbane.
124 Bin Demin, *Once in Broome*, p. 30.
125 Shnukal & Ramsay, 'Tidal flows', pp. 44–5.
126 Shibasaki, 'Billy Isao Shibasaki', p. 290.
127 Hismile Shibasaki, telephone interview with the author, 6 February 2007.
128 Throughout the Malay and Muslim world Islamic days run from sunset to sunset. As Friday is the most sacred day of the week it is customary to have special prayers on Thursday night, following *maghrib* (Arabic for the fourth daily prayer at sunset) (Balfour Ross, email to author, 3 November 2008).
129 Jamel Shibasaki in interview with Joan Staples, 17 April 1993, Thursday Island, Qld. Copy of interview and transcript in author's possession.
130 Balfour Ross, email to author, 29 October 2008.
131 Ibid.
132 The offerings of food, toys, spirits, cigarettes and other items also reflect Shinto practice. See Shnukal, 'Confluence', p. 256.
133 Seriba Shibasaki in interview with Joan Staples, 19 April 1993, Thursday Island, Qld. Copy of interview and transcript in author's possession.
134 This three-day period of mourning is for a loved one or close relative. A woman may mourn the loss of her husband for four months and ten days.
135 Shnukal, 'Confluence', p. 256.
136 Kathleen Hirakawa in interview with Joan Staples, 18 April 1993, Thursday Island, Qld. Copy of interview and transcript in author's possession.
137 Ganter, *Mixed Relations*, p. 212.
138 Shnukal & Ramsay, 'Tidal flows', p. 46.
139 Jamel Shibasaki in interview with Joan Staples, 17 April 1993, Thursday Island, Qld. Copy of interview and transcript in author's possession.
140 According to Paul Battersby, Anna Shnukal found evidence of two principal Malay villages or *kampong* formed in the late nineteenth century in Torres Strait, one at 'Malaytown' on Thursday Island and the other at Upai on Badu (Mulgrave Island). The latter was settled in 'a culturally appropriate way with the permission of the local custodians and served as a haven for Malays seeking to retain their cultural traditions'. See Battersby, *To the Islands*, p. 31.
141 Staples & O'Shea, 'Thursday Island's Asian heritage', unpublished paper in author's possession, p. 11.

TWO Telling it like it was

1 Bouma, Daw & Munawar, 'Muslims managing religious diversity', pp. 59, 69.
2 Marilyn/Fatima Robertson (née Khan) in interview with the author, 9 June 2007, Adelaide. Unless otherwise indicated, all quotations from Marilyn come from this interview.
3 Beatrice/Zanzibar Boerkamp (née Khan) in interview with the author, 9 June 2007, Adelaide. Unless otherwise indicated, all quotations from Beatrice come from this interview.
4 Mona Wilson (née Akbar) in interview with the author, 21 November 2005, Kyneton, Vic. Unless otherwise indicated, all quotations from Mona come from this interview.
5 Brahim, 'Recollections of the early days', p. 51.
6 Joanne Nasir in interview with the author, 17 December 2007, Darwin. Unless otherwise indicated, all quotations from Joanne come from this interview.
7 *Salam* (or *salaam*) means 'peace' in Arabic.
8 Peacock, 'Eva Salam Peacock', p. 280.
9 Sally Bin Demin in interview with the author, 5 September 2006, Broome. Unless otherwise indicated, all quotations from Sally come from this interview.
10 Bouma, Daw & Munawar, 'Muslims managing religious diversity', p. 57.
11 Deen, 'Muslim journeys'.
12 Bouma, Daw & Munawar, 'Muslims managing religious diversity', p. 59.
13 Kabir, 'Muslims in Western Australia 1870–1970', p. 554.
14 Quoted in Balint, 'The pearling families of Broome'.
15 Bin Demin, *Once in Broome*, p. 33.
16 Mark Bin Bakar, 'Mark "Mary G" Bin Bakar', p. 44.
17 Wilson, 'Mona Wilson's life story'.
18 Stevens, *Tin Mosques and Ghantowns*, p. 252.
19 Rajkowski, *In the Tracks of the Camelmen*, p. 52.
20 Anthea Demin in interview with the author, 5 September 2006, Broome. Unless otherwise indicated, all quotations from Anthea come from this interview.
21 Muslims believe that the Prophet Muhammad received his first revelations from God (through the angel Gabriel, or Jibril) during the month of Ramadan in the year 610 AD.
22 Stevens, *Tin Mosques and Ghantowns*, p. 193.
23 Mark Bin Bakar in interview with the author, 14 July 2005, Broome. Unless otherwise indicated, all quotations from Mark come from this interview.
24 Shirley Wilson (née Akbar) in interview with the author, 8 April 2006, Perth. Unless otherwise indicated, all quotations from Shirley come from this interview.
25 'Sarah' in interview with the author, 17 December 2007, Darwin. Unless otherwise indicated, all quotations from Sarah come from this interview.
26 Johari Bin Demin in interview with the author, 4 September 2006, Broome. Unless otherwise indicated, all quotations from Johari come from this interview.
27 Semah Mokak-Wischki in interview with the author, 15 August 2006, Brisbane. Unless otherwise indicated, all quotations from Semah come from this interview.
28 The word *Datu* (or *Dato*), used in Malaysia, Indonesia, Brunei and the Philippines, can refer to a political leader or chief; to a priest or medical practitioner; an aristocrat or noble; or to an elder or one's grandfather. The Indigenous–Malay descendants from Broome and Darwin tended to refer to their grandfathers as *Datu* whereas descendants in the Torres Strait used *Datu* and *Dato* interchangeably.
29 Halimah Mokak in interview with the author, 14 August 2008, Melbourne. Unless otherwise indicated, all quotations from Halimah come from this interview.
30 Rajkowski, *In the Tracks of the Camelmen*, p. 48.
31 Walker, 'Douglas Walker', p. 70.
32 Azeem (Johnny) Khan in interview with the author, 13 December 2007, Alice Springs. Unless otherwise indicated, all quotations from Johnny come from this interview.
33 Rajkowski, *In the Tracks of the Camelmen*, p. 48.
34 Dean Gool Mahomed in interview with the author, 23 April 2007, Port Augusta, South Australia.
35 Burton, *General History of Broome*, p. 38.
36 Quoted in Balint, 'The pearling families of Broome'.
37 Halima Binti Hassan Awal in interview with the author, 30 March 2005, Brisbane.
38 Brahim, 'Recollections of the early days', p. 51.
39 Peacock, 'Eva Salam Peacock', p. 280.
40 Esther Kite in interview with the author,

12 December 2007, Alice Springs.
41 Philip Jones in interview with the author, 4 December 2007, Adelaide. Unless otherwise indicated, all quotations from Philip come from this interview.
42 Rajkowski, *In the Tracks of the Camelmen*, pp. 51, 80.
43 Sunni Muslims consider that all types of fish are halal for consumption, but some Shi'ites are of the opinion that only fish with scales are appropriate.
44 Quoted in Hercus, 'Afghan stories', p. 62.
45 Dadleh, 'Fair devil sticky beak', pp. 110–1. The story of Abraham (Ibrahim) throwing his knife in the sea has no Qur'anic or other Islamic basis. As far as the slaughtering of animals is concerned, it is related to the drinking of blood, which is forbidden in Islamic law. This is why animals must be drained of blood before consumption. Fish do not have to be killed in this manner because they do not bleed in the same way as warm-blooded animals. The story of Ibrahim's willingness to sacrifice his son (in an act of obedience to God) appears in the Qur'an. Each year it is commemorated by Muslims in a festival known in Arabic as Eid al-Adha or the 'Festival of Sacrifice'. The three-day festival is held at the end of haj, the annual pilgrimage to Makkah, and involves the ritual slaughter of an animal (usually a sheep or goat), as a symbolic representation of the lamb Ibrahim sacrificed in the place of his son.
46 Stevens, *Tin Mosques and Ghantowns*, p. 202.
47 Dadleh, 'Fair devil sticky beak', p. 110.
48 Quoted in Hercus, 'Afghan stories', p. 62.
49 Cited in Hercus, 'Afghan stories', pp. 56–9.
50 Stevens, *Tin Mosques and Ghantowns*, p. 203.
51 Johnny Akbar in interview with the author, 20 April 2007, Quorn, SA. Unless otherwise indicated, all quotations from Johnny come from this interview.
52 Quoted in Hercus, 'Afghan stories', p. 62.
53 Pike, 'Two camel men', pp. 80–1.
54 Bin Demin, *Once in Broome*, p. 55.
55 Haram (prohibited or forbidden) actions and objects are the opposite of those deemed to be halal (permitted). Non-Muslims often associate the Arabic word *haram* with the English (borrowed from the Turkish) *harem*, the women-only quarters in a sultan's palace. The harem has been imagined in very lurid terms in European writing and art since the seventeenth century, as virtual brothels where nubile young women existed only for the sexual pleasure of their husband. In reality these women-only apartments were given the name 'harem' because they were forbidden to men.
56 Stevens, *Tin Mosques and Ghantowns*, p. 246.
57 Barker, *Camels and the Outback*, p. 77.
58 Peacock, 'Eva Salam Peacock', p. 280.
59 Majunia Bin Swani in interview with the author, 3 September 2007, Broome. Unless otherwise indicated, all quotations from Majunia come from this interview.
60 Assan (Ken) O'Shea in interview with the author, 16 March 2008, Caboolture, Qld. Unless otherwise indicated, all quotations from Ken come from this interview.
61 Balfour Ross in telephone interview with the author, 26 December 2005. Unless otherwise indicated, all quotations from Balfour come from this interview.
62 Stevens, *Tin Mosques and Ghantowns*, p. 249. This practice was given artistic expression in director Mojgan Khadem's 2001 film *Serenades*. In one scene an Afghan cameleer beats an Aboriginal man in a game of cards. Having run out of money the Aboriginal character offers the Afghan the sexual favours of his daughter – who later gives birth to the main character 'Jila'.
63 Stephen (Baamba) Albert in Mitch (Michelle) Torres (2001), *Saltwater Bluesman*, Film Australia Limited, Macumba Media Enterprises.
64 Bin Demin, *Once in Broome*, p. 145.
65 Stevens, *Tin Mosques and Ghantowns*, p. 239.
66 Quoted in Shaw (ed.), *Our Heart is the Land*, p. 66.
67 Eric Sultan in interview with the author, 21 September 2005, Alice Springs.

THREE **Keeping it in the family**

1 Saeed, 'Trends in contemporary Islam', p. 400.
2 Ibid., p. 400.
3 Saeed & Akbarzadeh, 'Searching for identity', p. 9.
4 When speaking of their Malay or Afghan heritage, the Indigenous people I met tended not to use the word 'Muslim'. They often referred to their forebears in the common parlance of the time as 'Mohammedans'. The term 'Mohammedan' (variously spelled Mahometan, Muhammadan, Mahommedan) has now been superseded by 'Muslim' or, less commonly, 'Moslem', but it was regularly used in Western litera-

ture, Western Christian Europe and in Australia until around the mid-1960s. Today many Muslims find the terms 'Mohammedan' (Muslim) and 'Mohammedanism' (Islam) offensive because they worship Allah, not Muhammad.
5. Assan (Ken) O'Shea in interview with the author, 16 March 2008, Caboolture, Qld. Unless otherwise indicated, all quotations from Ken come from this interview.
6. Balfour Ross in telephone interview with the author, 26 December 2005.
7. Ross, 'Islam on Thursday Island', p. 7.
8. Ibid., p. 7.
9. Balfour and June also moved to Malaysia because they found they could retire there under the 'Malaysia My Second Home' (MM2H) program, an initiative of the Malaysian Government.
10. Anna Kenny in interview with the author, 10 December 2007, Alice Springs.
11. Perera, 'What is a camp …?'.
12. Mona Wilson in interview with the author, 21 November 2005, Kyneton, Vic. Unless otherwise indicated, all quotations from Mona come from this interview.
13. Azeem (Johnny) Khan in interview with the author, 13 December 2007, Alice Springs. Unless otherwise indicated, all quotations from Johnny come from this interview.
14. Bin Bakar, 'Mark "Mary G" Bin Bakar', p. 38.
15. Mark Bin Bakar in interview with the author, 14 July 2005, Broome. Unless otherwise indicated, all quotations from Mark come from this interview.
16. Peacock, 'Eva Salam Peacock', p. 280.
17. 'Ali' in interview with the author, 15 July 2005, Broome. Unless otherwise indicated, all quotations from Ali come from this interview.
18. 'Patricia' in interview with the author, 15 July 2005, Broome.
19. Esther Kite in interview with the author, 12 December 2007, Alice Springs. Unless otherwise indicated, all quotations from Esther come from this interview.
20. Quoted in Shaw, *Ships of the Desert*.
21. Joanne Nasir in interview with the author, 17 December 2007, Darwin.
22. Johari Bin Demin in interview with the author, 4 September 2006, Broome. Unless otherwise indicated, all quotations from Johari come from this interview.
23. 'People of the Book' adhere to an Abrahamic conception of God; that is, they believe that God is an omnipotent, transcendent and eternal being who created the universe and everything in it.
24. Brahim, 'Recollections of the early days', p. 51. It is noteworthy that Septu's Muslim Malay father offered up special prayers every Thursday night. As mentioned in chapter 1, in the Muslim world Islamic days run from sunset to sunset and, since Friday is the most sacred day of the week, Thursday evening prayers are especially significant.
25. Ibid., p. 52. It seems that Septu's father selectively adhered to religiously sanctioned behaviour and attitudes. He was very uncompromising when it came to his son's christening, but he worked at the local pub. It is not known whether Septu's father consumed alcohol himself, but many Muslims believe that working at or frequenting pubs, hotels and similar venues is Islamically unacceptable.
26. Semah Mokak-Wischki in interview with the author, 15 August 2006, Brisbane. Unless otherwise indicated, all quotations from Semah come from this interview.
27. Halimah Mokak in interview with Dilara Reznikas, date unknown, Sydney. Partial copy of the interview in author's possession.
28. Dean Gool Mahomed in interview with the author, 23 April 2007, Port Augusta, SA. Unless otherwise indicated, all quotations from Dean come from this interview.
29. Halimah Mokak in interview with the author, 14 August 2008, Melbourne. Unless otherwise indicated, all quotations from Halimah come from this interview.
30. Rosie Sahanna in interview with the author, 2 September 2006, Broome.
31. Two other practising Indigenous Muslim men mentioned having Muslim forebears (one interviewee has a Sudanese father and the other a Syrian grandmother), but these family details were mentioned only in passing and appeared to have no influence on their decision to embrace Islam.
32. Ahwang is also recorded as 'Ah Wong', 'Ahwang Dai' and 'Jaffa Ahwang'. See Ganter, 'Living an immoral life', p. 19, and Shnukal, '"They don't know what went on underneath"', p. 105.
33. Halima Binti Hassan Awal in interview with the author, 30 March 2005, Brisbane. Unless otherwise indicated, all quotations from Halima come from this interview.

34 Halima Binti Hassan Awal in third interview with the author, 14 December 2009, Sydney.
35 Justin Agale in interview with the author, 27 November 2004, Sydney. Unless otherwise indicated, all quotations from Justin come from this interview.
36 According to his family, Goolam Badoola earned unique recognition from the Australian Government that gave him citizenship and landholding rights because he saved the residents of flood-bound Western Australian townships 'from a terrible death'. See O'Donnell, 'Family's fight for citizenship rights'.
37 'Marium' is a variant of the Muslim name Maryam or Mariam, which means 'maidservant of Allah'; a name presumably given her by her Muslim Malay father.
38 The Perth mosque, begun in 1905, was built largely with donations from Afghan cameleers. Goolam Badoola was one of those who contributed funds towards its construction. See Jones & Kenny, *Australia's Muslim Cameleers*, p. 173.
39 1918 letter of Marium Martin, now Mrs Badoola, to the Warden, regarding her marriage. State Records Office of Western Australia, Aborigines Department, Personal file 156/31: Indian Goolam Badoola and Family of Mount Magnet. All subsequent quotations from Marium come from this source. My thanks to Shaz Rind for allowing me to view his family's file and to Christine Choo for supplying me with a copy of it.
40 Quoted in O'Donnell, 'Family's fight for rights'.
41 Shahzad (Shaz) Rind in interview with the author, 27 November 2004, Sydney.
42 Quoted in Nimmo, 'Islam Dreaming'.
43 Ramiz's grandmother quoted by Ramiz, written correspondence with the author, 12 April 2010.
44 'Ramiz' in interview with the author, 15 December 2009, Sydney. Unless otherwise indicated, all quotations from Ramiz come from this interview.
45 Ramiz, written communication with the author, 8 April 2010.
46 Bouma, 'The settlement of Islam in Australia', pp. 72, 77.
47 Tuguy Esgin in interview with the author, 11 November 2009, Adelaide. Unless otherwise indicated, all quotations from Tuguy come from this interview.

FOUR **Marriage matters**

1 According to Anna Shnukal, unlike their mixed-race Aboriginal counterparts, Torres Strait Islanders did not grow up on missions and were generally not removed from their families because of their mixed parentage. Some Muslim-headed families in Torres Strait broke down because of the intervention of the authorities, expressed either through an insistence that the men return to their home countries after their period of indenture or a refusal to allow formal marriages, but most remained intact. Queensland's Aboriginals Protection and Restriction of the Sale of Opium Act (introduced on the mainland in 1897) did not apply to Islanders until 1904 and came in gradually. By then most of the early Muslim–Islander families had formed and were very stable (Shnukal, written correspondence with the author, 10 April 2010).
2 Hussain, 'Family law and Muslim communities', p. 165.
3 Rajkowski, *Linden Girl*.
4 Lallie's tribally given name was Nilba, but when she was referred to by the missionaries, police and other officials they used the name Lallie. See Rajkowski, *Linden Girl*, pp. 19–20, 38.
5 The Aboriginal people who were registered at the Linden ration depot (southern Western Australia) gradually became known as the 'Linden mob'. According to Rajkowski, the wider Aboriginal group with which they identified in the eastern goldfields no longer spoke their original languages and had evolved their own common language. They were given the name 'Wongai', a non-Aboriginal word. See ibid., p. 21.
6 Rajkowski, *Linden Girl*, p. 98.
7 Ibid., p. 183.
8 Shirley Wilson (née Akbar) in interview with the author, 8 April 2006, Perth. Unless otherwise indicated, all quotations from Shirley come from this interview.
9 Mona Wilson (née Akbar) in interview with the author, 21 November 2005, Kyneton, Victoria. Unless otherwise indicated, all quotations from Mona come from this interview.
10 Haddad, Smith & Moore, *Muslim Women in America*, pp. 19, 54.
11 Mark Bin Bakar in interview with the author, 14 July 2005, Broome. Unless otherwise indicated, all quotations from Mark come from this interview.

12 'Patricia' in interview with the author, 15 July 2005, Broome.
13 Zanzibar (Beatrice) Boerkamp (née Khan) in interview with the author, 9 June 2007, Adelaide. Unless otherwise indicated, all quotations from Beatrice come from this interview.
14 Dadleh, 'Fair devil sticky beak', p. 105.
15 Ibid., p. 105.
16 Miriam Dadleh in interview with Pamela Rajkowski, date and location unknown. Recording and transcript in the possession of the author. My thanks to Pamela for giving me access to this interview. Unless otherwise indicated, all quotations from Miriam come from it.
17 Dadleh, 'Fair devil sticky beak', p. 106.
18 Semah Mokak-Wischki in interview with the author, 15 August 2006, Brisbane. Unless otherwise indicated, all quotations from Semah come from this interview.
19 Wadud, *Qur'an and Woman*, p. 36.
20 Haddad, Smith & Moore, *Muslim Women in America*, p. 156.
21 Rajkowski, *Linden Girl*, p. 241.
22 Ibid., p. 247.
23 Hussain, 'Family law', p. 166.
24 Ibid., p. 166.
25 Rajkowski, *Linden Girl*, p. 248.
26 Hussain, 'Family law', p. 164.
27 Wilson, 'Mona Wilson's life story'.
28 Halimah Mokak in interview with the author, 14 August 2008, Melbourne. Unless otherwise indicated, all quotations from Halimah come from this interview.
29 Sally Bin Demin in interview with the author, 5 September 2006, Broome. Unless otherwise indicated, all quotations from Sally come from this interview.
30 Johari Bin Demin in interview with the author, 4 September 2006, Broome. Unless otherwise indicated, all quotations from Johari come from this interview.
31 Stevens, *Tin Mosques and Ghantowns*, p. 185.
32 Kathleen Hirakawa (née Seden) in interview with Joan Staples, 18 April 1993, Thursday Island, Qld. Copy of interview and transcript in the author's possession.
33 Assan (Ken) O'Shea, conversation with Kathleen Hirakawa (captured in an interview with Joan Staples, 18 April 1993, Thursday Island, Qld). Copy of interview and transcript in the author's possession.
34 Halimah Mokak in interview with Dilara Reznikas, date unknown, Sydney. Partial copy of the interview in the possession of the author.
35 Stevens, *Tin Mosques and Ghantowns*, p. 167.
36 Brahim, 'Recollections of the early days', p. 51.
37 Travisano, 'Alternation and conversion as qualitatively different transformations', p. 600.
38 Ibid., pp. 600–6.
39 Wohlrab-Sahr, 'Conversion to Islam', p. 353.
40 Peacock, 'Eva Salam Peacock', p. 279.
41 Ibid., p. 279.
42 Hussain, 'Family law', p. 169.
43 Peacock, 'Eva Salam Peacock', pp. 279–80.
44 Rajkowski, *Linden Girl*, p. 249.
45 Ibid., p. 249.
46 Dadleh, 'Miriam Dadleh', p. 67.
47 Azeem (Johnny) Khan in interview with the author, 13 December 2007, Alice Springs. Unless otherwise indicated, all quotations from Johnny come from this interview.
48 Jones, 'Reflecting on Australia's Muslim cameleer heritage', p. 10.
49 Majunia Bin Swani in interview with the author, 3 September 2007, Broome. Unless otherwise indicated, all quotations from Majunia come from this interview.
50 Joanne Nasir in interview with the author, 17 December 2007, Darwin. Unless otherwise indicated, all quotations from Joanne come from this interview.

FIVE Having faith

1 Andrew Grills quoted in Doogue, 'Servants of God'.
2 Phyllis Williams quoted in Gallacher, 'Borders? What borders?'
3 Justin Agale quoted in Doogue, 'Servants of God'.
4 Rambo, *Understanding Religious Conversion*, pp. 12–14; Rambo & Farhadian, 'Converting', p. 23.
5 Rambo & Farhadian, 'Converting', p. 23.
6 Flinn, 'Conversion', p. 51.
7 Rambo, *Understanding Religious Conversion*, p. 127.
8 ABS 2008.
9 Onnudottir, Possamai & Turner, 'Islam', p. 67.
10 Ibid., p. 65.
11 ABS 2010.
12 Rambo, 'Conversion', p. 75.
13 Rambo, *Understanding Religious Conversion*, p. 20.
14 Rambo, 'Conversion', p. 75.
15 Ibid.

16 Köse, 'The journey from the secular to the sacred', p. 305.
17 Alinta Smith in interview with the author, 18 December 2005, Sydney. Unless otherwise indicated, all quotations from Alinta come from this interview.
18 Troy Meston in interview with the author, 31 March 2005, Brisbane.
19 Eugenia Flynn in interview with the author, 6 December 2005, Adelaide. Unless otherwise indicated, all quotations from Eugenia come from this interview.
20 Mahmoud, 'Finding my purpose in life', p. 80.
21 Jackson, 'My conversion to Islam', p. 10.
22 Köse, 'Native British Converts to Islam', p. 352.
23 Köse, 'The journey from the secular to the sacred', p. 305.
24 Poston, 'Becoming a Muslim in the Christian West', p. 163.
25 Sulaiman-Hill, 'Kiwis on the straight path'; Poston, 'Becoming a Muslim', pp. 161, 163.
26 Jackson, 'My conversion to Islam', p. 10; Abu Bakr, 'Abu Bakr's way to Islam', p. 16; Anas, 'My long journey to Islam', p. 68.
27 Conroy, 'In search of peace', p. 44.
28 Poston, 'Becoming a Muslim', p. 163.
29 Justin Agale in interview with the author, 27 November 2004, Sydney. Unless otherwise indicated, all quotations from Justin come from this interview.
30 Anonymous interviewee quoted in Boz, 'True blue Muslims', p. 39.
31 Anonymous interviewee quoted in ibid., p. 42.
32 Zebiri, *British Muslim Converts*, p. 199.
33 Koya, 'Why British women are turning to Islam'.
34 Haddad, Smith & Moore, *Muslim Women in America*, p. 50.
35 Conroy, 'In search of peace', p. 46.
36 Forrest, 'My path to Islam', p. 2.
37 Boz, 'True blue Muslims', p. 32.
38 'John' in interview with the author, 11 August 2005, Melbourne. Unless otherwise indicated, all quotations from John come from this interview.
39 Anthony Mundine in interview with the author, 4 December 2006, Sydney. Unless otherwise indicated, all quotations from Anthony come from this interview.
40 Sulaiman-Hill, 'Kiwis on the straight path'.
41 Sultán, 'Choosing Islam', p. 327.
42 Köse, 'Native British converts', p. 348.
43 Jensen, 'To be "Danish", becoming "Muslim"', p. 404.
44 Poston, 'Becoming a Muslim', p. 163.
45 Ibid., p. 163.
46 We have seen that Lebanon and Turkey have together supplied about a third of all Muslim immigrants to Australia. The rest have come to Australia from more than sixty different countries of origin. See Bouma, 'The settlement of Islam in Australia', p. 77.
47 Gilliat-Ray, 'Rediscovering Islam', p. 317.
48 Muslims say 'Peace be upon him' after saying the name of a prophet of Islam as an act of reverence. In writing it is often abbreviated to 'PBUH'.
49 Islam, 'Why I chose Islam', p. 28.
50 Köse, 'Native British converts', p. 349.
51 Poston, 'Becoming a Muslim', p. 164.
52 'Jamila' in interview with the author, 25 April 2005, Sydney. Unless otherwise indicated, all quotations from Jamila come from this interview.
53 Poston, 'Becoming a Muslim', p. 164.
54 Rocky Davis in interview with the author, 17 August 2006, Sydney. Unless otherwise indicated, all quotations from Rocky come from this interview.
55 Rambo, *Understanding Religious Conversion*, p. 170.
56 It is not an essential requirement for witnesses to be present when a person is embracing Islam. Thus, even if an individual declares *shahada* in private, she or he is considered a Muslim in the sight of Allah. But in order to be recognised as a member of the Muslim community they must declare the *shahada* in the presence of two witnesses or before an imam of a mosque who has been authorised to issue a certificate of *shahada*. A fuller definition of one's entry into the community of Muslims would also include the six elements of belief; that is, belief in Allah, the angels, the divinely revealed books, the prophets, the Last Day and the Decree (see Dutton, 'Conversion to Islam', pp. 153–4). Although it is not required, Shi'a Muslims sometimes add the following declaration (reproduced here in English): 'I testify that the Commander of the Faithful, the Pure Leader, Ali, is the friend of Allah, the successor of the Messenger of Allah, and nothing can come between them.'
57 Al-Fawzaan, *The Declaration of Faith*, pp. 25–6.
58 Dutton, 'Conversion to Islam', p. 154.

59 Dannin, *Black Pilgrimage to Islam*, p. 239.
60 The sick, the elderly, those on a journey and women who are pregnant or breast-feeding are permitted to break the fast and make up an equal number of days later in the year.
61 Rambo, *Understanding Religious Conversion*, p. 145; Bourque, 'Being British and Muslim', p. 9.
62 Boz, 'True blue Muslims', p. 60.
63 Rambo, *Understanding Religious Conversion*, pp. 107–8.
64 Bourque, 'Being British and being Muslim', p. 14.
65 Humes, 'Led by the Creator', p. 75.
66 Boz, 'True blue Muslims', p. 53.
67 Sulaiman-Hill, 'Kiwis on the straight path'.
68 According to Irfan Yusuf, the differences between Sunni and Shi'a Muslims are less about doctrine and more about politics and community leadership. Shi'a Muslims believed that Ali, the cousin and son-in-law of the Prophet Muhammad, should have been his successor because he was a blood relative. But Sunni Muslims believed that leadership should be decided by the community democratically. See Yusuf, *Once Were Radicals*, p. 211.
69 Bourque, 'Being British and being Muslim', p. 7.
70 Ibid., p. 8.
71 Jensen, 'To be "Danish"', p. 393.
72 Ibid., p. 393.
73 Nazra Wali in interview with the author, 9 July 2008, Melbourne. Unless otherwise indicated, all quotations from Nazra come from this interview.
74 Quoted in Boz, 'True blue Muslims', p. 20.
75 Bourque, 'Being British and being Muslim', p. 16.
76 Boz, 'True blue Muslims', p. 20.
77 Reddie, *Black Muslims in Britain*, p. 190.
78 Bourque, 'Being British and being Muslim', p. 9.
79 Reddie, *Black Muslims*, p. 10.
80 Poston, 'Becoming a Muslim', p. 162; Sulaiman-Hill, 'Kiwis on the straight path'; Bourque, 'Being British and being Muslim', p. 9.
81 Poston, 'Becoming a Muslim', p. 169.
82 Dutton, 'Conversion to Islam', p. 156.
83 Boz, 'True blue Muslims', p. 58.
84 Rambo, *Understanding Religious Conversion*, p. 147.
85 Rambo, 'Conversion', p. 77; Bourque, 'Being British and being Muslim', p. 7.
86 Rambo, *Understanding Religious Conversion*, p. 161.
87 Ibid., p. 162.
88 Ibid., pp. 161–2.

SIX **Speaking to the converted**

1 Wohlrab-Sahr, 'Conversion to Islam', p. 352.
2 Dannin, *Black Pilgrimage to Islam*, pp. 4, 260.
3 Rambo, *Understanding Religious Conversion*, p. 37.
4 Alinta Smith in second interview with the author, 18 December 2005, Sydney. Unless otherwise indicated, all quotations from Alinta come from this interview.
5 'Ramiz' in interview with the author, 15 December 2009, Sydney. Unless otherwise indicated, all quotations from Ramiz come from this interview.
6 Nazra Wali in interview with the author, 9 July 2008, Melbourne. Unless otherwise indicated, all quotations from Nazra come from this interview.
7 Anthony Anderson in interview with the author, 19 August 2009, Ipswich, Qld. Unless otherwise indicated, all quotations from Anthony come from this interview.
8 Eugenia Flynn in interview with the author, 6 December 2005, Adelaide. Unless otherwise indicated, all quotations from Eugenia come from this interview.
9 Islamic religious art focuses instead on the glorification of God's word with beautifully written verses of the Qur'an, often accompanied by geometric and floral designs.
10 Quoted in Nimmo, 'Islam Dreaming'.
11 Ibid.
12 Justin Agale in interview with the author, 27 November 2004, Sydney. Unless otherwise indicated, all quotations from Justin come from this interview.
13 Rocky Davis in interview with the author, 17 August 2006, Sydney. Unless otherwise indicated, all quotations from Rocky come from this interview.
14 Emerick, *The Complete Idiot's Guide to Understanding Islam*, p. 90.
15 Shahzad (Shaz) Rind in interview with the author, 27 November 2004, Sydney. Unless otherwise indicated, all quotations from Shaz come from this interview.
16 Kraft, 'Cultural concomitants of Higi conversion', pp. 431–42.
17 Ibid., p. 434.
18 Rambo, *Understanding Religious Conversion*,

p. 38.
19 Kraft, 'Cultural concomitants of Higi conversion', p. 435.
20 Ibid., 436.
21 Ibid., p. 433.
22 Gausset, 'Islam or Christianity?', pp. 257–78.
23 Ibid., p. 271.
24 Reddie, *Black Muslims in Britain*, p. 213.
25 Flynn, 'More than men and historical narratives', unpublished paper in author's possession.
26 Bunbury, 'View from the North', Episode 5.
27 Loos, *White Christ Black Cross*, p. 157.
28 Willis, 'Riders in the chariot', p. 313.
29 Hall & Hall, 'Dreams, visions and Aboriginal spirituality', p. 39.
30 Quoted in Bunbury, 'View from the North', Episode 5.
31 Robb, 'Church and mission history', p. 71.
32 Cited in Loos, *White Christ Black Cross*, p. 155.
33 Loos, *White Christ Black Cross*, p. 155.
34 Ibid., p. 13.
35 Quoted in ibid., p. 157.
36 Sharp, *No Ordinary Judgement*, p. 156.
37 Ibid., p. 156.
38 Robb, 'Church and mission history', pp. 71–2.
39 Paulson, 'The value of Aboriginal culture', p. 89.
40 Rosendale, 'Aboriginal myths and customs', p. 101.
41 Gondarra, 'Aboriginal spirituality and the gospel', p. 43.
42 Gilbert, 'God at the Campfire', p. 64.
43 Yengoyan, 'Religion, morality, and prophetic traditions', pp. 234, 236, 248.
44 Robb, 'Church and mission history', p. 67.
45 The Qur'an (49:13) states (in translation): 'O mankind! We have created you male and female, and have made you nations and tribes, so that you may recognise each other.'
46 Robb, 'Church and mission history', p. 71.
47 Mitchell, 'Corrupt desires and the wages of sin'.
48 Robb, 'Church and mission history', p. 72.
49 Sulaiman Menzies in interview with the author, 19 July 2009, Sydney. Unless otherwise indicated, all quotations from Sulaiman come from this interview.
50 Willis, 'Riders in the chariot', p. 313.
51 Onnudottir, Possamai & Turner, 'Islam', pp. 61–2.
52 Patrick L. Dodson in Dodson, Elston & McCoy, 'Leaving culture at the door', p. 262.
53 Harris, 'Guidelines for so-called Western civilization and Western Christianity', p. 69.
54 Yengoyan, 'Religion, morality and prophetic traditions', p. 254.
55 Reddie, *Black Muslims in Britain*, p. 230.
56 Rouse, *Engaged Surrender*, p. 35.
57 'Jamila' in interview with the author, 25 April 2005, Sydney. Unless otherwise indicated, all quotations from Jamila come from this interview.
58 'John' in interview with the author, 11 August 2005, Melbourne. Unless otherwise indicated, all quotations from John come from this interview.
59 Rouse, *Engaged Surrender*, p. 141.
60 Ibid., pp. 208, 217.
61 Philips, *The Fundamentals of Tawheed*, p. 102.
62 Bourque, 'Being British and Muslim', p. 6.
63 Haddad, Smith & Moore, *Muslim Women in America*, p. 45.

SEVEN Sisters are doing it for themselves

1 Zebiri, *British Muslim Converts*, pp. 14, 43.
2 Haddad, Smith & Moore, *Muslim Women in America*, p. 42.
3 ABS 2008.
4 Zebiri, *British Muslim Converts*, p. 201.
5 Rouse, *Engaged Surrender*, p. 34.
6 Martin, *Encycolpedia of Islam and the Muslim World*, p. 721; Mernissi, *Women and Islam*, p. 101.
7 Mernissi, *Women and Islam*, p. 95.
8 Zebiri, *British Muslim Converts*, p. 108.
9 Badran, 'Feminism and conversion', p. 204; Zebiri, *British Muslim Converts*, p. 138.
10 Afshar, Aitken & Franks, 'Islamophobia and women of Pakistani descent', p. 169.
11 Haddad, Smith & Moore, *Muslim Women in America*, p. 9.
12 Alinta Smith in second interview with the author, 15 December 2009, Sydney.
13 Zebiri, *British Muslim Converts*, p. 210.
14 Rouse, *Engaged Surrender*, p. 63.
15 Haddad, Smith & Moore, *Muslim Women in America*, p. 53.
16 Bullock, *Rethinking Muslim Women and the Veil*, p. 199.
17 Zebiri, *British Muslim Converts*, p. 193.
18 Eugenia Flynn in second interview with the author, 10 June 2007, Adelaide. Unless otherwise indicated, all quotations from Eugenia come from this interview.

19 Wadud, *Inside the Gender Jihad*, p. 224.
20 Halima Binti Hassan Awal in third interview with the author, 14 December 2009, Sydney.
21 Halima Binti Hassan Awal in interview with the author, 30 March 2005, Brisbane. Unless otherwise indicated, all quotations from Halima come from this interview.
22 Nazra Wali in interview with the author, 9 July 2008, Melbourne. Unless otherwise indicated, all quotations from Nazra come from this interview. While Indigenous people can't see beyond her veil, according to Nazra, when members of the Muslim community see her without it 'they just say, "No, we can't accept you like that, you must go and put a scarf on now", so I get it both ways.'
23 The Arabic phrase *As-salaam 'Alaikum*, meaning 'Peace be upon you', is a universal greeting with which Muslims address each other. Arab Christians and Jews also use this greeting. The traditional response is *wa 'Alaikum As-salaam*, transliterated as 'And upon you be peace'.
24 Halima Binti Hassan Awal in third interview with the author, 14 December 2009, Sydney.
25 Afshar et al., 'Islamophobia', p. 175.
26 Haddad, Smith & Moore, *Muslim Women in America*, p. 10.
27 Rouse, *Engaged Surrender*, p. 34.
28 Zebiri, *British Muslim Converts*, p. 244.
29 Halima Binti Hassan Awal in third interview with the author, 14 December 2009, Sydney.
30 Zebiri, *British Muslim Converts*, p. 244.
31 Ibid., p. 191.
32 Mernissi, *Women and Islam*, p. 64.
33 Wadud, *Qur'an and Woman*, p. 1.
34 Zebiri, *British Muslim Converts*, p. 3.
35 Rouse, *Engaged Surrender*, p. xiv.
36 Ibid., p. 134.
37 Zebiri, *British Muslim Converts*, p. 202.
38 Halima Binti Hassan Awal in third interview with the author, 14 December 2009, Sydney.
39 Rouse, *Engaged Surrender*, p. 128.
40 Bassey, *Malcolm X and African-American Self-Consciousness*, p. 6.
41 Rouse, *Engaged Surrender*, p. 165.
42 McGinty, 'Formation of alternative femininities through Islam', p. 475.
43 Rouse, *Engaged Surrender*, p. 46.
44 Haddad, Smith & Moore, *Muslim Women in America*, p. 156.
45 Ibid., p. 156.
46 Wadud, *Qur'an and Woman*, p. 25.
47 Mernissi, *Women and Islam*, p. 119.
48 Haddad, Smith & Moore, *Muslim Women in America*, p. 145.
49 Emerick, *The Complete Idiot's Guide to Understanding Islam*, pp. 235, 251.
50 Wadud, *Inside the Gender Jihad*, p. 148.
51 In the Qur'an, Allah says (in translation): 'This day have I perfected your religion for you and completed My favour upon you and have chosen for you Islam as your religion' (5:3). This was one of the last verses revealed to the Prophet, marking what Muslims believe to be the completion of the Qur'an and the perfection of Islam.
52 Rouse, *Engaged Surrender*, p. 173.
53 Many Muslims interpret the exhortation to women to guard in their husbands' absence 'what Allah would have them guard', to mean that a Muslim wife must guard her husband's property and belongings, her modesty and chastity and her husband's honour and reputation.
54 Zebiri, *British Muslim Converts*, p. 231.
55 Emerick, *The Complete Idiot's Guide to Understanding Islam*, p. 234.
56 Zebiri, *British Muslim Converts*, p. 242.
57 Rouse, *Engaged Surrender*, p. 56.

EIGHT Malcolm X Down Under

1 Mamiya, 'Malcolm X', p. 145. After leaving the Nation of Islam, Malcolm X established two new organisations: Muslim Mosque Inc., a religious grouping, and the secular Organization of Afro-American Unity. See Reddie, *Black Muslims in Britain*, p. 46.
2 Mamiya, 'Malcolm X', p. 145.
3 Sulaiman Menzies in interview with the author, 19 July 2009, Sydney. Unless otherwise indicated, all quotations from Sulaiman come from this interview.
4 Justin Agale in interview with Dilara Reznikas, date unknown, Sydney. Partial transcript in author's possession.
5 'Abdul' in interviw with the author, 22 July 2009, location unspecified. All quotes from 'Abdul' are from this interview.
6 Haddad, Smith & Moore, *Muslim Women in America*, p. 49.
7 'John' in interview with the author, 11 August 2005, Melbourne. Unless otherwise indicated, all quotations from John come from this interview.
8 Haddad, Smith & Moore, *Muslim Women in*

America, p. 49; Zebiri, *British Muslim Converts*, p. 101.
9 Haddad, Smith & Moore, *Muslim Women in America*, p. 49.
10 Wadud, *Qur'an and Woman*, p. 37.
11 Rouse, *Engaged Surrender*, p. 10.
12 Wadud, *Qur'an and Woman*, p. 37.
13 Kidd, *The Forging of Races*, p. 75.
14 Carretta, 'Review of Colin Kidd's *The Forging of Races*', p. 122.
15 This letter, sent to Bilal Cleland of the Australian Federation of Islamic Councils, was posted on the Barutiwa News Service website but the URL is no longer active. A downloaded copy of the letter is in the possession of the author, and all quotations are taken from it.
16 Dannin, *Black Pilgrimage to Islam*, p. 263.
17 Quoted in Nimmo, 'Islam Dreaming'.
18 Dannin, *Black Pilgrimage to Islam*, p. 115.
19 Quoted in Nimmo, 'Islam Dreaming'.
20 Goodall & Huggins, 'Aboriginal women are everywhere', p. 408.
21 Sykes, 'Bobbi Sykes', p. 67.
22 Shahzad (Shaz) Rind in interview with the author, 27 November 2004, Sydney. Unless otherwise indicated, all quotations from Shaz come from this interview.
23 Reddie, *Black Muslims in Britain*, p. 165.
24 Emerick, *The Complete Idiot's Guide to Understanding Islam*, p. 235.
25 When asked where one finds paradise, the Prophet Muhammad reportedly answered, 'Paradise lies at the feet of the mother.' This is variously interpreted to mean that the mother is responsible for teaching her children the religious obligations that will win them Paradise, or that one earns Paradise by serving one's mother throughout her life.
26 Haley, 'Foreword' to X, *The Autobiography of Malcolm X*, p. 13.
27 Roda, 'Preface' to Bassey, *Malcolm X*, p. iii.
28 Bassey, *Malcolm X*, p. 40.
29 Gallagher, *Expectation and Experience*, pp. 24–5.
30 X, *The Autobiography of Malcolm X*, pp. 90–1.
31 Ibid., pp. 101–2.
32 Rocky Davis in interview with the author, 17 August 2006, Sydney. Unless otherwise indicated, all quotations from Rocky come from this interview.
33 X, *The Autobiography of Malcolm X*, p. 102.
34 Troy Meston in interview with the author, 31 March 2005, Brisbane. Unless otherwise indicated, all quotations from Troy come from this interview.
35 X, *The Autobiography of Malcolm X*, pp. 453–4.
36 Ibid., pp. 483, 493.
37 Quoted in Correy, 'Sheikh Rock from the Block', p. 3.
38 Reddie, *Black Muslims in Britain*, p. 166.
39 Quoted in Nimmo, 'Islam Dreaming'.
40 ABS 2010.
41 Ron Woodham, Commissioner of NSW Department of Corrective Services, letter to the author, 30 January 2010.
42 In 2005 about a third of the thirty-six inmates in Goulburn jail's Super Max facility were Muslim. This has prompted the unit's unofficial renaming as Goulburn's 'super mosque'. See Gibbs, 'Hard men turn to Islam to cope with jail'. Prisoners also call the Super Max, or High Risk Management Unit (HRMU), 'harm you'.
43 Rocky Davis in interview with Dilara Reznikas, date unknown, Sydney. Partial transcript in the possession of the author.
44 Davis in interview with Reznikas.
45 Davis in interview with the author, 17 August 2006, Sydney.
46 Davis in interview with Reznikas.
47 Barringer, 'Adult transformations inside a Midwest Correctional facility', p. 15.
48 Terry Sampson (Indigenous Muslim prison inmate), letter to the author, 15 December 2009. My thanks to Dr Soliman Gilany for putting me in touch with Terry.
49 Quoted in Masters, 'The Goulburn "Supermax"'.
50 Aziz Cooper in interview with the author, 11 March 2009, Melbourne. Unless otherwise indicated, all quotations from Aziz come from this interview.
51 Kerbaj, 'Radicals brainwashing Aborigines', p. 4.
52 According to Abdullah Saeed, the correct name for those who rely on the teachings of Muhammad ibn Abd al-Wahhab (so-called Wahhabis) is 'Salafis'. Salafis do not call themselves 'Wahhabis' because Muhammad ibn Abd al-Wahhab did not establish a new school of thought but revived the original teachings of the Prophet as practised by his companions and the earliest generations of Muslims. See Saeed, 'Trends in contemporary Islam', p. 398.
53 Quoted in Kerbaj, 'Radicals brainwashing Aborigines', p. 4.
54 Quoted in Nimmo, 'Islam Dreaming'. In

Nimmo's *Insight* report the surnames of Khalid and the other (male) Indigenous Muslim interviewees were not supplied.
55 Frank Cilluffo quoted in Cooper, 'Towards a model for the spiritual care of Muslim prisoners', p. 18.
56 In the Qur'an, Allah says: 'Verily we have honoured the children of Adam. We have provided them with transport on land and sea and have given them for sustenance things good and pure; and conferred on them special favours above many of those whom we have created' (17:70).
57 Gibbs, 'Hard men turn to Islam'.
58 Quoted in Gibbs, 'Hard men turn to Islam'.
59 Quoted in ibid.
60 Gibbs, 'Hard men turn to Islam'.
61 Anonymous former Muslim prison chaplain in interview with Dilara Reznikas, date unknown, Sydney. Partial transcript in the possession of the author.

Conclusion

1 Rahnema, 'Islam in diaspora', p. 32.
2 Wadud, *Inside the Gender Jihad*, p. 5.
3 Rahnema, 'Islam in diaspora', p. 32.
4 Aly, *People Like Us*, p. xvi.
5 Deen, *Caravanserai*, pp. 297, 303.
6 Ibid., p. 285.
7 Stratton, 'Dying to come to Australia', p. 184.
8 Perera, 'Our patch', p. 213.
9 Bernard Cohen quoted in Perera, 'What is a camp …?'.
10 Perera, 'What is a camp …?'.
11 Turner, 'Shrinking the borders', p. 9.
12 Burke, 'Security politics', p. 202.
13 Unnamed Indigenous spokesperson, quoted in Chandler, 'This is "Black Children Overboard", say elders'.
14 Marion Scrymgour quoted in SBS World News Australia, 'Indigenous MP slams Howard's "black Tampa"'.
15 Wadiwell, '"A particularly governmental form of warfare"', p. 165.
16 Henderson & Marris, 'PM sends in the troops', p. 1.
17 Imtoual, 'Religious racism & the media'.
18 Nazra Wali in interview with the author, 9 July 2008, Melbourne.
19 Imtoual, '"Taking things personally"', p. 213.
20 Quoted in Nimmo, 'Islam Dreaming'.
21 Quoted in ibid.
22 Morris, 'A new faith for Kooris', p. 9.
23 ABS 2010.
24 Eugenia Flynn quoted in Morris, 'New faith for Kooris', p. 9.
25 Morris, 'New faith for Kooris', p. 9.
26 Bolt, 'Traditional Aboriginal imam'. I thank Simon Caldwell for bringing this blog entry to my attention.
27 Circe, 'Islam destroys Aboriginality'.
28 Humphrey, 'Australian Islam, the new global terrorism & the limits of citizenship', p. 134.
29 Johari Bin Demin in interview with the author, 4 September 2006, Broome. Unless otherwise indicated, all quotations from Johari come from this interview.
30 Semah Mokak-Wischki in interview with the author, 15 August 2006, Brisbane. Unless otherwise indicated, all quotations from Semah come from this interview.
31 Sulaiman Menzies in interview with the author, 19 July 2009, Sydney.
32 Quoted in Nimmo, 'Islam Dreaming'.
33 Mansouri, 'Citizenship, identity and belonging in contemporary Australia', p. 159.
34 Anthony Mundine in interview with the author, 4 December 2006, Sydney.
35 Alinta Smith in interview with the author, 18 December 2005, Sydney. Unless otherwise indicated, all quotations from Alinta come from this interview.
36 Reddie, *Black Muslims in Britain*, p. 186.
37 Quoted in Nimmo, 'Islam Dreaming'.
38 Quoted in ibid.
39 Flynn, 'The hard questions!', p. 17.
40 Reddie, *Black Muslims*, p. 185.

Bibliography

ABS (2010), Table generated using Census of Population and Housing, Australia, 2006, TableBuilder <www.abs.gov.au/tablebuilder>, Canberra: Australian Bureau of Statistics, viewed 25 May 2010.

—— (2008), Customised report using Census of Population and Housing, Australia, 1996 and 2001, 26 August 2008.

Afshar, Haleh, Rob Aitken & Myfanwy Franks (2006), 'Islamophobia and women of Pakistani descent in Bradford: The crisis of ascribed and adopted identities' in Moghissi (ed.), *Muslim Diaspora*, pp. 167–85.

Al-Fawzaan, Saalih ibn Fawzaan (1998), *The Declaration of Faith*, Middlesex, UK: Message of Islam.

Aly, Waleed (2007), *People Like Us: How Arrogance is Dividing Islam and the West*, Sydney: Pan Macmillan Australia.

Anas, Umme (2004), 'My long journey to Islam' in Islam Australia's *My Path to Islam*, pp. 65–72.

Badran, Margot (2006), 'Feminism and conversion: Comparing British, Dutch, and South African life stories' in Karin van Nieuwkerk (ed.), *Women Embracing Islam: Gender and Conversion in the West*, Austin, TX: University of Texas Press, pp. 192–229.

Bakr, Abu (2004), 'Abu Bakr's way to Islam' in Islam Australia's *My Path to Islam*, pp. 15–20.

Balint, Ruth (2005), *Troubled Waters: Borders, Boundaries and Possession in the Timor Sea*, Sydney: Allen & Unwin.

—— (2001), 'The pearling families of Broome', *Hindsight*, Radio National, broadcast 2 September (part 1) and 9 September (part 2).

Barker, H.M. (1995), *Camels and the Outback*, Carlisle, WA: Hesperian Press.

Barringer, Tony A. (1998), 'Adult transformations inside a Midwest correctional facility: Black Muslim narratives of their Islamic conversion', unpublished doctoral dissertation, Northern Illinois University, DeKalb.

Bassey, Magnus O. (2005), *Malcolm X and African-American Self-Consciousness*, Lewiston, NY: Edwin Mellen Press.

Battersby, Paul (2007) *To the Islands: White Australians and the Malay Archipelago since 1788*, Plymouth, UK: Lexington Books.

Berndt, R.M. & C.H. Berndt (1954), *Arnhem Land: Its History and Its People*, Melbourne: Cheshire.

Bin Bakar, Mark (2002) 'Mark "Mary G" Bin Bakar' in Noel Trevor (ed.), *Why Not Broome*, Cable Beach, WA: Noel Trevor Enterprises, pp. 37–63.

Bin Demin, Sally (2007), *Once in Broome*, Broome: Magabala Books.

Bolt, Andrew (2007), 'Traditional Aboriginal imam', blog entry, 4 May <http://blogs.news.com.au/heraldsun/andrewbolt/index.php/heraldsun/comments/peta_stephenson_a_doctoral_fellow_at_the_university_of_melbournes_asia_inst/>, viewed 23 February 2010.

Bouma, Gary D. (1997), 'The settlement of Islam in Australia', *Social Compass*, 44(1): 71–82.

Bouma, Gary D., Joan Daw & Riffat Munawar (2001), 'Muslims managing religious diversity', in Saeed & Akbarzadeh (eds), *Muslim Communities in Australia*, pp. 53–72.

Bourque, Nicole (1998), 'Being British and Muslim: Dual identity among new and young Muslims', in Alan Jones (ed.), *University Lectures in Islamic Studies* (vol. 2), London: Altajir World of Islam Trust, pp. 1–18.

Boz, Tuba (2002), 'True blue Muslims: An anthropological study of Muslim converts in Melbourne', unpublished honours thesis, La Trobe University.

Brahim, Septu (2000), 'Recollections of the early days', in Anne Brewster, Angeline O'Neill and Rosemary van den Berg (eds), *Those Who Remain Will Always Remember: An Anthology of Aboriginal Writing*, Fremantle, WA: Fremantle Arts Centre Press, pp. 46–57.

Bullock, Katherine (2002), *Rethinking Muslim Women and the Veil: Challenging Historical and Modern Stereotypes*, London: International Institute of Islamic Thought.

Bunbury, Bill (2003), *View from the North*, episode 5: 'Religions old and new',

Hindsight, Radio National, broadcast 20 July <www.abc.net.au/rn/history/hindsight/features/north/epis_5.htm#top>, viewed 18 May 2010.

Burke, Anthony (2007), 'Security politics and Us: Sovereignty, violence and power after 9/11' in Perera (ed.), *Our Patch*, pp. 197–218.

Burton, Val (2000), *General History of Broome*, Broome, WA: Broome Historical Society.

Carretta, Vincent (2007) 'Review of Colin Kidd's *The Forging of Races: Race and Scripture in the Protestant Atlantic*', *Eighteenth-Century Studies*, 41(1): 121–23.

Chandler, Jo (2007), 'This is "black children overboard", say elders', *Age*, Melbourne, 27 June.

Chase, Athol (1981), '"All kind of nation: Aborigines and Asians in Cape York Peninsula', *Aboriginal History*, 5(1): 7–19.

Choo, Christine (1995), 'Asian men on the West Kimberley Coast, 1900–1940', *Studies in Western Australian History*, 16: 89–111.

—— (1994), 'The impact of Asian-Aboriginal Australian contacts in Northern Australia', *Asian and Pacific Migration Journal*, 3(2–3): 295–310.

Cigler, Michael (1986), *The Afghans in Australia*, Melbourne: Australasian Educa Press.

Circe (2008), 'Islam destroys Aboriginality – destructive Muslim fishermen', part 1 of 3, *Australian Islamist Monitor*, 21 May <www.australianislamistmonitor.org>, viewed 23 February 2010.

Clarke, Anne (2000), 'The "Moormans Trowsers": Macassan and Aboriginal interactions and the changing fabric of Indigenous social life' in Sue O'Connor & Peter Veth (eds), *East of Wallace's Line: Studies of Past and Present Maritime Cultures of the Indo-Pacific Region*, Rotterdam, Netherlands: A.A. Balkema, pp. 315–35.

Conroy, Hanan (2004), 'In search of peace' in Islam Australia's *My Path to Islam*, pp. 43–7.

Cooper, Aziz (2008), 'Towards a model for the spiritual care of Muslim prisoners in Muslim minority countries', unpublished conference paper presented at the National Centre of Excellence for Islamic Studies conference *Challenges to Social Inclusion in Australia: The Muslim Experience*, 19–20 November, University of Melbourne.

Correy, Joseph (2005–06), 'Sheikh Rock from the Block', *South Sydney Herald*, December 2005–January 2006, p. 3.

Dadleh, Miriam (1995), 'Miriam Dadleh', in Bruce Shaw, *Our Heart is the land: Aboriginal Reminiscences from the Western Lake Eyre Basin*, Canberra: Aboriginal Studies Press, pp. 66–7.

—— (1990) 'Fair devil sticky beak' in Adele Pring (ed.), *Women of the Centre*, Apollo Bay, Vic: Pascoe Publishing, pp. 99–114.

Dannin, Robert (2002), *Black Pilgrimage to Islam*, New York: Oxford University Press.

Deen, Hanifa (no date) 'Muslim journeys: Cameleers and hawkers', National Archives of Australia, Canberra <http://uncommonlives.naa.gov.au/contents.asp?sID=29>, viewed 28 February 2010.

—— (2003) *Caravanserai: Journey Among Australian Muslims*, Fremantle, WA: Fremantle Arts Centre Press.

Dodson, Patrick L., Jacinta K. Elston & Brian F. McCoy (2006), 'Leaving culture at the door: Aboriginal perspectives on Christian belief and practice', *Pacifica*, 19: 249–62.

Doogue, Geraldine (2006), 'Servants of God', *Compass*, Radio National, broadcast 1 January <www.abc.net.au/compass/s1543881.htm>, viewed 4 March 2010.

Dutton, Yasin (1999), 'Conversion to Islam: The Qur'anic paradigm', in Lamb & Bryant (eds), *Religious Conversion*, pp. 151–65.

Earl, George W. (1841), 'An account of a visit to Kisser, one of the Serawatti group in the Indian archipelago', *Journal of the Royal Geographical Society*, 11: 108–17.

Eliade, Mircea (ed.) (1987), *Encyclopedia of Religion*, New York: Macmillan.

Emerick, Yahiya (2002), *The Complete Idiot's Guide to Understanding Islam*, Alpha: Indianapolis, IN.

Evans, Nicholas (1992), 'Macassan loanwords in Top End languages', *Australian Journal of Linguistics*, 12: 45–91.

Flinn, Frank K. (1999) 'Conversion: up from evangelicalism or the pentecoastal and charismatic experience', in Lamb & Bryant (eds), *Religious Conversion*, pp. 51–72.

Flynn, Eugenia (2009) 'More than men and historical narratives: Challenging notions of Indigenous and Muslim interaction', unpublished paper.

—— (2009) 'The hard questions!', *Crescent Times*, 7, May, p. 17.

Forrest, Jill (2004), 'My path to Islam' in Islam Australia's *My Path to Islam*, pp. 1–3.

Gallacher, Lyn (2002), 'Borders? What borders?', *Encounter*, Radio National, broadcast 1 December <www.abc.net.

au/rn/relig/enc/stories/s736108.htm>, viewed 4 March 2010.
Gallagher, Eugene V. (1990), *Expectation and Experience: Explaining Religious Conversion*, Atlanta, GA: Scholars Press.
Ganter, Regina (2008), 'Muslim Australians: The deep histories of contact' <www.griffith.edu.au/__data/assets/pdf_file/0007/58309/Ganter.pdf>, viewed 17 May 2010.
—— (2006), *Mixed Relations: Asian-Aboriginal Contact in North Australia*, Perth: UWA Press.
—— (1998), 'Living an immoral life: "Coloured women and the paternalistic state"', *Hecate* 24(1): 13–40.
Gausset, Quentin (1999) 'Islam or Christianity? The choices of the Wawa and the Kwanja of Cameroon', *Africa*, 69(2): 257–78.
Gibbs, Stephen (2005), 'Hard men turn to Islam to cope with jail', *Sydney Morning Herald*, 19 November.
Gilbert, Kevin (1996), 'God at the campfire and that Christ fella', in Pattel-Gray (ed.), *Aboriginal Spirituality*, pp. 54–65.
Gilliat-Ray, Sophie (1999), 'Rediscovering Islam: A Muslim journey of faith', in Lamb & Bryant (eds), *Religious Conversion*, pp. 315–32.
Gondarra, Djiniyini (1996), 'Aboriginal spirituality and the gospel', in Pattel-Gray (ed.), *Aboriginal Spirituality*, pp. 41–53.
Goodall, Heather, & Jackie Huggins (1992), 'Aboriginal women are everywhere: Contemporary struggles', in Kay Saunders & Raymond Evans (eds), *Gender Relations in Australia: Domination and Negotiation*, Harcourt Brace Jovanovich: Sydney, pp. 398–424.
Haddad, Yvonne Yazbeck, Jane I. Smith & Kathleen M. Moore (2006), *Muslim Women in America: The Challenge of Islamic Identity Today*, New York: OUP.
Haley, Alex (1968), 'Foreword', *The Autobiography of Malcolm X (with the assistance of Alex Haley)*, Harmondsworth, England: Penguin Books, pp. 11–78.
Hall, William & Marjory Hall (1996), 'Dreams, visions and Aboriginal spirituality', in Pattel-Gray (ed.), *Aboriginal Spirituality*, pp. 37–40.
Hāmid, Ismáil (1982), 'A survey of theories of the introduction of Islam in the Malay Archipelago', *Islamic Studies* 21(3): 89–100.
Harris, Charles (1996), 'Guidelines for so-called Western civilization and Western Christianity', in Pattel-Gray (ed.), *Aboriginal Spirituality*, pp. 66–78.
Henderson, Ian, & Sid Marris (2001), 'PM sends in the troops', *Australian*, 18 October, p. 1.
Hercus, Luise A (1981), 'Afghan stories from the north-east of South Australia', *Aboriginal History*, 5.1: 39–70.
Humes, Abdur Rahman (2004), 'Led by the Creator', lecture presented at Curtin University, Perth, 12 April 2003; reproduced in Islam Australia's *My Path to Islam*, pp. 73–6.
Humphrey, Michael (2005), 'Australian Islam, the new global terrorism and the limits of citizenship' in Shahram Akbarzadeh and Samina Yasmeen (eds), *Islam and the West: Reflections from Australia*, Sydney: UNSW Press, pp. 132–48.
Hussain, Jamila (2001), 'Family law and Muslim communities' in Saeed & Akbarzadeh (eds), *Muslim Communities in Australia*, pp. 161–87.
Imtoual, Alia (2006), '"Taking things personally": Young Muslim women in South Australia discuss identity, religious racism and media representations', unpublished PhD thesis, University of Adelaide, South Australia.
—— (2005) 'Religious racism and the media: Representations of Muslim women in the Australian print media', *Outskirts: Feminisms Along the Edge*, 13; <www.chloe.uwa.edu.au/outskirts/archive/volume13/imtoual>, viewed 23 February 2010.
Isaacs, Jennifer (1980), *Australian Dreaming: 40,000 Years of Aboriginal History*, Sydney: Lansdowne Press.
Islam, Abdullah (2004), 'Why I chose Islam' in Islam Australia's *My Path to Islam*, pp. 25–9.
Islam Australia, *My Path to Islam: Australian Muslim Revert Stories*, Mount Druitt, NSW: Goodword Media.
Jackson, Jan (2004), 'My conversion to Islam' in Islam Australia's *My Path to Islam*, pp. 9–13.
Jensen, Tina (2008), 'To be "Danish", becoming "Muslim": Contestations of national identity?', *Journal of Ethnic and Migration Studies*, 34(3): 389–409.
Jones, Mary Lucille (1993), 'Muslim impact on early Australian life', in Mary Lucille Jones (ed.), *An Australian Pilgrimage: Muslims in Australia from the Seventeenth Century to the Present*, Melbourne: Victoria Press, pp. 31–48.

Jones, Philip (2007), 'Reflecting on Australia's Muslim cameleer heritage' in Jones & Kenny, *Australia's Muslim Cameleers*, pp. 9–15.

Jones, Philip, & Anna Kenny (2007), *Australia's Muslim Cameleers: Pioneers of the Inland 1860s–1930s*, Kent Town, SA: Wakefield Press.

Kabir, Nahid (2005), 'Muslims in Western Australia 1870–1970', *Early Days: Journal of the Royal Western Australian Historical Society*, 12(5): 550–65.

Kerbaj, Richard (2006), 'Radicals brainwashing Aborigines in prison', *Australian*, 17 August 2006, p. 4.

Khadem, Mojgan (2001), *Serenades*, Palace Films.

Kidd, Colin (2006), *The Forging of Races: Race and Scripture in the Protestant Atlantic World*, Cambridge: Cambridge University Press.

Koch, Grace (compiler and editor), & Harold Koch (translator) (1993), *Kaytetye Country: An Aboriginal History of the Barrow Creek Area*, Alice Springs: Institute for Aboriginal Development.

Köse, Ali (1999), 'The journey from the secular to the sacred: Experiences of native British converts to Islam', *Social Compass*, 46(3): 301–12.

—— (1995) 'Native British converts to Islam: Who are they? Why do they convert?', *American Journal of Islamic Social Sciences*, 12(3): 347–59.

Koya, Zakieh (2000), 'Why British women are turning to Islam', *Mahjubah* 19(3): 44–5; <www.islamwomen.org>, viewed 4 March 2010.

Kraft, Charles H. (1976), 'Cultural concomitants of Higi conversion: Early period', *Missiology: An International Review*, October 1976: 431–42.

Lamb, Christopher, & Bryant, M. Darrol (eds), *Religious Conversion: Contemporary Practices and Controversies*, New York and London: Cassell.

Lamilami, Lazarus (1974), *Lamilami Speaks: An Autobiography*, Sydney: Ure Smith.

Loois, Vivienne (1988), 'Afghans and Indians in Western Australia', in Anne Atkinson (compiler), *Asian Immigrants to Western Australia 1829–1901: The Bicentennial Dictionary of Western Australians*, vol. 5, Perth: UWA Press, pp. 397–402.

Loos, Noel (2007), *White Christ Black Cross: The Emergence of a Black Church*, Canberra: Aboriginal Studies Press.

McGann, Peter J. (1990), '"Malays" as indentured labour: Western Australia 1867–1900', *Papers in Labour History*, 5, pp. 35–54.

McIntosh, Ian (2008), 'Pre-Macassans at Dholtji? Exploring one of north-east Arnhem Land's great conundrums', in Veth, Sutton and Neale (eds), *Strangers on the Shore*, pp. 165–80.

—— (1997) 'The Birrinydji legacy: Aborigines, Macassans and mining in north-east Arnhem Land', *Aboriginal History*, 21: 70–89.

—— (1996) 'Allah and the spirit of the dead: The hidden legacy of pre-colonial Indonesian Aboriginal contact in north-east Arnhem Land', *Australian Folklore*, 11: 131–38.

—— (1994) *The Whale and the Cross: Conversations with David Burrumarra MBE*, Darwin: Historical Society of the Northern Territory.

Macknight, C.C. (2008), 'Harvesting the memory: Open beaches in Makassar and Arnhem Land', in Veth, Sutton and Neale (eds), *Strangers on the Shore*, pp. 133–47.

—— (1976), *The Voyage to Marege: Macassan Trepangers in Northern Australia*, Melbourne: MUP.

Macknight, C.C. (ed.) (1969), *The Farthest Coast: A Selection of Writings Relating to the History of the Northern Coast of Australia*, Melbourne: MUP.

Mahmoud, Asiya (2004), 'Finding my purpose in life', in Islam Australia's *My Path to Islam*, pp. 77–82.

Mamiya, Lawrence H. (1987), 'Malcolm X' in Eliade (ed.), *Encyclopedia of Religion*, pp. 144–5.

Manderson, L. (2001), 'Malay' in James Jupp (ed.), *The Australian People: An Encyclopedia of the Nation, Its People and Their Origins*, Cambridge: Cambridge University Press, pp. 579–80.

Mansouri, Fethi (2005), 'Citizenship, identity and belonging in contemporary Australia' in Shahram Akbarzadeh and Samina Yasmeen (eds), *Islam and the West: Reflections from Australia*, Sydney: UNSW Press, pp. 149–64.

Mansson McGinty, Anna (2007), 'Formation of alternative femininities through Islam: Feminist approaches among Muslim converts in Sweden', *Women's Studies International Forum*, 30(6): 474–85.

Martin, Marium (1918), 'Letter of Marium Martin, now Mrs Badoola to the Warden, regarding her marriage', State Records Office of Western Australia, Aborigines Department, Personal file 156/31: Indian Goolam Badoola and Family of Mount Magnet.

Martin, Richard C. (ed.) (2003), *Encycolpedia of Islam and the Muslim World*, New York: Macmillan Reference.

Masters, Chris (2005), 'Goulburn "Supermax"', *Four Corners*, ABC TV, broadcast 7 November, <www.abc.net.au/4corners/content/2005/s1499699.htm>, viewed 9 March 2010.

Mernissi, Fatima (trans. Mary Jo Lakeland) (1991), *Women and Islam: An Historical and Theological Enquiry*, Oxford: Basil Blackwell.

Milner, Anthony (2008), *The Malays*, West Sussex: Wiley-Blackwell.

Mitchell, Jessie (2007), 'Corrupt desires and the wages of sin: Indigenous people, missionaries and male sexuality, 1830–1850', in Ingereth Macfarlane (ed.), *Transgressions: Critical Australian Indigenous Histories* <http://epress.anu.edu.au/aborig_history/transgressions/mobile_devices/ch11.html>, viewed 5 March 2010.

Moghissi, Haideh (ed.), *Muslim Diaspora: Gender, Culture and Identity*, London and New York: Routledge.

Moorwney, M.J., & D.R. Hobbs (1997), 'The Asian connection: Preliminary report on Indonesian trepang sites on the Kimberley coast, NW Australia', *Archaeology in Oceania*, 32(3): 197–206.

Morris, Linda (2007), 'A new faith for Kooris', *Sydney Morning Herald*, 4 May, p. 9.

Mulvaney, D.J. (1989), *Encounters in Place: Outsiders and Aboriginal Australians 1606–1985*, Brisbane: University of Queensland Press.

Mulvaney, John, & Johan Kamminga (1999) *Prehistory of Australia*, Sydney: Allen & Unwin.

Nimmo, Julie (2003), 'Islam Dreaming', *Insight*, SBS TV, broadcast 27 February.

O'Donnell, Mick (2005), 'Family's fight for citizenship rights', *Stateline*, ABC TV, broadcast 4 March, <www.abc.net.au/stateline/wa/content/2005/s1317894.htm>, viewed 27 May 2010.

Onnudottir, Helena, Adam Possamai & Bryan S. Turner (2010), 'Islam: A new religious vehicle for Aboriginal self-empowerment in Australia?', *International Journal for the Study of New Religions*, 1(1): 49–74.

Palmer, Lisa (2007) 'Negotiating the ritual and social order through spectacle: the (re)production of Macassan/Yolngu histories', *Anthropological Forum*, 17.1: 1–20.

Pattel-Gray, Anne (ed.) (1996), *Aboriginal Spirituality: Past, Present, Future*, Melbourne: Harper Collins Religious.

Paulson, Graham A. (1996), 'The value of Aboriginal culture', in Pattel-Gray (ed.), *Aboriginal Spirituality*, pp. 81–93.

Perera, Suvendrini (2007), 'Our patch: Domains of whiteness, geographies of lack and Australia's racial horizons in the War on Terror' in Perera (ed.), *Our Patch*, pp. 119–46.

—— (2002) 'What is a camp … ?', *Borderlands e-journal*, 1.1 <www.borderlandsejournal.adelaide.edu.au>, viewed 2 March 2010.

Perera, Suvendrini (2007) (ed.), *Our Patch: Enacting Australian Sovereignty Post-2001*, Australian Research Institute, Curtin University of Technology, Perth: Network Books.

Philips, Abu Ameenah Bilal (2005), *The Fundamentals of Tawheed*, Riyadh: International Islamic Publishing House.

Pike, Jimmy (2002), 'Two camel men', in Eirlys Richards, Joyce Hudson & Pat Lowe (eds), *Out of the Desert: Stories from the Walmajarri Exodus*, Broome: Magabala Books, pp. 76–83.

Poston, Larry (1991), 'Becoming a Muslim in the Christian West', *Journal of Muslim Minority Affairs*, 12(1): 159–69.

Rahman, Fazlur (1987), 'Islam: An overview', in Eliade (ed.), *Encyclopedia of Religion*, pp. 303–22.

Rahnema, Saeed (2006), 'Islam in diaspora and challenges to multiculturalism' in Moghissi (ed.), *Muslim Diaspora*, pp. 23–38.

Rajkowski, Pamela (2005 [1987]) *In the Tracks of the Camelmen: Outback Australia's Most Exotic Pioneers*, Henley Beach South, SA: Seaview Press.

—— (1995) *Linden Girl: A Story of Outlawed Lives*, Kensington Gardens, SA: Market Media.

Rambo, Lewis R. (1987) 'Conversion' in Eliade (ed.), *Encyclopedia of Religion*, pp. 73–9.

—— (1993) *Understanding Religious Conversion*, New Haven, CT, and London: Yale University Press.

Rambo, Lewis R., & Charles E. Farhadian (1999), 'Converting: Stages of religious change', in Lamb & Bryant (eds), *Religious Conversion*, pp. 23–34.

Reddie, Richard S. (2009), *Black Muslims in Britain: Why are a Growing Number of Young Black People Converting to Islam?* Oxford: Lion Hudson.

Reynolds, Henry (2003), *North of Capricorn: The Untold Story of Australia's North*, Sydney: Allen & Unwin.

Richards, Eirlys, Joyce Hudson & Pat Lowe (eds) (2002), *Out of the Desert: Stories from the Walmajarri Exodus*, Broome: Magabala Books.

Robb, Lyndel (1996), 'Church and mission history', in Anne Pattel-Gray (ed.), *Martung Upah: Black and White Australians Seeking Partnership*, Melbourne: Harper Collins Religious, pp. 67–75.

Roda, Anthony (2005), 'Preface' in Magnus O. Bassey, *Malcolm X and African-American Self-Consciousness*, Lewiston, NY: Edwin Mellen Press, pp. i–v.

Rosendale, George (1996), 'Aboriginal myths and customs: Matrix for gospel preaching', in Pattel-Gray (ed.), *Aboriginal Spirituality*, pp. 99–106.

Ross, Bahauddin (1992), 'Islam on Thursday Island', *Australian Muslim Times*, 7 August, p. 7.

Rouse, Carolyn Moxley (2004), *Engaged Surrender: African American Women and Islam*, Berkeley: University of California Press.

Russell, Denise (2004), 'Aboriginal–Makassan interactions in the eighteenth and nineteenth centuries in northern Australia and contemporary sea rights claims', *Australian Aboriginal Studies*, 1: 3–17.

Russell, Susan (no date), 'Islam: A worldwide religion and its impact in Southeast Asia' <www.seasite.niu.edu/crossroads/russell/islam.htm>, viewed 17 May 2010.

Saeed, Abdullah (2007), 'Trends in contemporary Islam: A preliminary attempt at a classification', *Muslim World*, 97, pp. 395–404.

Saeed, Abdullah, & Shahram Akbarzadeh (2001), 'Searching for identity: Muslims in Australia' in Saeed & Akbarzadeh (eds), *Muslim Communities in Australia*, pp. 1–11.

Saeed, Abdullah, & Shahram Akbarzadeh (eds) (2001), *Muslim Communities in Australia*, Sydney: UNSW Press.

Salam Peacock, Eva (2004), 'Voices from Torres Strait: Eva Salam Peacock' in Shnukal, Ramsay & Nagata (eds), *Navigating Boundaries*, pp. 278–81.

SBS World News Australia (2007), 'Indigenous MP slams Howard's "black Tampa".

Scriver, Peter (2004) 'Mosques, ghantowns and cameleers in the settlement history of colonial Australia', *Fabrications*, 13(2): 19–42.

Searcy, Alfred (1909), *In Australian Tropics*, London: George Robertson & Co.

Sharp, Nonie (1996), *No Ordinary Judgement: Mabo, the Murray Islanders' Land Case*, Canberra: Aboriginal Studies Press.

Shaw, Adrian (2008), 'Ships of the desert', documentary, *AWAYE!*, Radio National, broadcast 20 September.

Shibasaki, Billy Isao (2004), 'Voices from Torres Strait: Billy Isao Shibasaki' in Shnukal, Ramsay & Nagata (eds), *Navigating Boundaries*, pp. 289–90.

Shnukal, Anna (2004), 'Confluence: Asian cultural contributions to *Ailan Pasin*' in Shnukal, Ramsay & Nagata (eds), *Navigating Boundaries*, pp. 247–63.

—— (2004) '"They don't know what went on underneath": Three little-known Filipino/Malay communities of Torres Strait', in Shnukal, Ramsay & Nagata (eds), *Navigating Boundaries*, pp. 81–121.

Shnukal, Anna, & Guy Ramsay (2004), 'Tidal flows: An overview of Torres Strait Islander–Asian contact', in Shnukal, Ramsay & Nagata (eds), *Navigating Boundaries*, pp. 33–51.

Shnukal, Anna, Ramsay, Guy, & Nagata, Yuriko (eds) (2004), *Navigating Boundaries: The Asian Diaspora in Torres Strait*, Canberra: Pandanus Books.

Sickert, Susan (2003), *Beyond the Lattice: Broome's Early Years*, Fremantle, WA: Fremantle Arts Centre Press.

Staples, Joan (compiler), & Ken O'Shea (supervisor) (1995), 'Thursday Island's Asian heritage: An oral history'.

Stephenson, Peta (2009a), 'Keeping it in the family: Partnerships between Indigenous and Muslim communities in Australia', *Aboriginal History*, 33: 97–116.

—— (2009b), 'Recreating community: Indigenous women and Islam' in Tanja Dreher & Christina Ho (eds), *Beyond the Hijab Debates: New Conversations on Gender, Race and Religion*, Newcastle upon Tyne: Cambridge Scholars Publishing, pp. 67–80.

—— (2009c), 'Typologies of security: Indigenous and Muslim Australians in the post-9/11 imaginary', *Journal of Australian Studies*, 33(4): 473–88.

—— (2007), *The Outsiders Within: Telling Australia's Indigenous–Asian Story*, Sydney: UNSW Press.

—— (2005), 'Aboriginal Muslims: The practice and politics of hybrid identities in a globalising world', in Russell West-Pavlov (ed.), *Who's Australia? Whose Australia? Contemporary Politics, Society and Culture in Australia*, Trier, Germany: WVT, pp. 83–98.

—— (2004) 'Islam in Indigenous Australia: Historic relic or contemporary reality?', *Politics and Culture*, 4, <http://aspen.conncoll.edu/politicsandculture/arts.cfm?id=55>, viewed 9 August 2010.

Stevens, Christine (1993), 'Afghan camel drivers: Founders of Islam in Australia' in Mary Lucille Jones (ed.), *An Australian Pilgrimage: Muslims in Australia from the Seventeenth Century to the Present*, Melbourne: Victoria Press, pp. 49–62.

—— (1989), *Tin Mosques and Ghantowns: A History of Afghan Cameldrivers in Australia*, Oxford: OUP.

Stratton, Jon (2007), 'Dying to come to Australia: Asylum seekers, tourists and death' in Perera (ed.), *Our Patch*, pp. 167–96.

Sulaiman-Hill, Ruqayya (2007), 'Kiwis on the straight path: Muslim conversion in NZ', *Aotearoa Ethnic Network Journal*, 2(2), <www.aen.org.nz/journal/2/2/AENJ.2.2.Sulaiman-Hill.pdf>, viewed 4 March 2010.

Sultán, Madeleine (1999), 'Choosing Islam: A study of Swedish converts', *Social Compass*, 46(3): 325–35.

Sutton, Philip W., & Stephen Vertigans (2005), *Resurgent Islam: A Sociological Approach*, Cambridge: Polity Press.

Swain, Tony (1993), *A Place for Strangers: Towards a History of Australian Aboriginal Being*, Cambridge: Cambridge University Press.

Sykes, Roberta (1984), 'Bobbi Sykes', in Robyn Rowland (ed.), *Women Who Do and Women Who Don't Join the Women's Movement*, Routledge & Kegan Paul: Melbourne, pp. 63–9.

Torres, Mitch (Michelle) (2001), *Saltwater Bluesman*, Film Australia Limited, Macumba Media Enterprises.

Travisano, Richard V. (1970), 'Alternation and conversion as qualitatively different transformations', in Gregory P. Stone & Harvey A. Faberman (eds), *Social Psychology Through Symbolic Interaction*, Waltham, MA: Xerox College Publishing, pp. 594–606.

Tsiolkas, Christos (2008), *The Slap*, Sydney: Allen & Unwin.

Turner, Graeme (2007), 'Shrinking the borders: Globalization, culture and belonging', *Cultural Politics: An International Journal*, 3(1): 5–19.

Veth, Peter, Sutton, Peter, & Margo Neale (eds), *Strangers on the Shore: Early Coastal Contacts in Australia*, Canberra: National Museum of Australia Press.

Wadiwell, Dinesh (2007), '"A particularly governmental form of warfare": Palm Island and Australian Sovereignty' in Perera (ed.), *Our Patch*, pp. 149–66.

Wadud, Amina (2006), *Inside the Gender Jihad: Women's Reform in Islam*, Oxford: Oneworld Publications.

—— (1999) *Qur'an and Woman: Rereading the Sacred Text from a Woman's Perspective*, New York: OUP.

Walker, Alan (1988), 'Macassan influences on the Aboriginal language and culture of northern Australia', *Indonesian Studies*, 5(1): 28–37.

Walker, Douglas (1995), 'Douglas Walker' in Bruce Shaw (ed.), *Our Heart is the Land: Aboriginal Reminiscences from the Western Lake Eyre Basin*, Canberra: Aboriginal Studies Press, pp. 69–70.

Warner, W. Lloyd (1969; rev. edn), *A Black Civilization: A Social Study of an Australian Tribe*, Gloucester, MA: Peter Smith.

—— (1931–32) 'Malay influence on the Aboriginal cultures of north-eastern Arnhem Land', *Oceania*, 2: 476–95.

Willis, Brian (1992), 'From indispensability to redundancy: The Afghans in Western Australia 1887–1911', *Papers in Labour History*, 9: 39–61.

Willis, Peter (1988) 'Riders in the chariot: Aboriginal conversion to Christianity at Kununurra', in Tony Swain & Deborah Bird Rose (eds), *Aboriginal Australians and Christian Missions: Ethnographic and Historical Studies*, Bedford Park, SA: Australian Association for the Study of Religions, pp. 308–20.

Wilson, Mona (2001), 'Mona Wilson's life story', interview with Julie McCrossin, *Life Matters*, Radio National, broadcast 29 June.

Wohlrab-Sahr, Monika (1999), 'Conversion to Islam: Between syncretism and symbolic battle', *Social Compass*, 46(3): 351–62.

X, Malcolm (1968), *The Autobiography of Malcolm X (with the assistance of Alex Haley)*, Harmondsworth, England: Penguin Books.

Yengoyan, Aram A. (1993), 'Religion, morality, and prophetic traditions: Conversion among the Pitjantjatjara of Central Australia', in Robert W. Hefner (ed.), *Conversion to Christianity: Historical and Anthropological Perspectives on a Great Transformation*, Berkeley and Los Angeles, CA: University of California Press, pp. 233–57.

Yusuf, Irfan (2009), *Once Were Radicals: My Years as a Teenage Islamo-Fascist*, Sydney: Allen & Unwin.

Zebiri, Kate (2008), *British Muslim Converts: Choosing Alternative Lives*, Oxford: Oneworld Publications.

Index

9/11 terrorist attacks 18, 98, 100, 160, 276, 277–78
    post-9/11 era 21, 100, 223, 260

'Abdul' 246, 249–50, 294
Aboriginal
    men 252
        initiation of 46
        as pearl-shell workers 49, 297
    women 252
        chaperoning of 46, 130
        married to Muslim men 16, 45–47, 71–72, 102–04, 113–15, 117, ch. 4
        supposed sexual availability of 17, 220, 227
Aborigines
    Chief Protector of 4, 67, 114–15, 124
    Christianisation of 196–202, 204
Aborigines Act 1905 (WA) 4, 124
adat 55–56
Adelaide 1, 44, 64, 67, 77, 83, 125, 127–28, 134–35, 170, 195
    cameleer-funded mosque in 64, 94, 131, 134
Afghan cameleers 10, 13, 14–15, 21, 35–47, 64–65, 75–76
    Aboriginal descendants of 2–6, 10, 43–44, 47, chs 2–4
    (threatened) removal of 4–6, 115, 127–28
    raised as Muslim 5, 62
    avoidance of alcohol by 79, 86–87
    avoidance of pork by 75–80, 86
    encounters with Aboriginal people 37–47, 88
    gambling of 88
    ghantowns 42, 44–46, 65, 67, 80, 87–88
    non-Aboriginal descendants of 98–99, 102
    mosques funded by 64, 94, 97–98
Afghan Cameleers and Pioneers Cultural Festival 2, 68–69
Agale, Justin 112–13, 117, 150–51, 158–59, 161–62, 166, 180, 188–90, 198, 210–11, 245–46, 250–51, 254–55, 257–58, 260, 268–69, 290, 292–93
Akbar, Jack 4, 5, 47, 67, 73, 123–25, 130, 132, 134, 143–44

Akbar, Jimmy 4
Akbar, Johnny 4, 84–85
akhirat 55
'Ali' 101
Alice Springs 1, 38, 44, 79, 89, 98
    Alice Springs Islamic Society 89
Anderson, Anthony 186, 190, 253–54, 256
Australia Day 7, 8
Australian Islamist Monitor 285
Australia's Muslim Cameleers: Pioneers of the Inland 1860–1930s 3, 98–99

Baluchistan 113, 115–16, 127
barakah 210, 292
Bin Bakar, Mark 66, 68, 73–75, 100–01, 103, 108, 126–27
Bin Demin, Johari 70, 83–84, 103, 108, 134, 148, 285–86
Bin Demin, Sally 52, 63, 65, 70–71, 86, 88, 132–33
    Once in Broome 52, 86, 88
Bin Hitam, Sherena 50
Bin Juda, Ambrose (Binjie) 8
Bin Juda, Rosemary (Mary) 8
Bin Swani, Majunia 66, 70, 87, 148
Bin Swani, Rose 66, 70
Bin Tahal, Wahap 94, 95, 110
Bin Walid, Khalid 249, 264–65
Binawel, Karim 7–8
Binti Hassan Awal, Halima 6–8, 52, 55, 78, 109–11, 221, 223, 226, 229
Birrinydji 31
Boerkamp, Beatrice/Zanzibar (née Khan) 5, 61–62, 78–79, 127, 138
Bolt, Andrew 11, 284, 289
Boz, Tuba 159–61, 177
Bahim, Septu 62, 78, 104, 139–40
Brisbane (Qld) 1, 7, 10, 64, 110, 221
    cameleer-funded mosque in 64
Broken Hill 97–98, 146
    Broken Hill Historical Society 98
    Afghan mosque 97, 146
Broome (WA) 1, 6, 48, 63, 65–70, 75, 77, 83, 86–88, 100–01, 104, 108, 112, 126, 132–34, 148, 286
Burrumarra, David 29–31

Cairns 7
Cape York Peninsula 7, 51, 198
Cooper, Aziz 267
Cummings, Nazmeena 102

Dadleh, Miriam 43, 82, 89, 128–29, 135, 144–45
Darwin 6, 29, 70–71, 75, 85, 107, 142, 195
Davis, Rocky (Shaheed Malik) 9, 168, 190–91, 202, 207, 257–58, 260, 262, 269–70, 284, 287
da'wah 95, 180, 226
deen 110, 173
Demin, Anthea 67, 71
Department of Native Affairs 4
dhabiha 81, 82
Dowling, Julie 43–44
Dutch East Indies (Indonesia) 6, 110

Eid al-Adha 94, 299
Eid ul-Fitr 68, 94
Elcho Island 29, 31
Esgin, Tuguy 118–20

Federation of Malaya 6
fiqh 210, 277
fitrah 112
Flynn, Eugenia 9, 156, 165, 169–70, 186, 195–96, 217–18, 220, 223, 229, 283–84, 291

Galiwin'ku 29
ghusl 169
Gilany, Soliman 265–67, 269, 271–75

Hadith 137, 171, 187, 236, 239
haj 94–95, 142, 169, 172, 225, 258, 260, 263, 271
halal 54, 81, 89, 123, 176, 226, 299
  food 7, 45–46, 54, 80–84, 116, 148, 225
haram 86, 89, 147, 172, 176, 299
hijab 7, 17, 146, 159, 214–24
  the verse of the hijab 215–16
  wearing of by Indigenous Muslim women 7, 17, 146, 216–25, 240, 243–44
Hirakawa, Kathleen 56–57, 136

ijtihad 224
Indigenous Muslim Support Network 9
Indigenous Muslims 9, 16–19, 109–20, chs 5–8
  accusations of renouncement of

Aboriginality 9, 290
  as positive role models 9–10
  depiction of in fiction 12–13
  men 153, 191, 214, 233, ch. 8, 292
  numbers of 153, 214, 233, 283
  prison converts 10, 17–18, 261–75, 283
  supposed security risk of 12, 18, 260, 269–75, 282–85, 287–89
  women 153, ch. 7, 246, 248, 255, 283, 292
Islam
  arranged marriages in 16, 124, 130–33, 184, 202
  arrival in pre-colonial Australia 13–14, 21
  burial practices in 28, 56–57, 116
  daily prayers in 28–29, 62–63, 69, 171, 267
  disavowal of racial distinctions in 12, 18, 177–78, 201, 249, 260, 265, 290
  Five Pillars of 106, 171–72, 209
  gender differentiation in 185, 229
  gender equality in 129–30, 231–32
  gender segregation in 7, 16, 133–38, 185, 216, 226
  negative stereotypes of 9
  polygyny in 46, 143, 144, 184, 202, 236–37, 255–56
  prohibition of drugs, alcohol and gambling in 10, 46, 55, 86–89, 172, 208, 268
  prohibition of pork in 15, 46, 55, 75, 172
  prophets in 189–91, 267
  reversion to 15, 111–13, 178, 184, 246, 274
  significance of the family in 17, 123, 227–28, 247

'Jamila' 167, 208, 217–18, 221, 223, 228, 233–38
'John' 162, 166, 174, 208–09, 247
Jones, Philip 43, 80, 98–100

Kaaba 28, 63, 172
Kaissis, Georgina 65
Kayu Jawa 24, 28
Kenny, Anna 43, 98–99
'Khalid' 270, 283
Khan, Azeem (Johnny) 5, 76, 100, 145
Khan, Cissie 5
Khan, Goolbegum 5, 62, 127, 138–39
Khan, Nameth 47, 61–62, 127–29, 144
Khan, Philip 5
Khan, Rameth (Rocky) 5, 79
kinverts and kinversion 15–16, 91, 106, 109,

118, 121, 123, 139, 141, 222, 290, 292
   Indigenous–Malay kinverts 93–97, 147–48
   Aboriginal–Afghan kinverts 97–100, 146
Kite, Esther 5, 79, 102
Koori Muslim Association 9, 295
Koran *see* Qur'an
Kuala Lumpur 79, 147

maghrib 29, 71, 297
Mahomed, Dean Gool 76, 106
mahr 114, 232
Makassan trepangers 13–15, 22–34, 60
   encounters with Aboriginal communities 24–34, 60, 285
   outlawing of trepang trade 25, 29
Makkah (Mecca) 7, 28, 62–63, 81, 84, 95, 142, 169, 172, 225, 258, 259
Malay pearl-shell workers 13–15, 21, 48–58, 64–65
   avoidance of pork by 77–78, 86, 104
   encounters with Aboriginal people 48–58
   gambling of 88–89
   Indigenous descendants of 6–8, 10, 50–58, chs 2–4
   in Broome 6, 48, 50, 58, 66, 100–01, 127, 132, 146, 148
   in Darwin 48, 50, 58, 105, 146
   in Torres Strait 8, 48, 50, 53–58, 94, 95, 97, 109, 142, 146, 297, 301
   Malaytowns 6, 58, 65–66, 68, 97, 297
Malaysia 48, 70, 93, 97, 132–34, 136, 148–49, 286, 295
Malcolm X 12, 17–18, 150, 205, 244, 250, 255–59, 271, 284
   autobiography of 150, 161–62, 191, 244–46, 262
   influence of on Indigenous men 12, 18, 150–51, 162, 191, 244–46, 250, 259–60, 262–63, 271, 284
Marege 24, 28
Marree (SA) 39, 44–45, 61, 69, 75–77, 80, 88, 106, 144, 146
masjid 169
maslaha 227
Matbar, Lallie 4, 5, 47, 67, 123–25, 134, 143–44
Mecca *see* Makkah
Menzies, Sulaiman 188, 205–07, 245, 247–48, 252–53, 257–61, 267–68, 270, 273, 287–88
Meston, Troy 156, 258, 260
Mokak, Halimah 74–75, 85–86, 104, 106–08, 132, 134, 136–37, 140, 142, 146–48, 286
Mokak-Wischki, Semah 10–11, 72–74, 79–80, 104–05, 129–30, 132–33, 139, 140, 142, 286–87
Moore River Native Settlement 4, 124
Mundine, Anthony 11–12, 162, 166–67, 191, 203, 251, 283–84, 289
Muslims
   born 173, 176–77, 225
   converts (non-Indigenous) 18, 164, 173, 176–77, 222, 225, 233
      African-American 184, 219, 221, 230–31, 249, 263
      Anglo-Australian 154, 156–60, 165–66
      British 154, 157, 160, 162, 213–14, 217, 253
      Danish 154, 162, 176
      New Zealander 154, 157–58, 162, 174–75
      Swedish 154, 162
      US 154, 157–58, 163, 214
      name change of 111, 179, 205, 290
      reaction of family to conversion 9, 174, 217
   negative portrayal of in media 2, 98–100, 159–60, 183, 213, 260, 274, 277
   Shi'a 175, 277, 289, 299, 304
   Sunni 175, 259, 269, 277, 289, 299, 304

Nasir, Joanne 62–63, 71, 73, 103, 148–49
Nation of Islam 256–59, 271
Neville, A.O. 4, 114, 124
niqab 225, 282

Oodnadatta (SA) 5, 129
O'Shea, Assan (Ken) 87, 92, 136

'Patricia' 101–102, 126
pearling luggers 8, 49, 77, 88, 97
perahu 23–24, 27, 48
Perth (WA) 1, 6, 14, 64, 114, 118–19, 124, 286–87
   cameleer-funded mosque in 64, 114
Peshawar 4, 43, 67, 69, 78, 81, 82, 84, 100, 102, 123, 138, 144–45, 295
Pike, Jimmy 85
Port Pirie 2
Prislam 270–71
Prophet Muhammad 12, 56, 62, 114, 123, 137, 165, 169–71, 178–79, 186–87, 189, 209, 215–16, 224, 226, 236, 251, 254–55, 267, 274

Qur'an 9, 54, 63, 75, 81, 86, 92–95, 101–02, 104, 106–07, 118, 129, 137, 141, 165–71,

173, 175, 179, 184, 186, 201, 203–05, 209, 215–16, 220, 224, 227, 231–32, 234–35, 239, 248, 249, 253–56, 260, 264, 266, 270–71, 287, 289

Rajkowski, Pamela 4, 43, 44–46, 75–76, 123, 125, 128, 135, 143–44
   Linden Girl 4, 123
Ramadan 6, 16, 68, 94–95, 106, 146, 172
'Ramiz' 116–18, 185, 190–91, 204
religious conversion 151–52
   macrocontext of 154–55, ch. 6, 276, 284
   microcontext of ch. 5, 183–84
   Rambo's stage model of 154–81
Renmark (SA) 4, 130, 134
Reznikas, Dilara 140, 245, 263, 273
Rind, Shahzad (Shaz) 113–16, 127, 191, 200–01, 203, 252–54
Robertson, Marilyn/Fatima (née Khan) 5, 6, 61, 77
Ross, Balfour 87, 93–97
   Society of Islam 93, 95–96

Sahanna, Rosie 108
Salam Peacock, Eva 63, 78, 87, 101, 142–43
salat 106–07, 110, 171
Sampson, Terry 263–64
'Sarah' 70, 75, 78, 92
shahada 106, 169, 171, 239, 263, 303
sharia 170, 210, 277
Shibasaki, Billy 54
Shibasaki, Hismile (Izzie) 54
Shibasaki, Jamel 54–55, 58
Shibasaki, Seriba 56
shirk 224
silat 65
Singapore 6, 11, 48, 63, 66, 101, 110, 142, 148, 286, 295
Smith, Alinta 155–56, 159, 162–65, 169–70, 173–74, 181, 185–88, 203–04, 207–08, 218–20, 223, 226–27, 229–30, 235–36, 289
Stevens, Christine 43, 46, 67, 83, 87–89, 140
   Tin Mosques and Ghantowns 83
Stolen Generations 72, 118–20, 126
Straits Settlements 6, 48
sujud 28–29, 62
Sulawesi 23, 27–28, 285
   Islam's arrival in 27
Sultan, Eric 89
Sunna 170–71, 224, 226–27

taqwa 251
tawheed 167, 189–90
trepang 23–24
The Outsiders Within 13
The Slap 12–13
Torres Strait Islands 9, 228
   Badu 167, 218
   Darnley 6
   Hammond 8
   Horn 7
   Mer 188–90, 198
      Malo's law 188–90, 198
   Thursday Island 1, 6–8, 14, 52, 58, 63, 78, 87, 92–95, 97, 109–10, 142, 221
   TI Cemetery 8, 94
Tsiolkas, Christos 12

umma 108, 174, 177, 248–49, 259

Wahhabism 2 69
Wali, Nazra 176–77, 186–88, 222, 224–26, 238–42, 281–82
Walitha'walitha 28–31, 33–34
White Australia Policy 146, 163
Wilson, Mona (née Akbar) 3–4, 62, 67–68, 81, 100, 103, 109, 117, 123, 125–26, 130–32, 134–35, 140, 143–44
Wilson, Shirley (née Akbar) 3–4, 69–70, 71, 73, 75, 78, 108–109, 123, 125, 130, 134–35
wudu 56, 71, 106, 117, 169
wurramu 31, 34
   ceremony 30–31, 33
   grave-post 32–33

Yolngu 30, 32, 34
   moieties of 30
   Warramiri people 29–31, 33

zakat 172, 209
zina 123, 131

www.ingramcontent.com/pod-product-compliance
Lightning Source LLC
Chambersburg PA
CBHW021343300426
44114CB00012B/1055